Visual Guide to

Hedge Funds

Since 1996, Bloomberg Press has published books for finance professionals on investing, economics, and policy affecting investors. Titles are written by leading practitioners and authorities, and have been translated into more than 20 languages.

The Bloomberg Financial Series provides both core reference knowledge and actionable information for finance professionals. The books are written by experts familiar with the work flows, challenges, and demands of investment professionals who trade the markets, manage money, and analyze investments in their capacity of growing and protecting wealth, hedging risk, and generating revenue.

Books in the series include:

Visual Guide to ETFs by David Abner
Visual Guide to Chart Patterns by Thomas N. Bulkowski
Visual Guide to Municipal Bonds by Robert Doty
Visual Guide to Options by *Jared* Levy
Visual Guide to Candlestick Charting by Michael Thomsett
Visual Guide to Financial Markets by David Wilson
Visual Guide to Elliott Wave Trading by Wayne Gorman and Jeffrey Kennedy
Visual Guide to Hedge Funds by Richard C. Wilson

For more information, please visit our Web site at www.wiley.com/go/bloombergpress.

Visual Guide to

Hedge Funds

Richard C. Wilson

Cover design: Wiley
Cover Image: Generic Chart © JAAP HART/ISTOCKPHOTO

Published by John Wiley & Sons, Inc., Hoboken, New Jersey.
Published simultaneously in Canada.

For general information on our other products and services or for technical support, please contact our Customer Care Department within the United States at (800) 762-2974, outside the United States at (317) 572-3993 or fax (317) 572-4002.

Wiley also publishes its books in a variety of electronic formats. Some content that appears in print may not be available in electronic books. For more information about Wiley products, visit our web site at www.wiley.com.

Library of Congress Cataloging-in-Publication Data:

ISBN 978-1-118-27837-6 (Paperback)
ISBN 978-1-118-41964-9 (ePDF)
ISBN 978-1-118-42133-8 (ePub)

Printed in the United States of America

10 9 8 7 6 5 4 3 2 1

Contents

How to Use This Book

The *Visual Guide to . . .* series is designed to be a comprehensive and easy-to-follow guide on today's most relevant finance and investing topics. All charts are in full color and presented in a large format to make them easy to read and use. We've also included the following elements to reinforce key information and processes:

- **Definition:** Terminology and technical concepts that arise in the discussion.
- **Key Point:** Critical ideas and takeaways from the full text.
- **Step-by-Step:** Tutorials designed to break down the steps in a multi-phase process.

- **Do It Yourself:** Worksheets, formulas, and calculations.
- **Smart Investor Tip:** Insights, hints, and ideas provided to help the reader better understand concepts.
- **Test Yourself:** A section where readers can test their newly honed knowledge and skills
- **Bloomberg Functionality Cheat Sheet:** For Bloomberg terminal users, a back-of-the-book summary of relevant functions for the topics and tools discussed.

Introduction

The goal of *The Visual Guide to Hedge Funds* is to provide you with the value of a $500 seminar on hedge fund investment strategies and fundamentals in exchange for your investment of time and purchase of this sub-$50 book.

This book was written for potential and current hedge fund investors, startup fund managers, hedge fund career professionals, and industry service providers such as attorneys, fund administrators, or consultants.

This book is required reading for the Certified Hedge Fund Professional (CHP) designation program, the leading self-paced training and certificate program for professionals dedicated to working and leading in the hedge fund space. (Note to CHP participants: All of the content within this book, including audio expert interviews, video modules, and whiteboard walkthroughs, may be covered on your examination.)

Many hedge fund books are written by investment consultants, portfolio managers, or analysts, and are heavy on the theory, math, and statistics. Our perspective in writing this book is made up of three parts: Direct Hedge Fund Experience, Family Office Relationships, and our 120,000 member association, the Hedge Fund Group (HFG). First, I have worked directly for many hedge fund managers ranging from startups to, more recently, multi-billion-dollar funds. Second, our team represents a few ultra-wealthy families who ask us to help them source investments; working as an extension of these families has changed our perspective on hedge funds and portfolio management. Third, through running the Hedge Fund Group association and hosting our Family Offices Group & CapitalRaising. com training workshops we have spoken with over 4,500 hedge funds, and we screen over 1,000 each year to identify the handful that we can partner with, help directly, or may want to represent to the family office and ultra-wealthy client base that we work with. Our quarterly travel destinations and relationships span the globe including places such as New York, Singapore, Tokyo, London, the Cayman Islands, São Paulo, and Monaco, so we have tried to incorporate global considerations in this book.

CHAPTER 1

Hedge Fund Daily Operations

Hedge funds have become a powerful force in finance. There are thousands of hedge funds operating today; an incredible expansion for an industry that was only in its infancy half a century ago. If the hedge fund industry was crawling and learning how to walk in the 1960s and 1970s, it is now fully grown, at times running circles around its more traditional peers in the investment world. In this chapter, you will learn how these alternative funds operate and how these vehicles have become ever more complex and sophisticated over the years.

As you will learn in this book, the hedge fund has evolved greatly in recent years and differs in many ways from its peers in traditional investment vehicles. Hedge funds are private investment partnerships, with only a couple exceptions where the fund is sponsored by a publicly traded investment firm. Hedge funds often employ significant leverage to maximize profits on investments (with increased risks to the portfolio and investors), and managers run many exotic and complex strategies from convertible arbitrage to quantitative-driven investments executed in the blink of an eye.

One common misconception is that hedge funds are "just another type of mutual fund." I asked Paul Udall, Investment Director at GAM, to share how he explains what separates a hedge fund like his from a mutual fund. "Very simply, a 'hedge' fund hedges the risk in the portfolio by taking short positions to offset the long positions. The aim of this is simply to reduce the risk of general market moves." There are many other attributes that separate hedge funds as a unique alternative investment class, but the core concept to understand, as Paul explained, is that hedge funds seek to limit risk with short positions.

Hedge funds are often described along two extremes: one stereotype is of the so-called "masters of the universe," hedge fund managers who occupy lavish offices all over Manhattan and employ hundreds of traders and analysts, all earning millions in

> **DEFINITION:**
> **Hedge Fund**
>
> An alternative investment fund, typically structured as a private investment partnership, that is restricted to accredited investors (investors with significant means and sufficient sophistication). Hedge funds are actively managed, invest in a variety of securities—sometimes highly complex or exotic ones—and typically operate with greater flexibility, higher leverage, more complicated strategies, and with less regulatory oversight than a traditional investment fund.

compensation on the billions that the hedge fund earns in profits. This depiction resembles Michael Douglas's famous Gordon Gekko character from the movie *Wall Street*. The other caricature is a lone trader, executing massive trades in his garage, reaping huge rewards while assuming equally huge risks. The truth, as is often the case, lies somewhere in the middle, and there is some truth in both extreme stereotypes.

Many hedge funds manage well over $1 billion in assets under management. These funds often occupy large Manhattan office spaces (as seen in Figure 1.1), run hugely complex trading operations, and many of these hedge fund employees will earn $1 million or more in compensation on a good year (and even on a bad year, for some funds). However, not all hedge funds are created equal and there are thousands of hedge funds that manage "mere" millions in assets under management and grind out modest gains for a small number of investors.

A sub-$1 billion dollar fund might be a startup with just $1 to $10 million under management or emerging managers who have been around a few years and have yet to hit it out of the park with returns big enough to attract institutional capital en masse. In *The Big Short* (Norton/Allen Lane), a terrific account of the financial crisis and the hedge funds that succeeded during that time, author Michael Lewis profiles a few managers in this low-to-middle tier of hedge funds. Michael Burry

Figure 1.1 Successful Hedge Fund Titan, Leon Cooperman, founder of Omega Advisors, Inc., Manages Billions from His New York Office
Photographer: Mackenzie Stroh/Bloomberg Markets.

is a hedge fund manager and one of the characters in Lewis's nonfictional story. Burry managed to make a killing shorting the financial crisis and housing bubble, but for years he was just trading during the night and in his spare time. He didn't fit the stereotype of a Wall Street titan, not with his shorts and informal style, but he possessed exceptional analytical skills.

As we explore in the next chapter, the size of a hedge fund determines the complexity and vastness of its resources and operations. Hedge funds range from the giant firms like Bridgewater Associates (which manages over $100 billion in AUM) to modest trading outfits that most investors have never heard of. The single-trader hedge fund may only have an analyst and an assistant on staff and the rest of the services, like auditing, accounting, legal, and so on, are out-sourced to industry service providers. More established, large firms will typically handle a lot of operational functions in-house and may employ dozens, even hundreds of employees. It is best to think of a hedge fund as a financial company, with all the day-to-day responsibilities and activities of a small to medium-sized business.

A hedge fund is a cohesive business with many moving parts that require numerous individuals to perform specific daily activities to allow the firm to generate returns and profit from management and performance fees. Each employee, from portfolio to risk managers, plays an important role in helping the firm operate on a daily basis. This chapter describes the roles in a hedge fund organization and how each role plays a part in the operation of a hedge fund.

Hedge Fund Manager

The principal of a hedge fund usually wears many hats. These include portfolio manager, asset allocation specialist, supervisor of portfolio managers, and sales representative. Each of these roles is important to the operation of a hedge fund.

Generally, when a hedge fund hangs out its shingle to start its business, the hedge fund manager is the key driver of returns. This person is usually the portfolio manager who is creating the investment strategies and the risk level associated with the fund. This portfolio manager is generally responsible for generating the hedge fund's past returns that create the bulk of the fund's track record. The hedge fund manager has a robust understanding of how to invest and how to manage the risks to the portfolio.

As the hedge fund expands, the fund manager's responsibilities grow, requiring that individual to play a more versatile role within the firm. Hedge fund managers supervise and meet with the other portfolio managers on a daily basis to discuss strategy as well as their profits and losses. Risk is another issue for the hedge fund manager as he or she needs to be abreast of the potential losses his/her firm could incur if the market takes a swing that negatively affects the position.

Asset allocation is a key ingredient to generating the most efficient risk-adjusted returns. If the firm is set up so that there is only one strategy and one manager, then asset allocation is more linear and easier to manage. For funds that have multiple managers and multiple strategies, this quantitative issue is key to performance. A hedge fund manager needs to allocate capital to the managers and strategies that are going to produce the best risk-adjusted returns. A combination of certain types of market environments and trader underperformance can create a situation where a hedge fund manager reallocates capital to a different portfolio. Some managers use qualitative allocation methods while others use quantitative methods.

Marketing and selling the services of a hedge fund is another role the hedge fund manager handles. As a hedge fund grows, the investor-relations team is formed, which removes some of the initial introductions that take place when marketing a firm. Most of the time, closing the deal is still left up to the hedge fund manager.

In summary, the principal of a hedge fund is involved in almost every aspect of the business—much like the CEO of a small business understands everything about his business. Most successful hedge fund managers that I have met were knowledgeable about every part of the firm, from the day-to-day portfolio management to how the reporting is distributed to investors by the investor relations team.

Portfolio Managers

Portfolio managers initiate, manage, and monitor risks associated with their portfolios. On a daily basis, managers evaluate their portfolio risk and look for additional opportunities that will allow their portfolios to generate robust returns.

The portfolio managers are responsible for generating returns and profits for a hedge fund and will meet with the hedge fund manager and fellow portfolio managers to discuss positions and potential trading ideas. Many hedge fund managers will use information gathered by their portfolio managers to initiate large positions based on the merits of the trading strategy.

On a normal business day, a portfolio manager will examine his positions and determine the risks that need to be managed. He will then calculate the profit and loss of the portfolio and compare that P&L to the one created by the controlling group.

During the course of a trading day, a portfolio manager will have conversations with analysts and other portfolio managers to gather information about current risks and potential future risks. If any trades are transacted, the portfolio manager will either enter the trades into a system that can monitor the trades and evaluate the risk, or notify an operational group of the details of the trade. Additionally, the portfolio manager will verbally confirm the details of the trade at the end of a trading day.

Traders

Portfolio managers work hand-in-hand with execution professionals who trade securities on regulated exchanges, as well as via over-the-counter (OTC) exchanges. Generally, the responsibilities of transacting are separated at hedge funds. Execution professionals provide market information that includes deal flow and options flow. The information is crucial to a portfolio manager as they can garner the sentiment surrounding a security. If a portfolio manager was looking to purchase large blocks of stock, it would be difficult if investors were already bidding up a stock and were lifting offers to enter positions.

Traders also control access to numerous types of algorithms, which allows traders to enter positions at an average weighted volume. On a daily basis, traders discuss market actions with other trading professionals and execute trades throughout the day.

One might think that hedge fund trading is highly complicated (and it can be) but the act of opening and closing positions is really fairly simple. We turned again to Paul Udall of GAM to share the process he uses to execute trades in his hedge fund. Paul explains, "It really is very simple; you call or email your broker to ask him to buy the shares for your account. They will go and source them. To sell them you simply call up the broker again, and he will go and find a buyer to take them off your hands."

Risk Management

Risk management is where individuals evaluate the risks of each trading book and the overall risk of the hedge fund on an aggregate basis; it is an independent area separate from portfolio management typically. Risk management uses a number of tools, which include evaluating the delta within each area to generate the Value at Risk of the entire hedge fund.

Value at Risk can be calculated using a number of approaches. Each methodology uses specific assumptions about return performance. Historical data is one of the more popular techniques but it assumes that history will repeat itself, and therefore historical data is presumed to be the most efficient method to test risk. Another option is to analyze the distribution of the returns and use variances and covariances across these risks. A third methodology is to use a simulation which generates a data series based on random sampling.

Every day, the risk-management group will run reports outlining the risks of the overall portfolio, as well as each trading book, and then discuss the risks with portfolio managers. The team discusses whether the risks are in line with or are above the level of risk allowed for a specific trading book. Risk management is installed within a fund to protect the hedge fund and its investors. Risk managers not only evaluate market risk, but also credit risks. A risk manager has to account not only for risks that could harm the portfolio but also such hard-to-predict events like the inability of a counterparty to pay money owed to the fund—an area of risk management that drew a lot of attention during the financial crisis when some of the largest investment banks struggled to make good on their debts and liabilities.

Chief Financial Officer

The chief financial officer (CFO) is responsible for the daily activities of capital flow throughout the hedge fund. Any money that comes in or out of a specific

KEY POINT

Not all securities are traded through well-known exchanges like the NYSE, Euronext, or London Stock Exchange. A hedge fund will often buy and sell securities through the over-the-counter market, meaning the buying and selling parties are transacting outside of the exchanges. This is where many hedge funds trade derivatives, commodities, and other securities beyond exchange-listed equities.

DEFINITION:
Value at Risk (VaR)

VaR is a methodology for determining the worst-case scenario given a number of assumptions made out of market and credit risks. Value at Risk started to gain popularity as a tool to measure financial risks during the mid-1990s, but its origins lie in the early developments of modern portfolio theory.

fund is monitored by the CFO. The hedge fund's CFO is responsible for multiple entities and vehicles; for example, the CFO is accountable for monitoring the money that is moved in and out of domestic and off-shore funds, often with different structures, tax treatments, and other considerations. On a monthly basis, the hedge fund reports their profit and loss to their investors. The specifics need to be signed off on by the CFO and the hedge fund manager. Chief financial officers at large hedge funds have to consider a multitude of factors that could affect the financial stability of the fund, such as potential redemption requests, collateral calls, poor performance, and compliance costs. Every day, hedge funds execute substantial trades that affect the firm's overall financial liabilities, so the CFO has to keep a constant eye on the financial picture to ensure that the fund is well capitalized and meeting all of its obligations.

Controllers

The controllers at a hedge fund play an accounting role and evaluate the profits and losses associated with each portfolio manager, as well as the hedge fund as a whole. Usually, the controlling group reports directly to the chief financial officer, who monitors the profit and loss statements generated by the controlling group.

Controllers will have daily interaction with portfolio managers, questioning the profits and losses created by each individual portfolio. The controllers will drill each portfolio down to specific individual trades to determine if the proper profit and loss was created, how the trades affect the portfolio's VaR, and other factors that could come into play if the trade moves in one direction or another. At many funds, the controlling group manages and monitors a reserve created by a portfolio that sets funds aside if a trade or deal will not be realized until sometime in the future.

Settlements

Settlements are an operational group that evaluates each trade and determines when cash is needed to be moved in and out of a hedge fund. When trades are transacted, the settlements division is responsible for confirming each trade and making sure each party agrees to the details of a transaction. On a daily basis, the settlements team not only confirms each detail of a transaction, but assists in the process of moving capital from one firm to another. When a trade settles, it is the responsibility of the settlements group to move and receive funds to ensure that the capital accounts of each firm are current.

Margin and Collateral

Margin groups ensure that the amount of capital posted for margin is correct. Margin is borrowed capital that is collateralized by securities or other assets. The margin group is responsible for calculating margin on a daily basis and transferring money to and from other entities based on changes in the underlying assets that are traded. On a daily basis, members of the margin group discuss the margin requirements with their counterparts and make daily transfers of capital based on margin agreements that are negotiated. As a hedge fund grows, margin professionals also generate new margin agreements with new counterparts.

Legal

The legal department at a firm is usually comprised of the general counsel along with associate lawyers and paralegals. Legal groups assist in regulatory processes and in specific types of transactions that need to be negotiated. If a hedge fund participates in over-the-counter transactions, the legal team will negotiate broader agreements, such as ISDA (International Swaps Dealers Association) agreements.

Each business day, the legal team discusses issues with outside counsel and compliance in an effort to protect the hedge fund from any regulatory issues, as well as to identify potential compliance issues on the horizon. If the hedge fund participates in nonstandard transactions, the legal team will be in constant discussions with the counterpart's legal teams in an effort to make sure that contracts are secure prior to the initiation of any transactions.

Compliance

Hedge fund compliance groups work to ensure that the hedge fund is complying with all the mandatory regulations that pertain to the trading of securities by each entity associated with their hedge fund. The compliance group will work with each individual trader to make sure that they have the proper authority to trade securities based on the filing status of the hedge fund. For example, in many cases each trader will need to have a FINRA Series registration to trade on behalf of the hedge fund and its clients.

Compliance groups work hand-in-hand with the SEC (Security Exchange Commission), FINRA (Financial Industry Regulatory Authority), the CFTC (Commodity Futures Trading Commission), and the OCC (Officer of Controller of the Currency). Compliance groups work with specific exchanges, and make sure that the trading undertaken by their hedge fund meets all the regulatory requirements issued by an exchange. Hedge fund compliance has emerged as a hot issue, with insider trading, the Dodd–Frank Act, and other recent compliance-related stories dominating the news in recent years.

Investor-Relations

Investor relations professionals at hedge funds wear many hats and usually have experience from other organizations, which may include client services, marketing, sales, and capital introduction. Senior members of the investor relations department at a hedge fund are usually familiar with the different types of clients who will invest in a hedge fund, including pension funds, funds of funds, and other institutional investors. They often assist hedge fund managers in the sales process by speaking to prospective clients about the fund strategy and the specific return profile.

Junior investor relations staff will respond to client questions about the fund, as well as questions regarding the general market and economic conditions that might affect the fund. Junior members work on the firm's quarterly newsletter or arrange for members of the firm to appear at industry conferences and other speaking engagements to help promote the funds.

An investor relations professional performs many tasks and has a variety of responsibilities. He or she will involve themselves in all aspects of the sales and client service activities of the fund.

To download several videos related to the focus of this chapter and to watch over 125 total video modules and expert audio interviews, please activate your free account here: http://HedgeFundGroup.org/Access.

Conclusion

As you learned in this chapter, hedge funds do not succeed or fail based on the trading prowess of a single manager. Hedge funds are more complex than a lone trader raking in money, and the largest hedge funds approach the complexity of investment banks. Even a medium-sized hedge fund will often have a compliance department, legal and tax issues, and carefully managed trading operations. Hedge funds can employ a chief financial officer, IT professionals, an investor-relations team, portfolio managers, and dozens of analysts and traders. I hope that this chapter demonstrates how hedge funds have evolved to become a more sophisticated and institutional industry.

Test Yourself

Answer the following questions.

1. This person or persons executes transactions for the hedge fund:
   A. Fund Manager
   B. Traders
   C. Chief Financial Officer
   D. Controllers

2. True or False: Hedge fund managers do not think about risk and delegate the risk-management task to a separate team.

3. Margin is:
   A. Capital used for a transaction.
   B. Another term for options and OTC trades.
   C. Borrowed capital that is collateralized by securities or other assets.

4. True or False: Investor-relations professionals are normally responsible for, and do not deviate from, one task.

5. True or False: On a day-to-day basis portfolio managers evaluate risk and look for new ways to generate returns.

6. Value at Risk is:
   A. A methodology for determining the worst-case scenario given a number of assumptions made out of market and credit risks.
   B. A ratio that shows the volatility within a fund.
   C. An evaluation of the percentage of funds deemed to be toxic by an auditor or governmental agency.
   D. The true cost of an investment using a risk factor determined by simulations of market tendencies.

7. True or False: A hedge fund's success is determined by the skills and success of the hedge fund manager.

8. Which group does *not* have regulatory oversight of hedge funds?
   a. FINRA
   b. SEC
   c. Consumer Financial Protection Bureau
   d. FEC

9. True or False: After a trade has settled, it is the responsibility of the settlement group to make sure that all legal and compliance regulations concerning the financial instrument have been met.

10. True or False: Controllers are responsible for looking into the profit and loss of a fund, often evaluating each specific trade.

Answers can be found in Appendix B.

CHAPTER 2

The Hedge Fund Life Cycle: From Startup to Titan

The hedge fund industry can be an alluring place for investors and traders who eye starting their own funds and for career professionals, but most people new to the space do not understand the structure. Today, there are over 20,000 hedge funds globally, with the majority of them based in the United States and Western Europe.

In the previous chapter, we learned how hedge funds operate and the different professionals who work together to make a successful hedge fund. One important note on the staffing of a hedge fund is that the staff's experience, size of each department, and abilities can vary significantly from fund to fund. An important determinant of a hedge fund's operational capabilities and staff is the firm's assets under management (AUM) and years of operation. As you will see in this chapter, there is a hedge fund life cycle, through which a hedge fund will experience growing pains (such as difficulty raising capital as a startup), pressure to stand out from the pack (and separate from other emerging managers), and finally an age of maturity (when hedge fund titans either continue to grow larger and outperform, or become satisfied at a certain size and risk level).

This chapter will provide an overview of the hedge fund startup, emerging hedge fund manager, and hedge fund titan areas, so that you are better armed with the facts on how the industry operates right now. For each area we will cover the total estimated global volume, total AUM, AUM as a share of total-industry AUM, the types of investors they typically attract, team size, and long-term trends that are affecting the health and performance returns of each size of funds.

Douglas F. MacLean, founder of Armor Compliance, a compliance consulting firm, and Armor Law Group, a hedge fund law firm, thinks that the most accurate term to describe the hedge fund industry right now is "Social Darwinism," or survival of the fittest. Hedge Fund Research has determined that although over half of hedge fund managers currently manage less than $100 million in assets under management, these assets from emerging managers represent only 1.4 percent of the industry's $2 trillion or so in assets. Thus, the big hedge fund managers are simply growing bigger and capturing more market share. Emerging managers, who are the large majority of managers, are having difficulty raising assets and gaining any market share. In addition, massive additional compliance requirements imposed on hedge fund managers by the SEC, the CFTC, and NFA as a result of the Dodd–Frank Act are making it harder and harder for emerging managers to win the Darwinism battle.

Hedge Fund Startups ($1M to $10M)

For the purposes of this book, hedge fund startups will be categorized as those firms that have less than a three-year track record and less than $10 million in assets under management. All hedge funds began as a startup, even the billion-dollar ones that dominate the industry today, so it is important to recognize that although these funds are small today, tomorrow they could be the next big hedge fund. However, hedge fund startups come from very humble beginnings, pooling capital from friends and family, pitching the fund to uninterested investors, struggling to set up the structure and navigating institutional hurdles like compliance, operating challenges, and standard auditing and accounting practices. Different investors view startups differently: for example, some investors frequently allocate capital to new funds because they want to get in on the ground floor with a new manager. As one of the early investors in a hedge fund, an investor can often push for extraordinarily good terms, including lower management and performance fees, greater transparency, input on the fund's management, and a structure that favors the Limited Partners (LPs).

I alluded to the idea that all funds started as small startups, and that is an important draw for investors because as a fund matures and the manager develops a reputation as a rising star in the industry it can be increasingly difficult for investors (especially smaller LPs) to command the manager's attention. Many large hedge funds have limited capacity and may close the fund to new investors or charge exceptionally strict terms on new capital; as early seed investors to a hedge fund, the LPs who took a chance on the manager are typically rewarded with that manager's loyalty. Therefore, a lot of hedge fund investors see allocating to startups as a necessary and sometimes lucrative exercise that is crucial to developing relationships with new managers, tracking industry performance, and forming long-term relationships with the next crop of top-tier managers.

Smart Investor Tip

Savvy investors who are comfortable investing in unproven new hedge funds can often secure preferred terms, such as reduced fees, and more input on the fund's investment strategy. Furthermore, if the startup performs well over time then the hedge fund will often reward early investors by continuing to allow them to invest, even if it means turning away larger institutional investors.

However, many investors have a different attitude toward startups. Some investors see investing in startup hedge funds as an unnecessary risk to the portfolio. Startup hedge funds present a number of potential issues, namely business risks and performance risks. On the business side, compared to larger, older funds, a new hedge fund will typically have none of the glamor that larger funds have, like first-class office space in Manhattan; less institutional risk management practices; a smaller or nonexistent compliance department; unsophisticated business management; and other business risks that tend to ward off very cautious investors. As an investor, it is unsettling to interview a startup manager and find it is a one-man shop, based in a home office, and that he is responsible for trading, complying with regulations, filing taxes, legal matters, and every other aspect of running a hedge fund. Investors have to wonder, does the manager have enough savings to support the fund if it endures a few bad quarters? How will he respond when the day-to-day operations grow too time-consuming while also managing the strategy? Will this fund be around in five years? What about five months?

Beyond the business risks of investing in a startup, investors then have to worry about how a startup will perform. Startups must compete with top-quartile hedge funds and face a number of disadvantages. In the early years, these funds must make investment decisions without the benefit of having access to all the latest research, data, and technology that top hedge funds possess. Top hedge funds often attend industry conferences, buy research on relevant markets, and travel around the world in search of trading opportunities. Will a startup be able overcome these barriers to entry and notch returns consistent with their larger peers? Another concern for investors is that the fee structure often incentivizes startups to take extraordinary risks. Startups often attract investors by offering lower management and performance fees. Of course, lower fees are good for limited partners, but some startups wander into unfamiliar territory in pursuit of outsized returns or establish highly leveraged positions in order to juice returns and generate big performance fees. In order to guard against this, investors often adopt strict controls on startups and monitor the strategy very closely, questioning even slight deviations from the hedge fund's stated investment strategy. In light of these risks, many investors prefer to see a multi-year track record of consistent, stable returns before committing capital to the manager.

Hedge fund launches are often very different depending on the manager. I am constantly approached by startups looking for fundraising help for their fund that only has $100,000 in seed capital, operates out of the manager's garage, and is ran by a single trader with little-to-no experience in the industry. On the other hand, there are a number of hedge funds that are launched every year by professionals who have worked for years at a trading desk at an investment bank or even as a portfolio manager to a top hedge fund. These funds are often viewed favorably by investors because they have at least some form of track record in their strategy. Additionally, these more experienced startup managers can usually attract seed investments from institutional investors, former clients or industry colleagues. This seed capital often makes it easier for additional investors to climb aboard because it allays any fears that they are "the first ones on the beach," and the fact that others have evaluated the fund and committed capital implies a level of investor confidence in the strategy and management team. Brand-new managers with limited trading experience, no seed capital outside the manager's own contribution, and little-to-no track record have a much harder time attracting capital than their more seasoned startup peers. It often takes a year or more of managing the strategy to convince a couple of investors to invest in the startup, so startups should be prepared for months and even years of low fee revenue and tough sales to cautious investors.

While it is easy to dismiss startup managers outright because they have limited experience and a low AUM, I've heard a number of successful managers talk about their early years trading part-time or working from home. For many investors, though, the idea of entrusting even $100,000 to a startup is daunting. Investors want to know that their managers are 100 percent devoted to successfully managing their capital. Wary and prudent investors often require garage funds to go through a rigorous and exhaustive screening process involving multiple interviews, on-site visits, detailed explanations of the strategy, and even personality tests. All of these precautions are aimed to mitigate the risks of investing in a startup. In the end, the startup phase is a form of natural selection: the funds that perform well and attract capital survive and the funds that cannot sway investors for whatever reasons ultimately close shop and move on.

Case Study

A couple of years ago, our firm was in early discussions with an individual who had recently left his portfolio management position at a top-quartile, multibillion-dollar hedge fund. He had stayed in touch with us and attended our events over the years and now that he was striking out on his own, he called on us for assistance raising capital for his next venture: a hedge fund startup.

He had a leg up on many startup managers in that he could turn to his affluent former colleagues and industry friends, as well as former investors. We rarely represent emerging managers because of the associated risks and the difficulty in raising capital from our particular investor network, but we took a long look at this fund for a number of reasons.

First, the fund manager was not a startup in the traditional sense; he spent years successfully managing outside capital at a well-known hedge fund firm. Unlike many new funds, he had a proven track record that he could show to skeptical investors. Second, he knew what it took to run a hedge fund; in our conversations it became clear that he was familiar with the operational aspects of managing a hedge fund. Many successful institutional portfolio managers focus primarily on performance and prefer to stay out of the back office operations. This becomes an issue when the manager launches a startup and all those operational challenges and responsibilities come front and center. It is important to us, and to any investors evaluating the fund, that the manager has a clear business plan and the structure in place to manage money, issue performance reports, comply with laws and regulations, and all of the other challenges. Relatedly, this startup manager already had a team of professionals on board and only a couple positions were still in the process of being permanently filled.

This manager's situation was a very different one than that of many startups that contact us. Yet this manager still faced an uphill battle to raise capital because there were some regulatory concerns involving his former employer. Fairly or unfairly, the fund manager was associated with that well-known hedge fund's problems and some investors likely took a pass for this reason alone. In this way, experience and track record is a double-edged sword: if you rely too heavily on your past hedge fund experience, you will be judged by the reputation of that firm, even if the questionable actions were taken by others and even after you left the firm. So, it can be an advantage to start from scratch. There are, of course, institutional barriers to entry for those who do not have a well-developed track record, but they also come with less baggage than a hedge fund manager departing a top firm.

Emerging Hedge Fund Managers ($10M to $300M)

Emerging hedge fund managers are those hedge funds that rise out of the initial startup phase by proving they can manage capital for outside investors. The challenge for these hedge funds is often retaining their early investors while growing the capital base through new investors. A startup will have attracted money primarily from family, friends, colleagues, and a few other investors; emerging managers, on the other hand, must broaden that net to new capital sources and institutional investors if the fund hopes to continue its growth. At the emerging manager level, new challenges arise as investors demand the same level of service, attention, and quality offered by other established hedge-fund peers. No longer can a hedge fund use its size and startup nature to excuse a lack of processes, limited resources, subpar reporting, and communication.

So, we can see that the increased assets under management for emerging managers come with new responsibilities, challenges, and expectations. For these reasons, the emerging-manager phase is one of the more perilous ones in a hedge fund's lifecycle. How a manager adjusts to this stage may determine whether that hedge fund falls by the wayside or becomes a shooting star rising toward the upper echelons of the hedge fund industry.

In terms of raw number of fund vehicles, the majority of the industry is made up of startups and emerging managers, but the larger titans of the industry really have the lion's share of the investible assets. This is a frustrating situation for many hedge fund managers, as investors want to see a higher AUM, of say $100M, $500M, or $1B, sometimes before investing, yet the fund manager cannot often reach those levels without attracting significant investor interest. Fund managers have to find ways of overcoming this capital-raising challenge in order to survive and have a chance at reaching the next level.

Hedge Fund Shooting Stars ($300M to $1B)

Shooting-star hedge fund managers are an important subsection of the hedge fund industry. In conducting interviews for my last book, I often heard family offices refer to managers in the $300M to $1B range as "the sweet spot." By this, they mean that rising shooting star managers are not too small and not too massive. As I previously alluded to, investors are often wary of a startup because they have such a short track record from which the investor can forecast future performance and evaluate the quality of the hedge fund. There is also the fact that start-ups have a small pool of only $1M to $10M, which may add significant risk to investors. Additionally, many startups try to grow quickly by executing risky, highly leveraged trading strategies that, when successful, produce eye-popping returns (and terrific performance fees for the GP) but, when unsuccessful, can lead to rapid severe losses for the portfolio. Investors often prefer to see the manager perform over a couple of years before allocating capital to a new fund.

On the other hand, you have the hedge fund titans managing billions of dollars in assets under management. Some investors are hesitant to invest in these hedge funds for a number of reasons including: concerns that a small investor will be neglected, fear that the fund will play it safe with weak performance but low risk to keep collecting fees, and that performance may suffer as the hedge fund grows too large and may exceed a strategy's capacity. It might surprise readers to learn that the biggest hedge funds routinely refuse interested investors for various reasons, rejecting tens of millions of dollars in capital and turning investors toward smaller hedge funds. More and more investors are telling managers that they do not want to fight to claim a slot in a hedge fund titan and then surrender to above-average fees, poor terms, and infrequent attention when there are shooting star-type established managers producing similar returns.

A number of investors I have spoken with see shooting-star managers as the sweet spot because the hedge fund manager is still driven to produce big returns, but not so hungry that they experiment with risky strategies or leverage trying to juice returns. I asked Edward Stavetski, a hedge fund investing expert who literally wrote the book on evaluating and managing hedge fund managers (*Managing Hedge Fund Managers: Quantitative and Qualitative Performance Measures),* whether large investors necessarily invest in the biggest hedge funds. While institutional investors are perceived to favor larger funds in the neighborhood of $1 billion or more in assets under management, Stavetski brings up some interesting points in favor of smaller funds. "One of the things we often look at is size, too. Our preference is always for small-size asset managers. People think that well, there is risk in them. I tell you that there is as much risk in a $1-billion manager as there is a $100-million manager because as they are looking for performance, they have got to take bigger risks to grow a $1 billion than a $100-million manager does." He continues, saying that $200 to $300 million in AUM is the "sweet spot" and that "at a certain level, they stop working on performance and start working on the management fee." This opinion illustrates an ongoing debate in the industry on the ideal hedge fund size.

Shooting stars with more than $300 million and less than $1 billion in AUM occupy a unique position in the hedge fund industry, one that is often viewed more favorably in recent years in comparison to startups, emerging managers, and titans. Shooting-star managers have substantial financial resources to invest in all of the following areas: competitive employee compensation; strong operational processes; the institutionalizing of legal, compliance, and accounting areas; the latest research and analysis; and most tools and technologies that are available to top-flight hedge funds and investment firms. These are not garage funds, but rather these firms are sophisticated trading operations, often with multiple offices around the globe that house dozens of employees.

From a performance standpoint, a shooting-star manager is often more attractive to investors than a startup because the former has a multiyear track record that they can point to and show how they have performed during various investing cycles and scenarios. Startups often compensate for the lack of performance history by running simulations to illustrate how the strategy would perform in years prior to the fund's launch, but these simulations are significantly less compelling than a real, audited track record. Shooting stars and some emerging managers can run through their previous returns and explain how they invested, what circumstances contributed to the performance, and what they learned from past experiences. In my business, we are hesitant to represent clients that launched after the financial crisis and recession, primarily because that difficult trading environment provides an excellent case study in how the manager performs, manages risk, and preserves capital. Additionally, a new manager might be riding a temporary boom cycle and it is hard to know how the fund would fare in a tougher investing climate. We, and many investors, like to see how a hedge fund performs over multiple years, different scenarios, and through at least a few trials that test the strategy and the manager's abilities.

Shooting-star managers are rarely satisfied. By this, I mean that I have only met a few of these hedge-fund managers who are happy managing $500M and uninterested in growing the fund. Part of this attitude is motivated by a desire to collect greater fees, but these managers more often are driven by ambition and the need to prove that their strategy is successful and to cement their reputation in the industry. This partly explains the momentum associated with these funds; many investors understand that these shooting-star managers are driven and motivated to outperform in order to reach the next AUM tier. Many shooting-star managers describe a sort of invisible barrier that stands between their current fund size and where they want to be (some emerging funds see $1 billion as the ideal size, others set their sights much higher). These managers' drive to claim their seats at the top of the industry has largely benefitted investors, as these hedge funds seek to win ever-greater commitments by consistently producing alpha and satisfying their investors. As you will soon read, the billion-dollar club is an exclusive and exceptional group of hedge funds and there are important advantages and disadvantages associated with this level of assets under management.

To add an additional perspective to this chapter we interviewed Joseph Di Virgilio, CIO of Ardour Capital. We asked Joseph about what it takes to succeed as a hedge-fund manager and here was his response:

> In our industry, there are no guarantees. Typically, in-depth knowledge of a sector, and/or a specific sub-segment along with a track record demonstrating one's skill sets and innovation in creating a unique investment strategy with acceptable risk/reward ratios, are critical. In addition, one needs to be able to sell the idea to investors and this is especially hard. I know many highly skilled individuals with great track records that have been unable to launch new products because of their inability to find investors. The space is very crowded but there is always need for new ideas, these after all contribute to the evolution of our industry.

We have used the term shooting star in this section because these hedge funds are awarded high expectations by investors. These hedge funds are expected to rise to the billion-dollar club, riding a recent wave of exceptional performance, or after years of consistent steady returns. Many times, we see shooting stars burn out under the intense heat of high expectations, portfolio risk, and investor demands. For those who survive, however, there is a special distinction in joining the billion-dollar club and earning your seat as a hedge fund titan.

Hedge Fund Titans ($1B+)

The hedge fund industry went through a transformation in the boom and bust that ended with the financial crisis in 2007. In the fallout, a high number of hedge funds had to close shop as the industry faced a number of headwinds including limited liquidity, depressed valuations, and redemption requests by limited partners, all of which resulted in staggering losses to many portfolios. Many of the hedge funds that survived the rough seas of the financial crisis with reputation and performance intact have grown even larger in the last couple of years. Investors view these funds favorably because they weathered the worst-case scenario and protected their investors' capital. These larger, multibillion-dollar hedge funds continue to attract massive amounts of capital and are among the most sophisticated investment funds in the market.

In many ways, hedge fund titans demonstrate a self-fulfilling prophecy: Investors pay high fees because larger hedge funds are perceived to be less risky and to perform better than other asset classes and even their peers in the industry; these hedge funds, in turn, typically apply that revenue toward improving operations and risk management and investing in the business. Hedge fund firms with more than $1 billion in assets under management collect hefty fees from their clients, enabling the firm to grow more sophisticated in a number of ways including: obtaining high-quality investment research, opening new trading offices to identify opportunities around the globe, hire and compensate additional staff, and grow the business in many other ways. At the titan level, hedge funds are closer to institutional investment banks than a lone trader and can afford all the bells and whistles that Wall Street can offer. For example, at the conferences I speak at, I've noticed an uptick in representatives from billion-dollar hedge funds, whereas years ago investment bankers, Wall Street traders, and industry analysts largely dominated the investment conferences. Now, it seems that every major hedge fund sends a representative to the top conferences because it helps the management team keep abreast of the latest trends, research, and trading strategies. It is a sign of the times and how large these hedge funds have grown and how far the industry has advanced since the days of A.W. Jones. This growth and sophistication also leads to a common criticism of multibillion-dollar hedge funds: they may grow fat off the fees.

I have often heard of investors wary of investing in larger hedge funds because they suspect that, at a certain point, hedge fund managers lose the "fire in the belly" that drove performance in the early years. Instead, some large hedge funds seem to play it safe, taking on less risk and producing moderate, uninspiring performance and collecting substantial management fees on the huge pool of assets under management. At the $100M to $500M level, a 1.5 to 2 percent management fee is seen as a reliable revenue stream used to cover basic costs like office space, payroll, and business expenses. For some hedge fund titans who manage several billion dollars, that 2 percent fee brings in millions of dollars every year no matter how the fund performs. Of course, these hedge funds have incentive to perform well because investors can easily move their money in pursuit of better returns, but there is less incentive to produce huge returns if it entails greater risk. If those investments lead to losses then there are no performance fees and less management fees as investors will likely flee the fund. So, investors are increasingly responding to this potential for titans to relax by pushing for better terms and fees and greater liquidity so they can easily transfer their capital if the manager is underachieving.

To download several videos related to the focus of this chapter and to watch over 125 total video modules and expert audio interviews, please activate your free account here: http://HedgeFundGroup.org/Access.

Conclusion

This chapter clearly shows that there are advantages and disadvantages among startups, emerging managers, shooting stars, and titans. Regardless, there are exceptions to every hedge fund stereotype and a titan fund can collapse while a startup can beat the market. A fund's size can determine how the market (read: investors) perceives the fund's ability to generate returns, along with other factors discussed in this chapter, such as research capability and business risks. But a fund's size *does not* necessarily determine how that fund will actually perform, it is only one consideration for investors in the due diligence and evaluation process.

Test Yourself

Answer the following questions.

1. True or False: Hedge funds almost never start by raising capital from family and friends.
2. True or False: Many barriers of entry exist to new start-up hedge funds.
3. Hedge fund titans are:
   A. Firms with more than $1 billion in assets under management.
   B. Firms with more than 10 percent control of a particular market sector.
   C. A hedge fund allocating more than $500 million in capital to portfolio companies on an annual basis.
   D. A firm with less than $1 billion in assets under management.
4. True or False: Emerging hedge funds are generally seen as less risky than start-up hedge funds.
5. One reason to invest in a titan hedge fund is:
   A. Titan hedge funds have survived rough financial periods and are very experienced compared to new funds.
   B. Titan hedge funds may have trouble retaining top talent due to the allure of starting a spin-off fund.
   C. Titan hedge funds have incentive to take less risk because of the huge management fees they collect from investors.
   D. Titan hedge funds typically charge higher performance and management fees than smaller hedge funds.
6. Which hedge fund is typically perceived to have the most risk involved?
   A. Titan hedge fund
   B. Start-up hedge fund
   C. Emerging hedge fund
   D. Shooting-star hedge fund

Answers can be found in Appendix B.

CHAPTER 3

Hedge Fund Investors

Businessweek published an updated look at the United States' accredited-investor population written by Scott Shane, the A. Malachi Mixon III Professor of Entrepreneurial Studies at Case Western Reserve University. It revealed there are "5 million to 7.2 million American adults who were accredited investors in 2008." Beyond the United States, there are millions more high-net-worth and institutional investors who are capable and willing to allocate to hedge funds and other alternative investments. The Family Offices Group association estimates that the family office investor group alone is estimated to manage more than $1 trillion in capital under management. There is an incredible pool of capital for hedge funds when you take into account the surge in sovereign wealth funds, corporate and public pensions, foundations, ever-growing university endowments, and other institutional investors that actively invest.

It was not until the mid-1990s that hedge funds started to be seriously considered by mainstream institutional investors and some high-net-worth (HNW) investors. Currently, most institutional investors have an allocation to hedge funds within their overall portfolio, and assets under management in the industry have never been higher.

I have been working with hedge fund investors for 10+ years and our team now employs 10 professionals who do nothing but research hedge fund investors such as pension funds, endowments, foundations, wealth management firms, and family offices. We will leverage this data and experience to provide you with an overview of the hedge fund investor space in this chapter.

Who Invests in Hedge Funds?

The investor table (see Table 3.1) is a convenient and practical way to look at the hedge fund investor groups. These estimates are based on our team's internal research and informed by my own experience

> **DEFINITION:**
> **Foundations**
>
> A foundation is a nonprofit organization that is dedicated to donating funds to a cause or sector of its choice. A foundation is often a vehicle to manage the wealth of an individual or family and its management team may invest in hedge funds and other asset classes in order to grow the foundation's assets under management and ensure the foundation's long-term viability for continued charitable activities and giving.

Table 3.1 Overview of the Hedge Fund Investor Universe: Key Sources of Capital for Hedge Funds

	Average Investment Size	Level of Sophistication	Inv. Team Size	Number of HF Investments	Uses Investment Consultant	Number of Investors Globally
High Net Worth	$250,000	Low	0	2	No	10 Million
Wealth Management	$500,000	Medium	2	4	No	100,000
Family Offices	$ 3M	Medium	2	7	Sometimes	15,000
Foundations	$ 10M	Medium–High	4	12	Yes	10,000
Pension Funds	$ 50M	High	12	15	Yes	4,000
Endowments	$ 50M	High	5	15	Yes	3,500
Insurance Plans	$ 50M	High	12	15	Yes	1,000
Sovereign Wealth Funds	$ 75M	High	25	25	Yes	65

visiting investors around the world and consulting with institutional investors every day.

I have met largely unsophisticated and mediocrely managed pension funds as well as high-net-worth individuals who were advanced and brilliant enough that they could easily run their own hedge funds with great success. The point is that there are exceptions to every general category, but Table 3.1 is a valuable tool that we use to segment the general investor categories. For the more visually inclined, you can also see in Figure 3.1. a pyramid representation of hedge fund investors.

The top of the pyramid ($1 billion AUM funds) represents large institutional investors. This investor group includes pensions, endowments, sovereign wealth funds, and other massive allocators. Managers controlling over $1 billion in AUM typically draw on a smaller number of investors who make very large capital commitments. In the next tier (the $100M to $1B AUM funds), investors are still largely institutional investors and money management firms, but the commitments are often smaller and the funds draw from a wide pool of investors to meet capital raising targets. The third tier ($10M to $100M funds) is comprised of few institutional investors, hedge fund seeders, funds of hedge funds, and high-net-worth individuals such as the managers' friends and family. At the bottom of the pyramid (the $100,000 to $10 million AUM managers), hedge fund managers seek capital from sources far and wide. Without a long track record and few committed investors, startups and small funds have

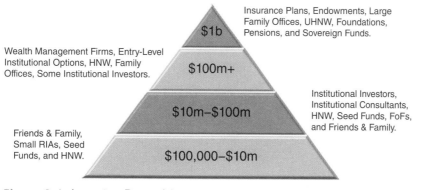

Insurance Plans, Endowments, Large Family Offices, UHNW, Foundations, Pensions, and Sovereign Funds.

$1b

Wealth Management Firms, Entry-Level Institutional Options, HNW, Family Offices, Some Institutional Investors.

$100m+

Institutional Investors, Institutional Consultants, HNW, Seed Funds, FoFs, and Friends & Family.

$10m–$100m

Friends & Family, Small RIAs, Seed Funds, and HNW.

$100,000–$10m

Figure 3.1 Investor Pyramid

a tough time raising capital and look for any seed investors or emerging manager specialists to take a flier on a new fund. This segment forms the widest section of the pyramid because its potential investor base is so wide. At the top of the pyramid, billion-dollar fund managers are often turning investors away (especially smaller investors), but at the bottom of the pyramid, new managers look to any potential investor and will approach hundreds (if not thousands) of potential LPs before securing a few small capital commitments.

Due to near-constant travel around the world to meet with hedge fund investors, I have developed extensive knowledge and research of where investors are based. I had my team compile this data to create the global map in Figure 3.2 of hedge fund investors.

Many hedge fund investors are based in Western Europe, major U.S. cities, and in second tier but growing centers of financial influence, such as Australia, Brazil, Canada, Middle East, and increasingly Asia. However, over the next 10 years, I expect that hedge fund investors will be located more and more in countries such as Turkey, Indonesia, and Nigeria as their middle- and upper-class populations expand and hedge funds look to new markets for investors. In many countries the laws surrounding hedge fund investments are starting to loosen up. For example, just a couple of years ago in Brazil a law passed allowing pension funds to invest in hedge fund managers based outside of Brazil.

Figure 3.2 is a map showing where single- and multi-family offices are based around the world. You can see here that while more family offices are clumped in locations such as Hong Kong and Zurich, the industry is globally diversified. Family offices are being started

DEFINITION:
High Net Worth

While the legal definition in each country is different, high-net-worth individuals are normally regarded as having investable assets in excess of $1 million. For hedge funds and private equity, high-net-worth individuals are considered viable investors if they can comfortably commit allocations of at least $1 million to a single fund; otherwise, alternative investments are usually best left to the ultra-affluent with more capital to invest and spread across a diversified portfolio.

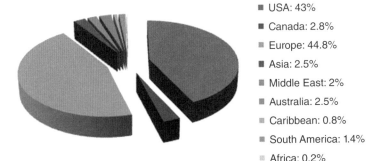

- USA: 43%
- Canada: 2.8%
- Europe: 44.8%
- Asia: 2.5%
- Middle East: 2%
- Australia: 2.5%
- Caribbean: 0.8%
- South America: 1.4%
- Africa: 0.2%

Figure 3.2 Family Offices Globally Map
Source: Family Offices Group

daily by the ultra-wealthy and wealth managers who serve that segment of the market. This is making family offices into the fastest growing investor segment for hedge funds. If you are looking for family office data and a free report please see our website: http:// FamilyOffices.com.

If you would like to learn more about family offices please read my bestselling book *The Family Office Book: Investing Capital for the Ultra-Affluent.* Two chapters are available at FamilyOfficesGroup.com/ Family-Office-Book.

Studies have shown that institutional investors prefer to invest in strategies that they can understand and easily comprehend the step-by-step investment process. This may seem like a reasonable expectation to those outside of the industry, but it is critical that hedge fund managers remember to explain their strategy with great detail and transparency in a way that investors can understand. Most hedge funds managers who claim to use a black box, a secret algorithm that nobody can understand, or a mostly gut-based trading mentality, do not typically succeed in raising enough capital to stay in business.

The Hedge Fund Investor Due-Diligence Process

Hedge fund investors typically take 10 to 20 months to conduct research on a hedge fund and make an investment. Sometimes this timeframe can be as short as three months but oftentimes it takes three to five years of relationship building and monitoring before the investor places capital with a manager.

1 Pager PDF   PowerPoint   Phone Call Review   Due Diligence Questionnaire Completed   On-Site Visit   CIO or Investment Committee Analysis

Figure 3.3 Fund Manager Selection

Typically investors move through the process depicted in Figure 3.3 while conducting due diligence on hedge fund managers.

All investors, except for high-net-worth individuals and the smallest of wealth management firms, use a thorough due diligence questionnaire that hedge fund managers must complete. Doing so allows investors to receive answers to many of their questions in writing before visiting the fund manager in person or making an investment. An example of what such a due diligence questionnaire may look like can be found at http://HedgeFundGroup.org/visual-guide.

Hedge Fund Investor FAQs

Hedge funds can be extremely complicated entities and many financial experts still lack a complete understanding of them. Here are some frequently asked questions I have encountered during my time in the industry.

1. **Do hedge fund investors want or demand *separately managed accounts* often?** Many investors who place over $20M with a fund manager will request a managed account, but it does involve some extra costs and oversight so this is not always done. To justify the extra cost you often need someone who monitors the account and makes use of the added transparency and control that is offered through such a structure, and that is not always possible.

2. **Do certain investors get fee breaks?** The short answer is yes. Early-stage investors may get to invest through a different share class, in return for equity in the hedge fund business itself, or a break in fees as long as they invest a certain minimum level of capital. As a hedge fund matures and grows up to $100M and $300M in size the amount of capital needed to get a break in fees typically rises. Hedge fund managers know that their capital raising life will be easier once they reach critical

hurdle assets under management levels, such as $100M, $300M, and $1B in assets under management (AUM), and that is why these fee breaks are provided. It is important to note, however, that funds be aware of most-favored-nations regulations and contract notes that may force them to provide their lowest fee investment option to some institutional investors. I recently met with a $15B+ hedge fund that has never given a single fee break to anyone since day one; they pride themselves on not cheapening their brand for any reason and have done so since they were founded over 10 years ago.

3. **Why does it take so long for investors to complete their due diligence on a hedge fund?** Since there are 20,000 hedge funds in the industry, it takes a large team a lot of time to make sure that they are not a fraud, that their strategy is unique and compelling, that the team is adequately incentivized to stay together for the long term, and that any single hedge fund stands up well when compared to the competition. One example of this is our own team, which recently undertook an exercise to identify three fund managers for family office investors. The process took us 14 months to find just three funds that we felt strongly about and that met our investment criteria.

4. **I have heard that there have been rampant cases of fraudulent hedge funds recently; is that true?** That is a myth. While only .5 percent of the industry is made up of dishonest or fraudulent hedge funds, those are the ones making the headlines that keep regulators up at night. This makes investors want to get to know a hedge fund manager over a long period of time to make sure they are consistent and can be trusted. The due diligence process is important and will always become more robust as additional best practices are adopted to avoid more unstable teams, frauds, and underperformers.

5. **Which investor types are investing the most new money into hedge funds right now?** Right now my team is seeing an expansion in the amount of capital being allocated to hedge funds within major institutional investors in pension funds, insurance plans, and sovereign wealth funds globally. This is being fueled by the difficulty that pension funds have meeting their capital obligations, combined with the challenge of finding yield and steady returns in a volatile marketplace. We are also seeing a slow global formalization of the family office concept, and these ultra-wealthy families that are being represented are dipping their toes into the hedge fund investment pool regardless of their geographical location. For example, I just recently had an hour-long conference call with an ultra-wealthy family client in Hong Kong who is trying to invest in a number of hedge funds this year or next. However, they have never done so before and desire guidance through the due diligence process to meet that goal.

6. **How can small hedge fund managers based in locations such as Europe or Brazil develop a global investor base?** The best strategy would be to identify just one or two target locations globally and to develop investor bases in those areas first. For example, I know of a Brazilian hedge fund manager who is only raising capital from a few select cities in the United States and Buenos Aires. Another example is my own firm: We work with investors globally but we have identified Brazil and Singapore as the two countries we spend the most energy on. The countries you choose should be based on what type of investors you are targeting; your ability to work with investors in that area due to current relationships, access to their contact details, and so on; and your ability to frequently have a team member in those locations to meet with the investors often. We discuss the capital-raising process more in the following chapter.

Any investor-relations professional will tell you that the key to raising capital is establishing and maintaining long-term relationships and understanding each investor's unique situation. Hopefully, this chapter has laid some of the initial groundwork for developing your understanding of hedge fund investors and moved you a step closer to meeting your capital-raising goals.

> ▶ To download several videos related to the focus of this chapter and to watch over 125 total video modules and expert audio interviews, please activate your free account here: http://HedgeFundGroup.org/Access.

Test Yourself

Answer the following questions.

1. Which investor typically does *not* have a high level of sophistication?
   A. Sovereign wealth funds
   B. Endowments
   C. Pension funds
   D. Non-Accredited Individual Investors
2. True or False: Ultra-high-net-worth individuals normally have upward of $30 million in assets.
3. True or False: A family office is an office that provides investing advice and portfolio management for high-net-worth individuals, businesses, and families.
4. Which investor typically does *not* have an investment team of 10 or larger?
   A. Pension funds
   B. Large endowments
   C. Small single family offices
   D. Sovereign wealth funds
5. True or False: No U.S. pension fund can invest in hedge funds.

Answers can be found in Appendix B.

CHAPTER 4

Hedge Fund Capital Raising

Hedge fund marketing and capital raising is a critical component of running a hedge fund but one often ignored by new fund managers who typically have backgrounds in trading, risk management, or portfolio management. This is partially why there are so many hedge funds started that close down because they never pass that $10M, $50M, or $100M in assets under management (AUM) level that they set out to reach. Raising capital is just as important as the investing component of running a hedge fund, since the trading cannot be done without capital. While that seems overly simplified and obvious, my experience would not suggest that it is so common to have built-in capital-raising abilities within a hedge fund team.

As you read in Chapter 3 about hedge fund investors, it can often take 10 to 20 months of research and consideration before an investor puts capital to work within a hedge fund they have learned about. This—combined with heavy regulation, licensing, and lack of experienced professionals in the area—makes it challenging for a hedge fund to execute capital-raising plans in any consistently successful fashion.

In my previous book on hedge funds, *The Hedge Fund Book: A Training Manual for Professionals and Capital-Raising Executives,* I provided some common mistakes and capital-raising best practices that funds can adopt and employ while working with investors.

In this chapter, I provide a visual guide to where a capital raiser should be spending time, several videos that provide you with proven capital-raising work models, and case studies of successful capital-raising campaigns and teams so you can see, step-by-step, how you can setup a capital-raising system that brings in new investors daily.

Note: Please re-read the disclosure regarding compliance at the beginning of this book. The state or country in which you reside, the type of fund, and the time at which you read this book are just a few of the factors that may affect which strategies you can use and to what degree. Please consult a compliance attorney or officer before executing these plans so your hard work is not wasted.

Daily Process

Whether you have one capital raiser or a team of 30, it is important that you meet with potential investors face-to-face more often than does your competition. The best way to ensure that your team raises more capital than the competition is to identify the top three most valuable activities and schedule those first every day. If you have a large team of 15 to 20 investor-relations professionals, like one $19B hedge fund I met with recently, then those activities will vary widely based on each person's role on the team. If you are like most hedge funds and have one or two people focusing on capital raising, then probably the most valuable activities will include meeting with potential investors, setting up meetings with potential investors, and following up via email and phone with all of the past investors you have met with to date. Many people get caught in a circle of leaving voicemails and sending emails that never get responded to, when they should be getting out and sitting face-to-face with as many qualified potential investors as possible.

In my own capital-raising efforts, I schedule 90 minutes daily for following up with past investors I have met with, and I leverage my team to help me schedule more investor meetings every week. In today's marketplace if you rely on raising capital via phone and email alone you will raise little to no capital.

Hedge Fund Warfare

In the long evolution of warfare, great military leaders did not debate whether to use either a naval vessel or a land unit, or an airplane versus a submarine. Instead, it is about the strategic use of as many assets as possible to move you toward your end goal. Similarly, in the case of raising capital, this way of strategically using all of your assets is the key to winning the attention of the limited number of hedge fund investors that exist so that your hedge fund raises enough capital to thrive.

You need every strategic asset available to win the capital-raising game. Many fund managers feel they are too busy to focus on raising capital; they spend three to five hours a week in this area and then show up to our full-day workshops frustrated with the whole process. As you read this chapter, try to avoid using excuses that you are "too busy" or "not experienced in that area" because those are the same reasons why none of your competition is using these strategies. If you don't want average results, you can't do what the average hedge fund manager does.

Here are 10 tools that you should be using to raise capital, assuming you employ them in a compliance-approved fashion:

1. In-person meetings.
2. Direct mail follow-up with information on your offering after you meet in person.

3. Email and phone follow up.
4. A Customer Relationship Management (CRM) system to store investor relationship details and preferences.
5. Public speaking and/or your own training seminars or workshops.
6. Video and audio materials that can be sent to potential or current investors to help build the relationship.
7. A monthly newsletter that adds value and doesn't just provide your investment view or pitch your offering.
8. Writing a blog, a column, guest articles, or publishing your own book.
9. Identifying strategic partners and connectors who can introduce you consistently to potential investors. Find these gatekeepers in your local market, or for your targeted investor type.
10. Association memberships and leadership.

You may already be employing four or five of these strategies but most hedge funds I meet are not consistently applying many of these approaches to developing investor relationships. If you compromise on what you use to attract investors you will also compromise your level of capital raised.

If you are looking for more tools and strategies please check out our webinar and workshops series on http://www.CapitalRaising.com, where you can also download a report on "The Top 7 Capital Raising Mistakes."

The 1 Percent Rule

Everyone knows there is a lot of life in the ocean, but what is not readily apparent is that a very small percentage of the ocean contains over 98 percent of its living organisms. The same goes for hedge funds—the top few funds attract the lion's share of investors at each level of assets under management. What you want to do is create a nutrient-rich environment in which you raise capital for your fund. This means building a strong team, creating a compelling competitive advantage, surveying the competition to make sure your offering is unique, developing a brand within your niche investor base or local investor community, and meeting with each potential investor you are targeting at least five to seven times. In capital raising the Holy Grail is reaching the point where more people know you than you know them. In the previous discussion on Hedge Fund Warfare we provided some clues on how to make sure investors know you. This is not easy to accomplish but it does pay dividends and can be a strategic long-term advantage if you can establish yourself as the expert in your tightly defined niche investment strategy.

Hedge Fund Investor Avatar Focus

It is critical to use a sophisticated CRM system to track your investor leads and follow up with them in a professional manner. As you can see in Figure 4.1, we use a CRM in our own business that allows us to

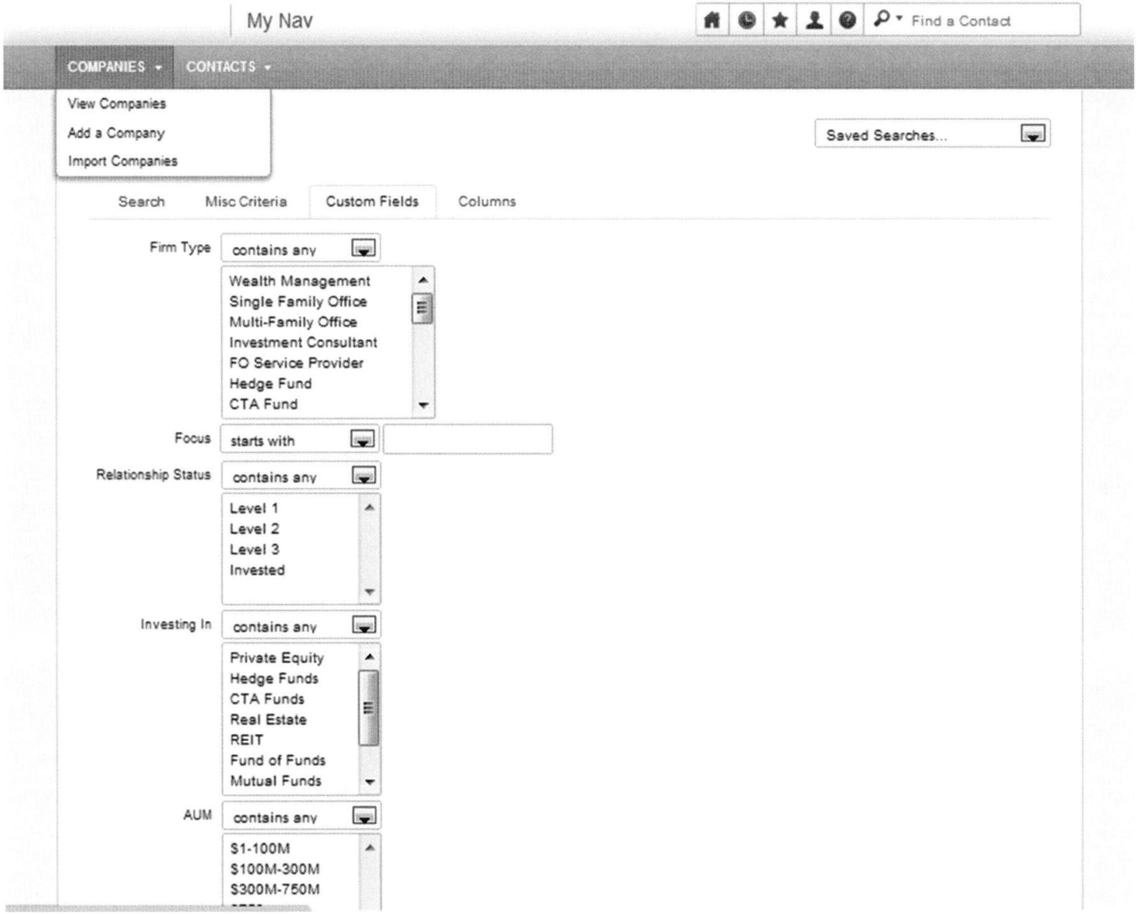

Figure 4.1 A Look at Our CRM

track investors, clients, and industry contacts. You can see from the screenshot that we can sort by various factors and obtain a resulting set of data with name, email, address, and more. This particular search was related to family offices in a particular region. Many hedge funds will use a CRM to help maintain contact with potential and current investors, then when their investor relations team or portfolio managers are on the road, they can set up a road show to update these investors.

One powerful way to grow your CRM and reach more potential investors is to use a database of investors. Our team has spent hundreds of hours researching LPs and compiling our database of investors to make the capital raising process more efficient; you can order the Family Office Database at http://FamilyOffices.com.

Capital-Raising Channels

Once you have more than one capital raiser on the team you will face decisions on how to split up their energy among the investor base. I believe it is first most fruitful to break apart a small team of two-to-four professionals by investor channel type, such as retail versus institutional or family office versus pension fund, and so on. The other way to organize a team is by geography, such as the United States west coast and east coast, or Europe, Asia, North America, and so on. Ideally your team will eventually be large enough to do both, but most funds don't make it to that point. The benefit of having an investor channel focus is that the individual or team assigned to that area can quickly learn lessons on how the investor likes to be approached, what conferences they frequent, and what their top objections or hot button issues are. The benefits of geographical focus include culture navigation and ease of travel, so it is practical to meet with investors several times a year.

Emulation before Innovation

It is critical for fund managers to study their competition and emulate their best practices before attempting to innovate. There is no need to re-create the wheel on how back-office work, or fund formation, is done. Investors want to see that 95 percent of your fund is boring—it looks like a collection of industry best practices that are reliable, proven, and commonly seen by the investor. However, there has to be 5 percent of the offering that leaps out at the investor, hits them between the eyes, creates a sense of scarcity, and demonstrates that genuine value is being created at this hedge fund. If you try to innovate before you emulate you will waste your time, appear arrogant or uninformed, and burn investor bridges before they are even fully built.

Placement Agents and Third-Party Marketers

Third-party capital-raising teams attempt to raise capital for hedge fund managers, often for several different funds at the same time. The business model is over 30 years old and serves an important role in reaching global investors, or niche types of investors such as family offices. Since many fund managers get into the business to execute their investment plans and not because they are strong capital raisers, third-party marketers play an important role in helping grow a fund's assets under management. In many cases funds would have to be closed if it wasn't for the help of a third-party marketer.

Third-party marketing firm teams range in size from one member to more than 30 professionals.

Examples and Case Studies

I have met with dozens of third-party marketers, worked for a third-party marketing firm, and operated my own so there are many pitfalls to avoid and lessons learned to share in this area. I have narrowed those down to five key takeaways for anyone looking to hire a third-party marketer or work in the space:

1. Never pay large upfront retainers to get things started; however, I do believe in ongoing retainers to show commitment on both sides. I have heard horror stories of funds paying $50k to $200k upfront for marketing material help and an engagement fee and then nothing at all coming of that.
2. Avoid working with a firm that has a 3:1 or higher fund-manager-to-capital-raiser ratio. In other words, if you work with a single professional raising capital, they should probably have no more than three clients, and most of the time two clients should keep them very busy.
3. Avoid small third-party marketing shops with no track record. Yes, everyone has to start somewhere but you do not want to be their learning curve as they figure the process out. Ask for references, capital raised in the past three years, current clients, and so on.
4. Do your homework on how long it takes to raise capital; most third-party marketing relationships fall apart due to mismanaged expectations. Who will be going on the road shows? Who is managing the existing investor relationships after those come in? How long will it take to raise capital in this environment, or a worse economic environment, if that occurs? What happens if no capital is raised after 24 months of hard work?
5. Trust your gut while deciding whether to trust a third party or not; you will be working closely with this person and if they become hard to deal with, impatient, unprofessional, or rushed during the upfront-negotiation stage slow things down and make sure this is someone you want partnering with your brand. The same goes for third-party marketers; you hurt your own brand and reputation if you hitch your wagon to a team that rubs investors the wrong way or wastes their time.

In the past few years there has been a backlash by some institutional investors, such as pension funds and endowments, on the use of placement agents. Several widely reported scandals involving pay-to-play deals with placement agents contributed to the bad reputation that the placement-agent industry received. After many lawsuits, regulator-imposed penalties, bans, and lengthy court battles, the use of placement agents has been highly scrutinized by investors and investment funds. Still, placement agents endure as an important part of the capital-raising process, and the resurgence of this industry today suggests that these third parties serve an essential function in the capital-raising process. As any placement agent can tell you, the industry operates under a strict regulatory watch, and a representative's clean public record with the Financial Industry Regulatory Authority (FINRA) or a relevant regulator is more important than ever. The industry appears to have weathered the storm, and the placement agencies that survived have emerged with tighter compliance controls and a new appreciation for following the rules.

As one would expect given the thriving hedge fund industry in the last decade, the future of the third-party marketing industry is bright. Here are some of the drivers of its growth:

1. **Growing Global Wealth:** Many fund managers have little or no global investor relationships, and they often hire regional placement agents who have face-to-face relationships with investors in the region.
2. **Capital Raising Team Costs:** Increasing costs of identifying and retaining experienced capital raisers. Most experienced and proven capital raisers demand minimum salaries of $300,000 and total compensation of $500,000 to $1M+ each. This is a sizable investment for a small to mid-sized fund manager, and many funds on their way up to $1B in assets under management don't have as much free cash as they would like.
3. **Hedge Fund Industry Expansion:** There are more hedge funds now than ever before, and assets under management have reached record highs as well. Globally, hedge funds are being started more frequently in the Middle East, Africa, and Asia than at any other point in the history of the industry. Our team at the Hedge Fund Group (HFG) association has felt this momentum as well—our membership has grown from 75,000 to 100,000+ members within just 12 months—and we don't believe the industry is going to slow down any time soon. The more hedge funds are started, the more managers there will be who need help with their capital-raising campaigns.

Hedge Fund Marketing and Capital-Raising FAQs

The Hedge Fund Group receives emails and phone calls every week from traders and hedge funds asking for advice on marketing and raising capital. The following is a sampling of the three most common questions we have answered related to hedge fund capital raising.

1. **Our team has very limited resources. We have just three principals in the fund and nobody dedicated to raising capital. We have**

approached 10 third-party marketers that all refuse to work with us because of our two-year track record and having just $8M in assets under management. Since we can't afford to hire a full-time capital raiser, and third-party marketers won't work with us, what should we do to raise capital? Most third-party marketers want to represent $30M+ or $100M+ fund managers with three-plus-year track records. I would recommend not wasting more time trying to outsource this issue and instead find someone who believes in your strategy and offer them equity or a percentage of fees collected on capital they raise plus a small base salary of just $1k to $3k per month to show that you are committed to keeping them around and supporting them. There are many professionals out there looking to prove their capital-raising abilities. Unless you can add some strategic advisory board members or dedicate one of your existing principals to raising capital, I see this as your only viable option for getting the job done.

2. **What is the seed-capital marketplace like right now?** The number of seed-capital providers has halved since the 2008 financial collapse. Now it is more common to see seeding of funds at the $10M to $30M level instead of the $75M to $300M levels we saw before. More than ever, seeders are looking for investment strategies that they can understand where the competitive edge in the investment strategy comes from regardless of how great the returns appear to be. More due diligence is done now than before as well, so expect the seeding process to last for six to nine months or more.

3. **How many investors can one capital raiser target at any one point in time?** The type of investor you target will change the answer to this question but most capital raisers will be most effective while targeting 100 to 300 potential investors at any one point in time. I just met with one $30B+ alternative investment firm that attempts to cover 2,000 total investors. This fund has 20 total investor-relations professionals but only four client-facing professionals and the other 16 professionals acting in more of a support role. The four client-facing professionals are thus responsible for the bulk of the work in meeting with and communicating to 2,000 investors, and the only way this huge fund can cover that ground is with a big supporting team to help make sure that these four people get to every meeting and have the best chance at closing with committed capital to the fund. Most funds in the $30M to $500M size range that I have met with, however, have just one or two capital raisers and they are targeting around 300 investors at any one point in time. It is extremely difficult to have capital-raising success with only the part-time efforts of your fund managers, so for even very small funds I would say that you need at least one full-time professional managing your investor relations and meeting with prospective investors.

Conclusion

Many capital raisers are underappreciated by management, even to the point that some hedge funds go out of business due to lack of assets under management and under-capitalization. When you start a hedge fund you are starting a small business, and like every business at least 50 percent of the equation is making sure that you can bring in new customers or, in this case, investors to the table. To review the suggestions from this chapter you can increase your chances of success in raising capital by:

1. Employing all of the weapons of hedge fund capital-raising warfare.

2. Focusing on prioritizing and having the discipline to target your daily capital-raising activities.
3. Considering employing a third-party marketer or placement agent to help you gain access to certain investor classes or investors in specific geographical locations, such as the Middle East.
4. Setting up systems so your capital-raising processes manufacture investors.
5. Using a CRM to follow up with potential investors in an organized, consistent fashion that respects everyone's time and past conversations held.
6. Deciding on your investor avatar and focusing your capital-raising energy and marketing materials around that target group.

To download several videos related to the focus of this chapter and to watch over 125 total video modules and expert audio interviews, please activate your free account here: http://HedgeFundGroup.org/Access.

Test Yourself

Answer the following questions.

1. According to the author, the best way to ensure that your team raises more capital than the competition is to:
   A. Identify the top three most valuable activities and schedule those first every day.
   B. Issue press releases every month.
   C. Reach out to all your friends and family to solicit capital commitments.
   D. Require employees to work overtime and weekends.

2. True or False: Writing a blog, a column, guest articles, or publishing your own book are recommended ways to develop relationships with investors.

3. True or False: Third-party marketing for hedge funds is illegal in the United States.

4. Which of these is NOT a suggested capital-raising practice in this book?
   A. Developing a daily process
   B. Creating a Hedge Fund Investor Avatar
   C. Cold-calling
   D. Using multiple capital-raising channels

5. True or False: This Visual Guide recommends that it only takes one investor-relations professional to cover 2,000 investors at any one moment.

Answers can be found in Appendix B.

CHAPTER 5

Long/Short Equity Strategy

The long/short equity fund is one of the most well-known hedge fund strategies and has helped define the concept of a hedge fund. The long/short strategy is most well-known for a number of reasons. First, the long/short strategy was one of the first hedge fund strategies ever used. Alfred Winslow Jones, widely recognized as the father of hedge funds, launched his hedge fund using a combination of long positions and short positions, summed up with the long/short strategy moniker.

Alfred Winslow Jones, born September 9, 1900, is credited as the inventor of the modern hedge fund. As detailed in Sebastian Mallaby's *More Money than God*, Jones's story is anything but typical: He began his career working on a tramp steamer and then decided to join the Foreign Service. He spent the first half of the 1930s in the U.S. embassy in Berlin before travelling to Spain during the Spanish Civil War. Upon returning home to the States, Jones earned his doctorate degree in sociology from Columbia University and worked

for *Fortune* magazine—an important step toward his hedge fund career (Mallaby, 2010b).

As a contributor to *Fortune*, Jones began reporting on finance and investing, ultimately leading to his decision to launch his own investment company, A.W. Jones & Co., based on a revolutionary idea: long investments in equities expected to rise in market value paired with short investments in companies expected to do the opposite. Jones shorted equities perceived to be overvalued (and due for a fall) by borrowing the stock and immediately selling it with the intention of buying the same stock at a later date (when the price has hopefully declined), returning it to the lender and pocketing the difference in the market value of the stock. By adding the short component to his portfolio, Jones was able to hedge out risk to his long portfolio and reduce the fund's exposure to a general market decline. Additionally, in what are now hallmarks of hedge funds, Jones used leverage (borrowed money) to maximize his investment gains and he charged his

DO IT YOURSELF

Try this example. Wilson Capital Partners borrows 100 shares of Apple, Inc. from a willing lender at a share price of $700. The fund will immediately sell the shares to short the company. Now, Wilson Capital Partners has $70,000 and owes the lender 100 shares of Apple, Inc. by a predetermined date at the then-current market value for the shares. Over time, shares of Apple decline 10 percent and the new share price is $630. At this point, Wilson Capital Partners decides to lock in the gains by repurchasing the shares on the open market for a total of $63,000—(CMR per share) $630 x (number of borrowed shares) 100 = $63,000. When the shares are returned to the lender, Wilson Capital Partners has earned a gross profit of $7,000—the initial sale price of $70,000 minus the repurchase price of $63,000.

investors a performance fee (taking a percentage of the gains). Jones's innovations at his hedged fund laid the groundwork for the industry we see today and especially the long/short hedge fund strategy.

The core of the long/short equity strategy is a portfolio of investments that includes both long and short positions. A long position is when the investor holds a security that he expects will appreciate in value. A short position is when the investor borrows capital and takes the opposite bet: that a particular security will decline in value.

In practice, this strategy is more complex than simply betting that a stock will rise or fall in value. Rather, the hedge fund will analyze a number of securities on both a technical and a fundamental basis and determine whether the stock is undervalued or overvalued, or due for any shift in its market value.

Identifying the Opportunity

There are a number of strategies used by investors to generate a trading opportunity within a long/short equity construct. While some strategists use discretionary strategies to generate returns, others are more focused on statistical methodologies to capture alpha.

By measuring a fund's alpha an investor can measure a hedge fund's excess returns against a relevant benchmark such as the S&P 500. A hedge fund with negative alpha has trailed the comparative benchmark, and investors will view that unfavorably; a hedge fund producing positive alpha has outperformed the market.

Discretionary Strategies

A strategist might believe that a particular stock is trading below what the investor believes is its fair value, and therefore he anticipates a correction; or it could be that the stock is overpriced and he assumes the opposite, a reversion to a more accurate valuation. Discretionary trading uses a number of different techniques to determine the eventual price of a stock.

Long/short positions, which can be viewed as a spread of one stock divided by another, can reflect one stock being undervalued, one stock being overvalued, or a combination of both. In some cases, both stocks can be overvalued or undervalued, but, for example, an investor can also believe that both are undervalued and will revert to a mean, but one stock will outperform—this can also be the case if both stocks are overvalued.

Short positions are often used as a hedge against the long portfolio, so a manager may select a basket of equities that he expects to appreciate. Then, in order to offset his risk, he will select a number of stocks, often in the same industry as his long positions, that will likely fall in value over time. This basket-spread approach means that a manager is wagering on a relative value change between two baskets of similar stocks.

The manager will *short* the stocks in the short position, most often by borrowing the stock, selling it at current market value (CMV), then purchasing the same quantity of shares at a later date when the current market value has (hopefully) declined in order to return the shares to the lender. The difference between the initial sale price and the cost of the subsequent re-purchase of the shares is the profit (or loss) on the transaction. The maximum gain is limited to the floor of the share price ($0 per share), but the maximum loss is theoretically infinite, as the share price could rise infinitely before the shares can be repurchased and returned to the lender.

The stocks in a long/short portfolio may be selected for a variety of reasons. Most commonly, the hedge fund manager will evaluate stocks to determine the corporation's real value and compare that to how the stock is valued in the market. If there is a significant deviation between the current market value and the value that the hedge fund assigns to the stock, then the hedge fund manager will look to invest accordingly with the expectation that the stock will eventually move to a more realistic valuation.

The key to a long/short strategy is to evaluate the relative value of one stock compared to another. If a manager is correct that a stock is undervalued and it reverts back to a more realistic value, then the manager can still lose money if the short position increases in market value (a loss if the market value exceeds the initial sale price) more than the long position appreciates.

There are two leading thought processes employed when finding candidates for a long/short equity strategy. The first is that a manager finds an undervalued stock and would like to hedge that long exposure with an index, as the manager believes the stocks will outperform the index. The second is that a manager finds a pair of stocks, and believes that the ratio of one stock to another will move in a specific direction.

In both cases, the manager believes they can generate alpha in a market-neutral strategy while eliminating the beta of the benchmark. The theory behind a market-neutral trading strategy is one in which the standard deviations of returns are mitigated by the market-neutral position.

Performance

According to data from Hedge Fund Research, Inc. (2013) over the past 14 years the Sharpe ratio on long/short equity strategies is approximately 1.12 compared to a Sharpe ratio of a long-only strategy targeting the S&P 500 index. Long/short equity strategies have a 71 percent correlation to U.S. stocks but produce a return profile that is much higher, 12.75 percent compared to an annualized return of 8.93 percent. The standard deviations of the returns are 9.18 percent for long/short equity while they are much higher at 14.97 percent for U.S. equities (Altegris, n.d.).

The Sharpe ratio is a measure of the average annualized return divided by the standard deviation of the returns; it is an excellent tool to gauge the risk-adjusted returns of a hedge fund strategy. Any strategy that has a Sharpe ratio above 1, means that the returns that are generated are more efficient than the risk that is taken to produce those returns. When a Sharpe ratio is below 1, it means that the volatility of the returns are higher than the average returns, which means that the risks of producing those returns are greater than actual returns.

Quantitative Strategies

Nondiscretionary strategies are strategies that follow fixed rules and attempt to generate income from long/short equity trades based on statistical anomalies that exist within the equity markets. This type of relative-value trading does not depend on the overall direction of the broader markets and instead produces returns based on the relationship between two stocks.

The combination of long and short positions transacted by simultaneously purchasing a stock and shorting stock aims to benefit from the change in the ratio of two or more stocks. Stocks are not the only assets that can be used to generate returns using a pair methodology. Developing a sound pair-trading strategy generally involves looking for two or more assets that are highly correlated, such as stock in corporations that operate in the same business or industry.

Pair Strategies

Pair trades are attractive because one stock is considered fairly inexpensive relative to another stock that functions within the same industry. Pair strategies avoid a high beta to the broader market indexes, such as the S&P 500 index, given that the risk is a relative-value risk, uncorrelated to market direction. This type of trading strategy allows investors to diversify their portfolios by allocating capital to an uncorrelated market relative to stocks, bonds, and cash.

There are a few types of pair-trading strategies, including statistical mean reversion pair-trading strategies and discretionary pair-trading strategies. Both of these strategies are focused on finding robust relative value between two or more stocks.

Mean reversion pair-trading strategies examine the historical relationship between two assets that are highly correlated and have high relative co-integration. A high correlation means that the returns of two assets move in tandem with each other.

Pair-trading strategies that focus on mean reversion seek to benefit when highly correlated stocks experience a divergence in returns over the short term. Investors can back-test the relationship between two specific stocks within the same industry to determine if a specific standard deviation from a historical mean of their spread represents attractive levels to purchase one stock and simultaneously sell short another stock.

Risk management will need to be incorporated into a pair-trading strategy. Investors should understand that the ratio between two stocks could diverge beyond historical standard deviations, generating negative returns if an investor picks a bottom or top in a pair ratio.

Finding Pairs of Stocks

The first step in finding pairs of stocks to trade is to look for stocks that operate similar businesses. This could include any set of stocks, including retail, staples, utilities, technology, industrials, or financials.

One of the issues that can arise from pair trading is related to dividends. Investors need to understand that if they short sell a stock, they are liable for the dividend that is paid to investors that are long that stock. This concept should be incorporated into a strategy if the investor is planning to hold a pair over the dividend date.

An example of two stocks that fit a mean reversion pair methodology are Visa Inc. and MasterCard Inc. Both of these companies operate similar businesses and generally have highly correlated returns. The ratio of these companies' stock prices historically trade in a range, but when the ratio moves a specific standard deviation from a medium-term moving average of the ratio, a pair trade can be initiated to take advantage of the divergence.

A mean-reversion strategy, such as the one depicted in the graph in Figure 5.1 with MasterCard and Visa, would look to purchase Visa and short sell MasterCard when the ratio moved to 2 standard deviations below the 20-day moving average of the ratio. The strategy would take profit on the trade when the ratio moved back to the 20-day moving average of the ratio. The reverse would be true when the ratio moved to 2 standard deviations above the 20-day moving average. An investor would sell MasterCard and buy Visa at that point and look to take profit when the ratio reverted back to the 20-day moving average of the ratio.

The backbone of quantitative strategies is the ability to find as many pairs as possible or a basket of pairs in an effort to generate as many trading opportunities as possible. Finding pairs of stocks that are highly correlated, in which the ratio of one price to another moves beyond 2 or 3 standard deviations from its historical means, requires a sophisticated software program that can calculate the mean and standard deviation of the ratio between the returns and evaluate the profit and loss that comes from these two stocks once the ratio moves beyond a specific standard deviation.

How the Long/Short Strategy Works

We have already covered the general idea behind a long/short strategy, but in this section we will look at how this strategy is executed. A long/short hedge fund strategy is most simply explained as a strategy of buying undervalued stock, expecting the stock's market value to appreciate, and selling (shorting) overvalued stock, expecting the stock's market value to decline.

To execute this trade, a hedge fund manager must be competent in short selling, the practice of borrowing a security from a dealer and selling it, then buying the security at a later date to return the security to the lender. When short selling, the seller hopes that the shorted stock will decline in value after it is sold short. Then, when the seller has to return the stock to the dealer, he will be able to buy the stock at a discount. The short seller can then pocket the difference between the price at which the security was initially sold and the price that it is later repurchased.

Smart Investor Tip

Correlation is used to measure how closely securities move in line with one another with a correlation coefficient ranging between −1 and +1. Correlation measures the relationship between two securities and how closely or distantly they move in line with one another. Perfect positive correlation implies that one stock moves in perfect tandem with another stock in the same direction with exactly the same return profile. Negative correlation means that if one stock moves in either direction the stock that is negatively correlated will move in the opposite direction. If the correlation is 0, the movements of the securities are said to have no correlation, and the returns move in a random direction.

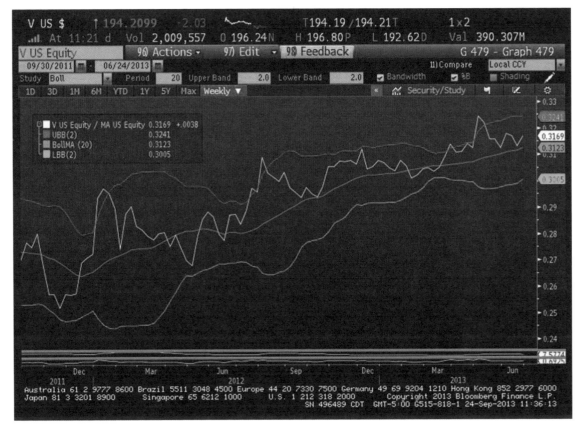

Figure 5.1 Visa versus MasterCard Mean Reversion
Source: © 2014 Bloomberg L.P. All rights reserved.

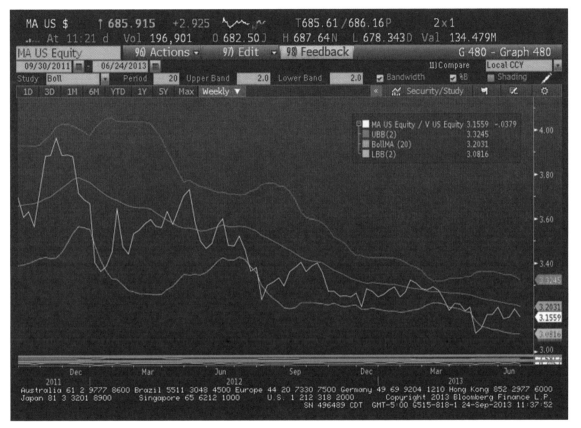

MA US $ ↑ 685.915 +2.925 T685.61 /686.16P 2 x 1
At 11:21 d Vol 196,901 O 682.50J H 687.64N L 678.343D Val 134.479M
MA US Equity 90) Actions ▾ 97) Edit ▾ 98) Feedback G 480 - Graph 480
09/30/2011 - 06/24/2013 11)Compare Local CCY
Study Boll Period 20 Upper Band 2.0 Lower Band 2.0 ☑ Bandwidth ☑ %B ☐ Shading
1D 3D 1M 6M YTD 1Y 5Y Max Weekly ▼ « Security/Study

MA US Equity / V US Equity 3.1559 -.0379
UBB(2) 3.3245
BollMA (20) 3.2031
LBB(2) 3.0816

Figure 5.1 *(Continued)*

Short selling involves a high degree of risk. An investor who buys a stock long has limited risk because the potential loss is known; a stock can only fall to zero so the loss is limited to money initially invested to buy the stock. In a short sale, the investor's risk is said to be unlimited because the potential loss is theoretically unlimited as the stock could rise infinitely past the market price at which the investor borrowed the stock. Since he still owes the stock that he borrowed, the trader must buy back the stock at what can be a substantial premium.

Additionally, since hedge funds are not restricted in their long/short ratio, they can assume greater potential short exposure by exceeding the 130:30 long/short ratio to which most traditional investment funds must adhere. Although there is a degree of risk in short selling, the ability to short is yet another tool for the hedge fund manager and can enable more sophisticated trading and risk management. Whereas a mutual fund or institutional investor may be limited in their ability to short a stock, a hedge fund is willing and able to profit from an overvalued stock or to hedge against long exposure in the event of a market downturn.

While there is certainly a high degree of potential risk in executing a long/short hedge fund strategy, the combination can also help manage risk exposure in the portfolio. As I just hinted, a hedge fund will often adopt a short position as a hedge against systemic risk to the portfolio. Since most hedge fund stock portfolios are long to varying degrees, it is advantageous for many hedge funds to adopt short positions to protect the portfolio against a downturn in an industry or the entire economy.

The Process of Short Selling

When a long/short manager short sells a stock they are required to borrow a stock from a prime broker. The prime broker either owns the stock or can borrow the stock themselves and in turn lend it to the hedge fund manager.

The ability for a prime broker to offer borrowed stocks can be the difference between a profitable execution of a solid long/short strategy and the inability to place a trade.

Short positions are sometimes more calculated than simply reducing long exposure, like those of David Einhorn's Greenlight Capital, a well-known hedge fund that has developed a reputation for savvy shorting. Einhorn and his team spend as much as a year studying a particular company, and then place a substantial wager either in favor of or against that company's performance.

One of the most notable examples of Greenlight Capital's successful shorting was the short sale of Lehman Brothers, Inc. stock in the months leading up to the financial crisis and Lehman Brothers' filing for bankruptcy. For Einhorn's fund, this trade was not only a bet against an investment banking powerhouse, but also a (perhaps unintended) hedge against the economic downturn set off by Lehman Brothers' bankruptcy filing. For most traders, the decline of Lehman Brothers and the unraveling of the financial industry was a dark time that signaled a substantial period of losses; for Mr. Einhorn and other short sellers, extraordinary gains were made, often helping to offset losses on long positions. This is one of the biggest draws to long/short hedge funds: the ability to make money for investors in both bull and bear markets.

Alternatives to Shorting a Stock

In addition to shorting stocks, many long/short hedge funds use derivatives to initiate long/short positions. A derivative is a security that derives its value from the performance of underlying assets, such as stocks, currencies, and indexes. For example, a futures contract on WTI oil derives its value from the physical oil delivered in Cushing, Oklahoma. Derivatives cover many products including currencies, commodities, equities, and debt. The risk management of a long/short equity shop is focused on the delta of stock positions. The delta is the theoretical exposure to a change in a stock's value. Shorting a stock is one way of creating a negative delta, but this can be accomplished with options as well as futures.

A put option is the right but not the obligation to sell stocks at a specific price, known as the strike price, on or before a certain date, which is known as the expiration date. When an investor purchases a put, they pay the seller of the option a premium and have the right to sell the underlying stock prior to expiration.

Exchange-traded options on stocks, which are the most popular way to purchase or sell an option, are listed as contracts, where one contract represents 100 shares of stock.

The delta on an option contract changes with time along with the underlying prices of the stock that it affects. This means that the market neutral aspect of a long/short strategy can change as the market moves, unless the manager actively alters the long position in the stock.

Another alternative to shorting a stock is to sell short a futures contract on a stock or an index. Futures contracts are derivatives representing the obligation to sell or buy a stock or stock index at a specific date in the future. Generally, futures have a specific notional value that can be matched to a stock's notional value to generate a market neutral position. Futures contracts are traded through a futures clearinghouse, which have member firms that can facilitate trading through their brokerage arms.

Access to Long/Short Strategies

Access to long/short equity funds has increased significantly over the past decade. Mutual funds and exchange-traded funds (ETFs) and notes allow investors access to funds that engage in long/short equity strategies.

ETFs trade throughout the day over an exchange like stocks, and most are designed to passively track the performance of an underlying index. They are typically the cheapest and sometimes the most tax-efficient structure, yet the overall level of long/short equity assets managed in ETF-form is not as robust and does not produce the risk-adjusted returns provided by the top hedge funds.

Fee Structure

Hedge fund fee structures within the long/short equity space are routinely 2 and 20: a 2 percent annual management fee on assets under management combined with a 20 percent performance fee charged on profits, after expenses. The average fees, according to Morningstar's *Long–Short Equity Handbook*, are approximately 1.50 and 19.00 percent, respectively.

Investors with more money invested will typically negotiate a lower overall percentage fee.

For context, mutual fund and ETF fees are reported as expense ratios, which calculate operating expenses as a percentage of fund assets. Transaction costs incurred by the fund, however, are generally not included in the calculation of the net expense ratio. The average annual reported net expense ratio of a long/short equity mutual fund is 2.15 percent as of September 30, 2011, according to Morningstar. The rise in hedge-like mutual funds with similar characteristics to standard hedge funds has put further pressure on hedge funds to reduce fees. Greater competition from market-neutral hedged mutual funds is a developing trend

that investors and fund managers should keep an eye on in the coming years (Horejs, 2011).

Taxes

Long/short equity hedge fund investors must file a K-1 partnership tax form, which could take months to obtain and could also result in non-tax-deductible expenses. Hedge funds generally produce estimated K-1 forms by April and finalized K-1s by June of the following year. Hedge funds structured as limited partnerships generally pass-through the net tax characteristics of their underlying investments and are taxed each year regardless of distributions. Both unrealized and realized gains can be taxed, generating phantom profits that create a tax liability.

Specialization versus Generalization

The stocks they invest in often distinguish long/short hedge funds, whether by the size of companies or the industry focus. The hedge fund may invest in a particular area of expertise like healthcare companies, financial firms, technology firms, and so on. This element of expertise is critical to persuading investors that the hedge fund has an edge in the marketplace. A long/short strategy is successful only if the manager has an ability to accurately value a company or predict market swings and events. That ability is enhanced if the hedge fund employs a number of stock specialists in a sector who are particularly adept at valuation and forecasting for that group of corporations.

Another way that a long/short hedge fund may specialize is by investing in a particular size of corporation; for example, small-, mid-, or large-cap companies. This allows the hedge fund to target a particular niche of the stock market, rather than looking very broadly at companies of all sizes and industries. Hedge funds often target nonhousehold-name companies or small-cap equities because these companies are believed to be less analyzed and therefore there may be a greater opportunity for investors in stocks flying under the radar. Consider, for example, Apple, Inc. Apple's stock has one of the highest trading volumes of any stock on the market; because of this, there are analysts paid to do nothing except scrutinize Apple and a few of its competitors. How likely is it, then, that a hedge fund will find an important item in the earnings report or recognize a factor likely to significantly affect the stock price? Compared to the chances of such a discovery in analyzing a less studied corporation, the odds are slim.

This does not mean that hedge funds cannot profit by buying or shorting Apple stock or other popular large-cap equities; indeed, many hedge funds have profited handsomely from trading some of the most popular stocks. But for a hedge fund with limited manpower and resources, it often makes sense to allocate analytical attention to those stocks that the team is most likely to have a particular edge in trading.

Who Runs a Long/Short Hedge Fund?

Stocks are affected by a number of different factors including broader market conditions, investor sentiment, macroeconomic events, company-specific events like legal issues or earnings reports, and many more potentially important variables. Thus, it is not as simple as calculating a stock's price-to-earnings ratio or book value and then determining whether the stock is accurately valued; a long/short strategy requires a sophisticated, analytical eye to accurately forecast events that could affect the stock or, most commonly, to determine whether a stock is trading above or below its value. Long/short fund managers are particularly adept at investing in equities. Additionally, as mentioned earlier, long/short equity managers are trading relative value, and need to understand both sides of their trade.

We asked Julien Sallmard, a portfolio manager at a global multibillion-dollar fund, how to start a long/short career and what it takes to run a long/short hedge fund. He told us, "I think that a long/short manager should have two main attributes: a strong analytical background and very disciplined risk management. I personally started my career as an analyst for an investment bank, which provided me with the necessary valuation tools and understanding to analyze companies on a daily basis. Risk management comes with time and experience rather than a specific training. A graduate finance degree is a prerequisite given the analytical background needed to work in fundamental long/short."

Risks

Despite being categorized as a market-neutral strategy, equity long/short strategies are not without risks. These strategies have market-spread risks, as opposed to outright directional risks. Long/short strategies also come with the liquidity risks of trading two or more stocks as opposed to one stock. Additionally, equity long/short strategies have some unique inherent risks. The main one is that the portfolio manager must correctly predict the relative performance of two stocks, which can be difficult.

Pair risks that are based on long-term correlation can break down permanently. Given that a ratio of one stock price to another is normally distributed—meaning that the spread of the two stocks are not bounded by zero—the ratio of one stock to another can continue to move with or against a portfolio manager's position to an infinite extent. Individual stock returns, on the other hand, are log-normal distributed, meaning that the stock price is bounded by zero.

Neal Hornsby, MBA, Director of D-Risk Pty Ltd and Head of Risk at PM CAPITAL Limited, has over 25 years within the fund industry in Australia and the Asia Pacific and is an experienced risk and compliance manager. So, we asked Neal about the potential risks that hedge funds consider when trading in equities.

Richard Wilson: What are the major types of equities trading risk that hedge fund managers face and what tools can be used to face those risks?

Neal Hornsby: For the most part, hedge fund have the same trading risks at work as any other fund, with three exceptions: The first is that of leverage, the second is shorting and the third being a potentially higher exposure to counterparty risk. Tools for the management of leverage is fundamentally ensuring that you maintain leverage that a) is appropriate to the economic environment and b) has the downside somewhat protected; shorting presents some interesting problems given the exposure is, at least in theory, unlimited. Controlling this is limited to having made the right decisions and managing the Value at Risk amongst other things ensuring that all shorts are covered and have a contingent exit strategy.

In handling counterparty risk, the board should pay particular attention to the amount of rehypothecation that they have allowed under the Prime Broker arrangement and attempt to match this to its risk appetite or at most, to that allowed by the SEC (i.e. 140 percent of the loan amount (as at 2013)).

Leverage

Long/short equity managers use leverage to enhance their returns. Leverage, as it exists within a long/short equity structure, is borrowed capital that uses the purchased equities as collateral. Leverage provides significant risks to a long/short hedge fund strategy, as quick sharp movements of a spread between two stocks can generate losses that are enhanced by leverage. Of course, leverage also allows long/short funds to juice returns with borrowed money.

Why Invest in a Long/Short Hedge Fund?

A long/short equity hedge fund can provide investors with the opportunity to invest in a diversified portfolio of both long and short stocks. For many investors, short selling is too difficult, too risky, or not practical, but a hedge fund presents a structure that enables the investor to hedge against the risk of a downturn. Many investors express concerns that the gains made in their traditional investment portfolios are often erased by cyclical downturns in the market. Thus, the notion that a long/short hedge fund could preserve capital in a negative cycle—and even notch gains during that time—is very appealing.

Conclusion

Long/short equity funds are the most popular and widely allocated funds within the hedge fund space. The roots of all hedge funds come from the long/short equity fund, as early managers used hedges on long positions to mitigate risk and maximize risk-adjusted returns.

Long/short equity funds began as qualitative funds that used discretionary analysis to initiate trades. Over the past two decades, quantitative funds have infiltrated the hedge fund environment, generating returns from highly sophisticated models that find statistical anomalies within the equity markets. Pair trading is one of the most common quantitative long/short equity strategies, as there are many companies that compete within the same industry that experience highly correlated returns. The evolution of buying long and selling short does not appear complete, as new hedge funds find innovative ways to morph the strategy and generate alpha.

Over the past decade, the long/short equity strategy has branched out into mutual funds, exchange-traded notes, and exchange-traded funds. Although the expense ratios on these funds make the fees more affordable, the historical returns of these funds fall short of the more attractive hedge funds, ensuring that (at least in the near future) hedge funds will remain the preferred vehicle for the long/short strategy.

To download several videos related to the focus of this chapter and to watch over 125 total video modules and expert audio interviews, please activate your free account here: http://HedgeFundGroup.org/Access.

Test Yourself

Answer the following questions.

1. The average fee structure for a long/short fund is
   A. 2/20
   B. 1/10
   C. 1.5/20
   D. 1.5/19

2. True or False: Alpha is a return on an investment after adjusting for risk.

3. True or False: Because long/short strategies are categorized as market neutral, they are without risk.

4. Derivatives:
   A. Are financial instruments that derive their value from an underlying asset, like a stock or bond.
   B. Have actual, tangible value.
   C. Are financial instruments that derive their value from market fluctuations and are unrelated to stock exchanges.
   D. Are complex stocks that pay dividends in a format that compounds the interest continually.

5. True or False: When buying a call option, an investor believes the stock price will rise.

Answers can be found in Appendix B.

CHAPTER 6

Global Macro Strategy

Global macro hedge funds take a macroeconomic approach to investing and employ multiple trading strategies to invest in a variety of securities and financial instruments. Global macro portfolio managers are also unique in their broad research and analysis, incorporating both fundamental and technical analysis to inform investing decisions and strategies. A global macro fund typically applies an investing focus that allows the fund to invest opportunistically around the globe in a number of different investments including foreign currencies, commodities, stocks, bonds, indexes, and derivatives. Global macro fund managers generally have a wide range of experience that allows the fund manager to confidently trade in foreign markets, often through complex financial transactions.

Discretionary versus Systematic

In the world of global macro hedge funds, there is often a dividing line between two branches of the sector; discretionary and systemic, similar to the discretionary and quantitative distinction covered in Chapter 5. A discretionary global macro manager will often employ a number of different trading strategies in order to profit from global trends and events. This is in contrast to a systemic global macro manager, who prefers to follow advanced algorithms and generate returns on data-driven trades. The discretionary manager uses a set of tools that are interpreted differently each time a trade is placed, relying on his discretion to determine if the risk is worth the reward. The systematic trading manager has fixed rules, relying more on historical returns and models to guide decisions.

Fundamental Analysis

Fundamental analysis is the process of using economic data, political news, monetary policy, or company earnings to evaluate the current market environment in an effort to predict the future movement of financial securities. Fundamental analysts will pour over numerous reports and releases to try to gain some insight into the future direction of the markets.

For example, an analyst might believe that given the current economic situation in Europe, the European Central Bank (ECB) is more likely to reduce interest rates. Holding this view, a portfolio manager might take a long position in Euribor (short-term European debt instruments) in the hope that the ECB will cut rates, thus driving up the price of the security.

Technical Analysis

An analyst employs technical analysis to evaluate past price movements and historical data to form a prediction of future movements in the price of a security or sector. Many technical analysts believe that all the current information that is available is already incorporated into the price of a financial security. Armed with this belief, a technical analyst will evaluate past behavior of price action to look for clues that will give a portfolio manager an edge in determining the future movements of a financial product.

Discretionary Technical Analysis

Technical analysis as viewed within the global macro arena can be looked at as objective or subjective. Subjective technical analysis is an art that focuses on patterns and levels to generate opportunities to initiate and manage trading positions. An example of subjective technical analysis is support and resistance levels.

A support, as seen in Figure 6.1A, describes a level where price action is supported by buyers of a security and prices are having a difficult time moving below the high-demand level. Buyers are looking to initiate positions at this level and sellers are unsuccessful at driving the price lower. Many analysts use trend lines or moving averages to determine support levels, and base their risk management on these levels.

Resistance, as seen in Figure 6.1B, describes a price level that is supplied by sellers and where price action cannot easily move above. Sellers are looking to initiate positions at these levels and buyers are unsuccessful at driving the price above these areas. Similar to support, many traders use trend lines or moving averages to determine subjective resistance levels.

Both support and resistance levels are used by discretionary traders to help initiate positions and manage risk. To initiate a position, a trader might look for prices of a security to move above resistance to determine that a market has broken out. That same trader might look for support levels to determine a specific

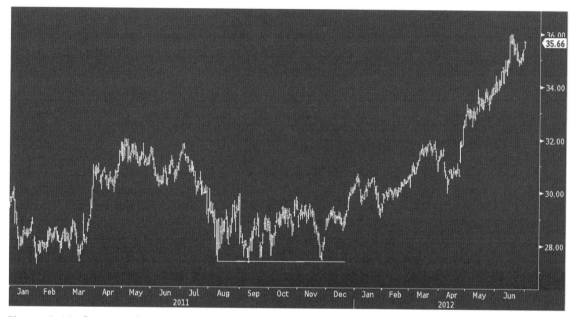

Figure 6.1A Support Level

level that he will use to stop out of the position if the security moves against him.

Another type of discretionary technical analysis is patterns recognition. Patterns use historical price-action recognition to forecast the potential future movements of specific markets. Analysts use historical prices that generally reflect potential continuation or reversals and offer clues about potential future movements. An example of a discretionary pattern is a triangle, seen in Figure 6.2.

Triangles reflect price action that is consolidating, prior to a market breakout. During a triangle pattern, prices generally move within a well-defined range, making lower highs and higher lows as the triangle is formed. The price action reflects positioning by traders as they wait for an impetus for future movement. As price action continues to consolidate, market participants attempt to find equilibrium. While the market is forming a triangle, volume begins to dip as the tug of war between bulls and bears rages on.

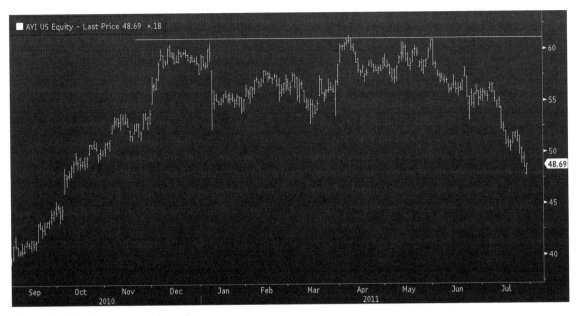

Figure 6.1B Resistance Level
Source: © 2014 Bloomberg L.P. All rights reserved.

The symmetrical triangle is a continuation pattern, which means that the resolution to the pattern is a breakout that flows with the trend, as you can see from the triangles in Figure 6.3.

When macro traders use discretionary technical analysis, they are attempting to use a combination of their experience and a historical view of price action to find tools that will help them initiate positions and minimize risk.

Systematic Technical Analysis

Many systematic traders use price action to determine the future direction of a financial security. To accomplish this, system traders will backtest a specific market using a historical time series of that security. The backtesting process is generally rigorous where the analyst generates algorithms to find out if the specific rules and criteria will generate profits in all types of market conditions.

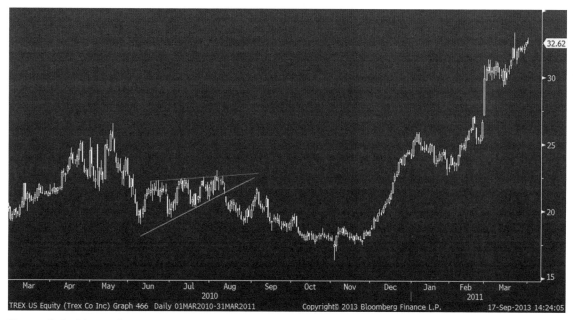

Figure 6.2 Discretionary Trading Pattern
Source: © 2014 Bloomberg L.P. All rights reserved.

There are numerous algorithms used by sophisticated, quantitative macro traders including a number of strategies that are based on trend following, momentum, and pattern recognition. One of the most common macro strategies using technical analysis is trend-following analysis. A trend-following system might use a combination of moving averages and momentum to determine if a trend is in place

A moving average gives traders and analysts an idea of the price changes within a window of time. For example, a 10-day moving average is the average of the past 10 days; on the eleventh day, the first day is dropped from the calculation of the average. If a moving average is climbing, the trend of the market is generally climbing; when a moving average is falling, the trend is usually declining.

Systematic technical traders will look for different moving averages and use a crossover method of one moving average over or under another and combine that with specific types of momentum indicators,

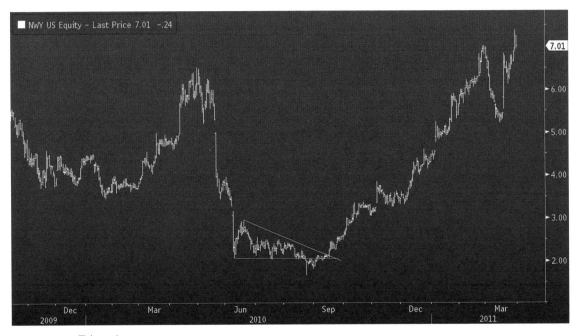

Figure 6.3 Triangle
Source: © 2014 Bloomberg L.P. All rights reserved.

such as the MACD (moving average convergence divergence index) created by Gerald Appel. For example, an upward trend could be defined when a five-day moving average of a security crosses above the 20-day moving average of a security in Figure 6.4.

Momentum as described by Appel's MACD is when a spread (a shorter-term moving average minus a longer-term moving average—the default for Appel is the 12-day moving average and the 26-day moving average) crosses above the nine-day moving average of the spread. This buy signal, when combined with a moving average crossover, is a powerful systematic technical signal.

Systemic traders often evaluate historical price relationships to build a framework within which they can operate comfortably by following what history

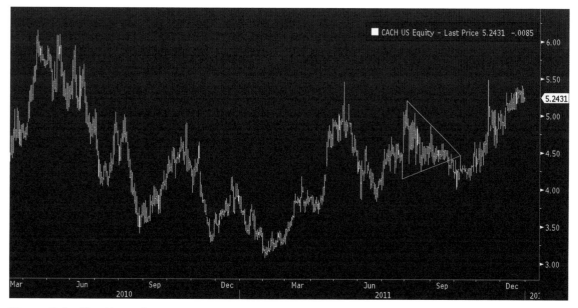

Figure 6.3 *(Continued)*
Source: © 2014 Bloomberg L.P. All rights reserved.

suggests will occur. Discretionary traders, on the other hand, will often stray from or directly challenge price action in favor of the fundamentals. This distinction is important in separating the two trading strategies within global macro investing.

As stated above, discretionary global macro managers incorporate a number of different tools to discover and execute trades. A discretionary trader may use a combination of technical and fundamental analysis. For example, the manager could use fundamental analysis to predict an event that would change European Central Bank policy to generate a view of where the currency might shift. This trader might combine this with levels of support and resistance to generate a transaction.

While there is some contrast between systemic and discretionary global macro managers, the line between the two trading strategies will sometimes blur, especially in a complex global macro trade that is based on a combination of assumptions, fundamental

Figure 6.3 *(Continued)*
Source: © 2014 Bloomberg L.P. All rights reserved.

and technical analysis, experience, and other factors that can come into play.

Global macro has become more popular in an increasingly complex global financial system. An investor in today's interconnected financial system may see his investments affected by a weather event in Africa or a European country's fiscal crisis.

For investors hoping to hedge against this risk (and, ideally, profit from macroeconomic events worldwide), a global macro fund may be a smart choice.

However, many global macro funds have underperformed in the most recent years, as you can see in the Figure 6.5 comparison. This is largely due to unforeseen economic events, such as the global financial crisis and recession, and the sovereign debt crisis in Europe. Global macro funds are thought to protect investors against being caught off guard by these events but even some of the brightest minds in macro investing appear to have mistimed or underestimated these situations. Still, there are a number of global macro

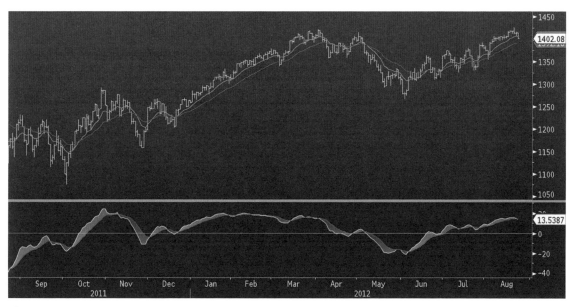

Figure 6.4 Moving Average Convergence Divergence Index
Source: © 2014 Bloomberg L.P. All rights reserved.

Fund Type	Last Valuation (MTD)	1 Month Return	Year to Date (YTD)	1 Year	3 Year
Macro Hedge Funds	8/30/2013	−1.0672$	−3.2902%	−2.7663%	−2.1564%
S&P 500	8/30/2013	−3.143%	14.4988%	−16.6838%	−15.8955%

Figure 6.5 Historical Performance of Global Macro Strategy Hedge Funds versus Standard & Poor's 500 Index 2010 to 2013
Source: © 2014 Bloomberg L.P. All rights reserved.

funds that performed well during an extremely volatile time period, and investors will undoubtedly look upon these managers favorably in a continued era of instability and uncertainty.

Leverage

Leverage is one of the most important factors contributing to the performance of a global macro fund. Leverage, as previously explained, is the process of borrowing capital to enhance positions. Most prime brokers allow investors to collateralize the securities they are trading (which are, in turn, backed by the assets themselves) so that the investors only need to put up a portion of the capital required to purchase the asset. Global macro funds often rely on leverage to make massive wagers on foreign currencies, interest rates, and other assets, taking significant risks in markets that would make most average investors nervous. The use of leverage has helped generate incredible gains for macro funds and also contributed to some spectacular losses when foreign markets shifted, trades soured, and lenders began making margin calls, forcing traders to close positions at a loss.

Most products that are traded within the capital-market environment are leveraged vehicles, such as derivatives.

Derivatives

As discussed in Chapter 5, derivatives are products that derive their value from another asset's value.

Derivatives have many benefits to the global macro trader. Instead of tying up a large quantity of capital to take a position in a German bond, a trader can instead purchase a futures contract on the German bond and enjoy any capital appreciation while only posting approximately 10 percent of the total notional value of the bond.

Over-the-Counter Products

Many trades are transacted as derivatives without the protection of a clearing house or a regulated vehicle. These products are referred to as over-the-counter products (OTC), and entail counterparty risk. Trades are completed between two willing partners who set the parameters of trading a specific instrument. The Bank of International Settlements pegs the total size of the OTC derivatives market at $633 trillion, a breathtakingly massive figure that shows how important derivatives are to our financial system (Bank of International Settlements, 2013).

Options

Options provide traders with leverage above and beyond futures contracts, but require knowledge of options pricing in order to effectively generate a profitable trade. Options have a time component to them, known as the time-to-maturity, which means that not only does a portfolio manager need to be correct about the price that the underlying asset moves to, but also how quickly the price will move to that level.

Options generally exist on all types of assets within the global macro space, including currencies, commodities, stocks, and fixed income.

Types of Products

A global macro hedge fund employs a strategy that focuses on economic and monetary policy changes that will create directional changes in equity indexes, interest rates, currencies, and commodities. The financial instruments used within the global macro environment range from ETFs (which track specific index changes) to cash positions.

A global macro strategy is generally considered a discretionary strategy where a manager uses a number of different tools to form an investment thesis. For example, a global macro manager might use U.S. growth prospects to take a position where he believes U.S. interest rates will increase at a quicker pace than what is currently implied in the market.

Currencies

Currency strategies generally focus on the relative strength of one currency versus another. A currency is usually quoted as an exchange rate in the form of a currency pair. A currency pair is one country's currency relative to another country's currency.

Currency traders follow trends within the global economic environment as well as monetary policy. Traders will focus on the interest-rate differential, which is the difference between one country's interest rates and another country's interest rates. The most liquid currency pairs are the major currency pairs, which include the U.S. dollar as part of the security that is traded. Cross-currency pairs are those that do not include the dollar, and emerging market currency pairs are those that come from developing countries.

One major advantage of a strategy that is focused on currencies is the leverage that is available within the currency markets. It is not uncommon for a currency trader to find leverage that is 200 to 1, which allows a manager to enhance his returns, while taking significant risks.

Currency instruments include ETFs, which follow specific currency pairs, futures contracts, and over-the-counter currency pairs.

Interest-Rate Trading

Portfolio managers who actively trade interest rates within the context of a global macro strategy usually invest in sovereign debt instruments. This includes U.S. Treasury instruments, Japanese debt instruments, and European debt instruments. The majority of these types of instruments are traded in either the ETF space, the derivative space, or with cash bonds. Leverage within the debt markets is substantial, allowing investors to enhance returns while assuming a certain degree of risk. Strategies include outright directional risk, calendar spread risk, and intermarket spreads.

Many interest rate traders combine sovereign interest-rate trading with currency trading as the two products overlap. Some will take a position in an interest-rate differential and hedge their coupon pick-up with a rolling hedge of a currency position.

Stock Index Trading

Equity Index investment managers use equity indexes to speculate on the direction of global stock markets with a view toward growth or contraction. In general, index strategies are directional, but some managers trade spreads. For example, a manager might consider trading the S&P 500 versus the NASDAQ or an intracountry spread, such as a U.S. exchange versus a German exchange.

Commodity Trading

The commodity space is a vast investment arena where portfolio managers can take positions in many different products. The most liquid products are within the petroleum and precious metal environments, which include crude oil and gold. Crude oil is a fungible product that trades both physically and financially around the globe. It is the largest source of energy on the planet and trades based on supply and demand along with perceptions of growth. Gold is one of the most liquid commodities traded against the American dollar.

Other areas of focus in the commodity space include grain commodities—such as wheat, corn, and soybeans—along with soft commodities, such as coffee, sugar, and cocoa.

Many global macro traders will take intercommodity spread positions where they will purchase one commodity and simultaneously sell another commodity in an effort to benefit from a change in the spread between the two assets.

Who Runs a Macro Fund?

Macro fund management teams are typically trained in multiple investing strategies from fixed income to currencies and large-cap equities. In theory, the greater range of abilities that a manager has, the better chances he will have to profit off a trade on a particular macroeconomic trend or event. For a single trade, a manager may use knowledge from several disciplines. For example, a manager may use his knowledge of economic and government policy to anticipate the response by Japan's central bank to a currency crisis; then, the manager can find a number of investments that will be affected by such a shift in policy and even how other companies and investment firms will respond to this event. That then enables the manager to protect the portfolio in case of such an event occurring and position the fund to profit handsomely from the change in policy.

To effectively pull off such a trade, the manager must employ several different areas of expertise including economic policy, politics, monetary policy, banking, and foreign currency, just to name a few areas. George Soros, the renowned hedge fund investor, is perhaps best known for his global macro trade that "broke the pound" in 1992. To short the pound, Soros used his knowledge of government policy (especially central banking and political pressures that influenced the British government), currency movements, and interest rates. This unique global macro trade netted over $1 billion for Mr. Soros and cemented his status as an investing legend (Litterick, 2002).

Managers who have this toolkit will also be able to hedge specific types of exposure by hedging their exposure. Many hedge fund managers are interested in taking positions that are outside of their domestic domain using local currencies. The ability to understand whether the portfolio will receive risk-adjusted gains by either hedging exposure or leaving it naked requires a view on not only the underlying asset, but also the local currency.

Why Invest in a Global Maoro Fund?

Global macro funds seek to profit from macroeconomic trends, events, and patterns. These events could include: severe economic downturns like the one that recently occurred in parts of Europe, most notably Greece; a financial crisis such as the collapse of Long Term Capital Management and Lehman Brothers; an unexpected weather event like a drought or hurricane; or the "lost decade" of economic stagnation in Japan. These large-scale events can have a tremendous effect on the global economy from shifts in interest rates to crop yields. At times,

global macro fund managers will surf these trend waves, riding momentum in a particular market or asset.

Other times, a manager may buck a trend, trusting that his fundamental analysis of the situation is accurate and that it will eventually be proven as the trend shifts in his favor. The Soros trade illustrates this point well: The Bank of England started spending reserves to prop up the pound against speculators like Soros. But even as the pound recovered somewhat and some short sellers feared that the Bank of England could fend off the attack, according to author Sebastian Mallaby, Soros and his team trusted their analysis and continued to short the currency, to "go for the jugular," as Soros famously told his partner Stan Druckenmiller (Mallaby, 2013a).

Global macro managers are in a unique position to profit from these events because they are typically capable of trading confidently in a vast array of financial instruments and strategies and are not limited by a strict mandate or investment structure. For example, a mutual fund manager who recognizes a short opportunity cannot capitalize on that because, under the Investment Company Act of 1940, mutual funds are prohibited from selling short (United States Securities and Exchange Commission, 1972).

Hedge funds are allowed to sell securities short and thus could take advantage of the opportunity, but what if the hedge fund's strategy is focused on domestic small-cap equities and the opportunity is in shorting a large European financial institution? Investors may not allow a hedge fund manager to stray too far from his niche area of expertise and strategy, so a wide focus for global macro funds can be a distinct advantage over narrow-focused hedge funds.

Conclusion

Global macro funds enjoy the flexibility to engage in risk taking in multiple assets classes that stretch across the globe. Managers in this sector look for trends that are in place or ones that are about to start, in an effort to take leveraged positions that will generate robust returns. Generally, global macro managers hire a number of portfolio managers who specialize in specific asset classes, which allow the fund to benefit when a trend is in place.

Global macro funds can be categorized as systematic or discretionary, but many times the lines that separate the two styles are blurry. Global macro managers trade a plethora of investment products which include debt instruments, currencies, commodities, equities, and derivatives.

Test Yourself

Answer the following questions.

1. Global Macro Funds commonly seek to profit from each of the following EXCEPT:
   A. Trends
   B. Events
   C. Patterns
   D. Stagnation
2. Managers use stock indexes to:
   A. Speculate on the growth of global stock exchanges.
   B. Place available capital in.
   C. Understand the housing market.
   D. Speculate on whether an investor will invest capital.

3. True or False: A global macro strategy is a strategy involving long and short positions based on global economic and political situations and events.
4. True or False: Currency traders almost never leverage.
5. True or False: A 10-day moving average is the average stock price of the past 10 days.

Answers can be found in Appendix B.

CHAPTER 7

Event-Driven Strategy

The event-driven hedge fund seeks to generate returns by accurately assessing, predicting, and trading on corporate events. The hedge fund will often target corporations in a particular sector or market capitalization, and analysts will scrutinize the corporations for trading opportunities, such as mergers and acquisitions (M&A), major changes in the business, earnings reports, restructurings, bankruptcies, financial distress, new product launches, and other events that impact the value and market price of a particular corporation. Event-driven strategies include merger-arbitrage strategies, distressed-debt strategies, capital-structure arbitrage, special situations, and activist strategies.

Who Runs an Event-Driven Fund?

Event-driven hedge funds are typically managed by an experienced team of traders, often with a specialization in a particular sector. The manager must be able to quickly analyze and capitalize on new information. For many event-driven trades, time is of the essence and the competitive edge is the ability to either foresee an event and position the fund to profit when the event comes to fruition, or to quickly react to an event while the market is still digesting the news and the pricing opportunity still exists.

When a public corporation seeks to make an acquisition, the news of the event could dramatically affect the stock price of both the acquiring corporation and its target. However, if the deal requires shareholder approval then it could be derailed by a shareholder contingency that organizes against the proposed acquisition. The fund's management team must be prepared for these types of impactful events and have a deep understanding of all areas of corporate activity relevant to the strategy.

An example of an event-driven manager reacting to an event is when a company's reorganization plan is announced. The event-driven fund could position

> **DEFINITION:**
> **Event-Driven Strategies**
>
> A strategy used by hedge fund managers to exploit and profit from changes and events that occur within a company or given market.

itself to profit if the news is well received or not by the markets; this could be achieved by utilizing different financial instruments, but most commonly through purchasing an asset tied to that company's value. The fund may short the stock if it believes that the reorganization will be unsuccessful in the long term, or even if the manager believes the stock will tank one day and then recover once the plan is better understood and analyzed over the ensuing days. So, we can see why an event-driven hedge fund manager must be talented not only in predicting and reacting to events, but also in finding unique, profitable ways to trade based on the event.

How to Invest Around Events

An investing strategy based on events carries inherent risk and difficulty. A trader must accurately predict the time and scope of such events. However, managers can utilize certain strategies and leveraging methods to minimize risk while exposing a fund to large returns. Some options available to managers include options strategies, capital-structure arbitrage, and distressed debt.

Options Strategies

There are numerous financial instruments that provide a trader with opportunities before and after events. If a fund manager believes an event will alter the course of the price of a stock, he or she can initiate options positions that provide a specific type of speculation based

on unfolding events. Specific options structures can be created prior to and or after an event to capitalize on a stock's price action.

For example, if company X bids for company Y at $100 per share, and a hedge fund manager expects a positive outcome for the sale, a merger arbitrage opportunity can be available, and he or she can take a position that will allow them to benefit from a specific outcome using options. Let's assume the price of stock Y is trading at $95; the manager can purchase a $95 call and finance that call with the sale of a call from the purchaser's stock (company X). The risk is similar to risk associated with a failed merger arbitrage, but in the case of options the losses can be more extreme along with the gains given the leverage provided by options. Of course, this is a simplified example and in many cases, a merger arbitrage trade will be centered on a more complex deal with more factors for a fund manager to consider such as the timing of the transaction, whether it is a stock-for-stock merger, etc. These complicating factors, which can be hard to predict, are what create the merger arbitrage opportunity for a savvy fund manager.

Capital-Structure Arbitrage

Capital-structure arbitrage involves taking market-neutral positions on both sides of the same issuer. For example, an investor could take a long position in senior debt and simultaneously short sell common stock.

A long debt versus short equity strategy in anticipation of a rights issue or long senior debt versus short junior debt in anticipation of a debt restructuring are examples of an impetus that would pay off using capital-structure arbitrage. Another strategy is to play holding companies versus subsidiary companies. This situation will only exist if the parent and child are both publically traded companies, or a secondary market provides access to a company's stock. Specific types of corporate events such as mergers, acquisitions, and spinoffs can generate different outcomes, which can be analyzed and speculated on by event-driven hedge fund managers who have expertise in this area.

Distressed Debt

The debt of a distressed corporation provides an excellent opportunity to speculate on future corporate events. This is the case with companies that may be experiencing severe operating or financial difficulties, and may or may not be in the process of restructuring through bankruptcy, or the sale of assets, or a debt for equity swap. Event-driven hedge fund managers are looking to identify where the market is undervaluing potential returns in certain situations, such as restructuring or liquidation.

Restructuring funds typically make new investments in troubled companies. Issues can range from operational problems to financial distress. Many times, hedge funds will want an activist role or a position of contract, with a view to improving the balance sheet and operations for a subsequent sale.

Distressed debt funds purchase the debt of companies in distress with a view to participating in any increase in value after reorganization. Strategies relative to distressed debt include passive trading, and many levels of control. These funds capitalize on opportunities generated by overleveraged, financially distressed, or poorly managed companies.

Risks

The risks associated with each event-driven strategy are different and can generate risk-adjusted returns that are on the tails of the risk distribution. Merger arbitrage has a weak risk-to-reward profile on the face of it. The issue is that the probability of an outcome has to outweigh the loss from a transaction given that the risk usually outweighs the reward. Generally the reward is well-known since the high price of a target is what the acquirer has stated he will pay. The price of a failure is unknown and, unless hedged in some way, could be substantial.

Regulation has recently become an issue for event-driven funds, as the financial crisis created obstacles for short sellers. Regulation disallowed short positions for a period of time and created a headwind for event-driven investors. For example, in the financial crisis of 2008, a number of countries banned short selling on some financial stocks, and more recently, European countries have banned short selling in an effort to stop the bleeding during the EuroZone debt crisis. These actions have been controversial and debates over the merits of short-selling bans continue to this day (New York Federal Reserve, 2012).

> **Smart Investor Tip**
>
> Regulatory interventions have been imposed on market participants with short notice in other countries to prevent short selling or other trading activity perceived to be harmful to a country's sovereign or financial interests. European countries recently imposed short-term, short-selling bans to protect domestic financial institutions. Investors should be mindful of the potential for sovereigns to quash an otherwise sound trading strategy and expose the fund to losses.

Why Invest in an Event-Driven Hedge Fund?

Event-driven hedge funds often place nondirectional bets because the events affecting a single corporation are rarely tied to the overall market movement, unless the corporation has exceptionally high beta with the major indices or a large enough market capitalization to sway the major indices, like Apple or Exxon, as in the example of merger arbitrage where a hedge fund manager is selling the purchaser's stocks and buying the company that is going to be acquired. Therefore, investors may find an event-driven fund attractive because the fund seeks to profit from a variety of events and is a potential diversification from overall market risk. Most importantly for investors in event-driven hedge funds is the potential to profit from a number of corporate events.

Another way that this strategy may offer investors diversification is that it trades on a wide range of corporate events and will not limit its focus strictly to merger arbitrage or distressed-situation investing. This allows the fund to trade on multiple opportunities and not limit the strategy to a narrow niche that could have limited trading volume from month to month, such as merger arbitrage, a strategy that can be difficult to execute in economic downturns when M&A activity is exceptionally low.

The correlation of distressed-debt situations to the broader markets is relatively low, which allows investors to diversify their assets. Event-driven strategies have a payout that is binary in nature. As opposed to returns that can vary in size, the payout of an event is either positive or negative. The amount that is made or lost is usually quantified prior to transacting a trade that is based on an event in an effort to insure there is no risk or ruin.

Using the example of a merger arbitrage trade, an investor who sells the acquirer's stock can experience the pain of a short squeeze if the acquisition does not go through. Many times a stock can move substantially higher, which can be hedged by other financial derivatives. By shorting a stock and purchasing an out-of-the-money option as a stop loss, a manager will limit his loss in the case that the trade does not go as planned.

Unlike the average investor in a corporation, a hedge fund employs a number of analysts to research companies. This allows a hedge fund to go above and beyond what an individual investor could handle. The analysis that is performed by evaluating the company's financials and participating on conference calls with the company gives a hedge fund detailed insights into a corporation's value and how its current market value might change based on future corporate events. This type of constant attention to and scrutiny of a company is not possible for most investors, especially nonprofessional investors.

Another advantage to investing in event-driven hedge funds is that hedge funds have a plethora of tools available in their belt that are simply not available to most investors. These tools include the use of

Test Yourself

Answer the following questions.

1. True or False: Event-driven hedge funds often place nondirectional bets.

2. True or False: Average individual investors and hedge funds have access to the same research and information.

3. Event-driven strategies are:
   A. Strategies that are based on the past earnings of a stock compared to a related index.
   B. Strategies that exploit and profit from changes that occur within a company or market.
   C. Strategies that involve going long a sector but short in individual companies.

4. True or False: The correlation of distressed-debt situations to the broader markets is relatively low.

5. Capital structure arbitrage:
   A. Involves placing bets on companies with an excess of capital on hand with the hopes that the capital will be invested into research and development.
   B. Involves taking market-neutral positions on both sides of the same issuer.
   C. Is the practice of meeting before an arbiter to redefine the capital structure of a firm.
   D. Is an investment strategy where the key objective is capital preservation rather than growth.

Answers can be found in Appendix B.

leverage, shorting stocks, options and swaps, a variety of complicated financial instruments such as credit-default swaps and other products typically reserved for hedge funds and institutional investors, limits on positions in public companies, and other unique instruments that allow hedge funds to profit from an event in a variety of ways.

This endeavor not only requires a plethora of exceptional intellectual tools, but additionally the need for relationships within the institutional financial area that allow analysts and portfolio managers opportunities to execute specific views using complicated financial instruments.

For the typical investor, these types of instruments and transactions are either too risky or too complicated and are best left to the experts who are actively monitoring the corporation and experienced in utilizing an array of complicated financial instruments.

There is certainly a great deal of risk involved in the event-driven strategy. To tie in the aforementioned example of an acquisition requiring shareholder approval, a hedge fund that bought the stock based on the news of the acquisition with the expectation that the stock price would rise could suffer a severe loss on the investment if the deal failed to secure shareholder approval.

Event risk is inherent in the event-driven strategy, and there are many different risks specific to the company such as bankruptcy, losses, and regulatory decisions. The results could have an extreme impact on the hedge fund and on investor returns, and these risks can often be difficult to anticipate.

Conclusion

Event-driven trading strategies focus on specific corporate events and the financial instruments they can use to capitalize on those events. The most popular event-driven strategy is merger arbitrage, but there are many event-driven strategies focused on events like a bankruptcy, product launch, or corporate reshuffling.

Event-driven hedge funds use experienced portfolio managers and analysts who have expertise in specific sectors to draw on their experiences to determine which way a corporate situation will unfold. The manager must be able to quickly analyze new information and evaluate the specific types of investment vehicles needed to execute a trading idea. For many event-driven trades, time is of the essence and the competitive edge is key to a successful investment.

Event-driven strategies are generally uncorrelated to other hedge fund strategies and stock and bond markets. Each corporate situation plays out differently and there are a number of factors, including regulation, that help event-driven funds generate uncorrelated returns. Event-driven funds have risks that are carefully analyzed by hedge fund managers to determine if the risk of a trade outweighs the reward. Given the risks associated with event-driven funds, many asset allocators keep their allocations to event-driven funds to a minimum.

CHAPTER 8

Fixed-Income Strategy

A fixed income hedge fund strategy is one where the investment manager focuses his attention on fixed-income products that range from sovereign bonds to distressed debt. The fundamental aspect of a fixed-income product is that it is a debt security where the issuer must repay the debt as well as a fixed coupon rate to compensate the buyer of the product. The coupon is the fixed-interest rate on the security and thus provides an income component to the holder of a fixed-income product.

Fixed-income assets are typically issued by a corporation or government, which uses the issuance to raise money from buyers (lenders). The issuer is thus borrowing money from the buyers of a debt security and must pay for that privilege in the form of a fixed interest (a set rate that the issuer pays security holders) until the time at which the principal is fully repaid. Fixed income securities include mortgage certificates, government issues such as treasury bills and agency bonds, corporate bonds, municipal bonds, preferred shares, and other securities that pay a steady, predetermined interest rate until principal repayment.

How Do Fixed-Income Securities Work?

The fixed-income market is a global market as well as a local market. Most investors view interest rates as the rates at which a sovereign government borrows money, or the amount they receive from depositing money at their local bank. In general, sovereign debt has the most liquid interest rates.

Interest rates move as a function of market forces. Market participants that purchase and sell fixed-income products use monetary policy as their guideline to gauge the value of specific interest-rate products.

Monetary policy is the process by which a central bank controls the supply of money by targeting an interest in an effort to stabilize prices and promote growth. Each central bank has a goal for their monetary policy that includes mandates such as maintaining relatively stable prices and low unemployment. Monetary theory provides insight into how to manage optimal monetary policy.

Central banks will be accommodative in times when growth is slow and prices are stable, and will lower interest rates to increase growth and employment. Central banks will become less accommodative when growth is robust and prices are rapidly moving higher. In these times the central banks will typically increase interest rates, as the Federal Reserve did under Paul Volcker's leadership in the 1980s. By changing interest rates, the central banks are changing the levels at which banks lend to one another, as well as the rate at which they will lend to banks.

In general, a central bank will have a greater effect on the levels of short-term interest rates, while market forces will have a stronger influence on long-term interest rates. Short-term interest rates generally affect bank deposit rates, such as the prime rate, while long-term rates, such as mortgages, are influenced by market participants.

Figure 8.1A illustrates the relationship between bonds and interest rates, as you can see in the inverse price relationship between the Federal Funds Effective Rate and the price of a five-year U.S. Treasury Note. The price of a fixed-income security, such as a bond, fluctuates in the opposite direction relative to interest rates. As interest rates move higher, the price of the bond moves lower. As rates increase, investors demand more compensation to purchase a bond with a relatively lower interest rate compared to other bonds. Hence, bond prices and interest rates are inversely related, as you can see in Figure 8.1B.

Changes in interest rates are generally described by the change in a basis point, which is one-thousandth of a percent. There are 100 basis points for every 1 percent change in yield. When describing the interest-rate risk of a portfolio or financial instrument, the nomenclature refers to the dollar value per basis point, which is referred to as DV01.

Duration

The term *duration* is a measurement of the time scale of cash flows related to a bond. The longer the duration of an interest-rate product, the higher the exposure to interest rates. For example, a 30-year bond will have a higher exposure to interest rate movements than a three-month treasury bill. Duration also measures the price sensitivity to yield. Modified duration is the price sensitivity for a unit change in yield. When discussing modified duration, units are referred to as the percent change in price per one percentage point change in yield per year.

Convexity

Convexity is a measure of the sensitivity of the duration of a bond to changes in interest rates. Price convexity is a second derivative of the price of the bond with

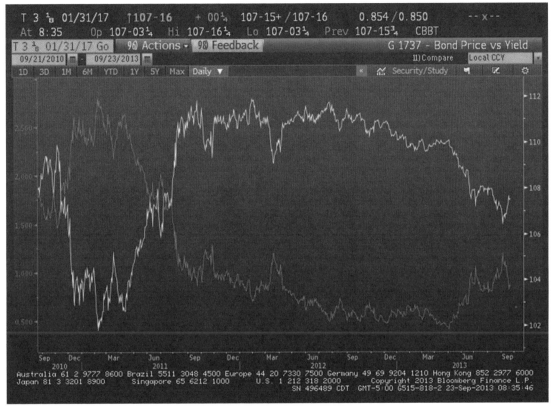

Figure 8.1A Federal Funds Index Versus Five-Year Treasury Note
Source: © 2014 Bloomberg L.P. All rights reserved.

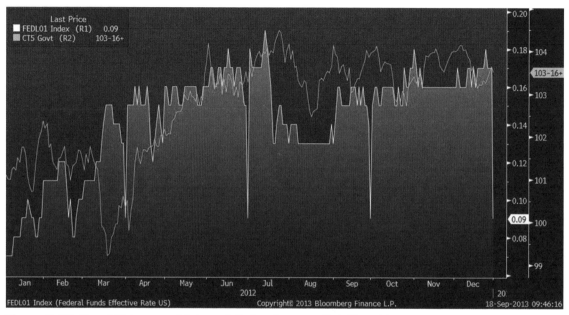

Figure 8.1B Bond Prices and Interest Rates Inverse Relationship
Source: © 2014 Bloomberg L.P. All rights reserved.

respect to interest. In general, the higher the convexity, the more sensitive the bond price is to decreasing interest rates and the less sensitive the bond price is to increasing rates.

Basic Strategy

By holding a fixed-income product such as a bond or a note, an investor is expecting to receive the principal fully repaid, while accruing interest from coupons that are paid on a regular basis by the issuer. Coupons are generally paid on a semiannual basis, but there are times when an issuer will pay coupons annually, quarterly, or monthly. There are also bonds called zero coupon bonds that pay the investor (lender) the sum of all the coupon payments when the principal is returned after the bond matures.

Types of Fixed-Income Products

A fixed-income strategy can utilize multiple products. By purchasing sovereign products, corporate bonds, and municipal bonds, an investor or asset management firm can effectively place investments with a known risk and return. The section below outlines the different products available to investors and hedge funds and how they are utilized.

Sovereign Products

Sovereign products are generally considered the most liquid products within a country. This does not mean that sovereign products are always liquid, but it does mean that they provide significant liquidity within each country.

A sovereign bond is a bond issued by a country. The issuer is the treasury of that country, and the credit rating is backed by the full faith of the country's treasury.

United States Treasury Securities are government-issued debt facilitated by the United States Department of the Treasury. These debt-financing instruments are issued in the form of Treasury Bonds, Treasury Bills, and Treasury Notes—they are often simply referred to as treasuries.

Although sovereign bonds are generally safe and liquid, there have been recent cases, such as the debt crisis in Europe, where the ability of a country to pay its debt came under question and they needed to be bailed out by another central bank. This occurred in

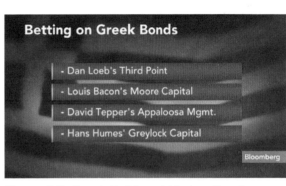

Figure 8.2 Greek Debt and Hedge Funds
Source: © 2014 Bloomberg L.P. All rights reserved.

Greece, Ireland, Portugal, and Cyprus. In each of these cases, the European Central Bank needed to provide liquidity to the country's central bank to avoid a default. Several large hedge funds held Greek debt (see Figure 8.2).

Hedge funds usually trade sovereign bonds as a global macro play or an emerging market play. There are also a number of strategies that use intercountry spreads to express an interest rate view.

How Sovereign Interest Rates Are Viewed

Many times, investors who take a view on sovereign bonds are examining the country's economic situation and the likelihood that the central bank will change their interest-rate policy based on new information. For example, if a hedge fund manager believes that the U.S. economy is beginning to gain traction and rates will likely climb in the near future, he might consider selling a bond or note to capitalize on a potential rise in interest rates. On the other hand, if an investment manager believes that a country's economics are weakening, the manager might purchase bonds to capitalize on declining yields.

Corporate Bonds

Corporate bonds are investment products that are issued by corporations to raise capital. Bonds at the corporate level are usually at the top of the capital structure and present the best investment protection during default or bankruptcy.

Similar to sovereign bonds, corporate bonds pay a coupon to investors, and generally have yields that are at a premium to sovereign bonds. The reason for the higher yields on corporate bonds is the potential for default is generally higher than a country.

Corporate bonds can be callable, which means that the issuer has the right to redeem the bond and will likely do that if the interest rates they can borrow at are lower at the callable date than the original issue date.

Some corporate bonds have a convertible feature. These convertible bonds thus give the investor the right but not the obligation to convert the bond into common stock. If investors believe the stock will climb and return a value better than the coupons issued by the bond, he will convert the bond into a stock.

Corporate bonds are rated by rating agencies that give investors an idea of the credit quality of the corporation, as you can see in Figure 8.3. The three largest credit rating agencies are Moody's, Standard & Poor's, and Fitch. Ratings range from AAA investment grade to high-yield junk. A lower credit rating generally spills over into a higher interest rate.

Municipal Bonds

Municipal bonds are bonds that are issued by a municipality such as a city or a town, in an effort to raise capital for normal operations or specific projects. Municipal bonds have the benefit of tax-free returns to investors located in the state or city that is issuing the bond. Generally, all municipal bonds are federally tax free. When compared to interest on sovereign bonds or corporate bonds, this adds an additional benefit. Many states and cities offer their residents tax-free returns on municipal bonds.

Municipal bonds are very beneficial to individuals who are in a high tax bracket. For example, a New York resident who pays 35 percent tax on federal income and 7 percent on state income will have a return profile as follows: The 6 percent tax-free yield would be equivalent to a return of 10.4 percent on a taxable corporate or government bond because the interest earned on a municipal bond is exempt from federal taxes and most state and local taxes.

Historically, the yield on municipal bonds is lower than sovereign or corporate bonds because of the tax benefit associated with these types of bonds. Municipal bonds are considered to have more credit risk than government bonds but less credit risk than corporate bonds.

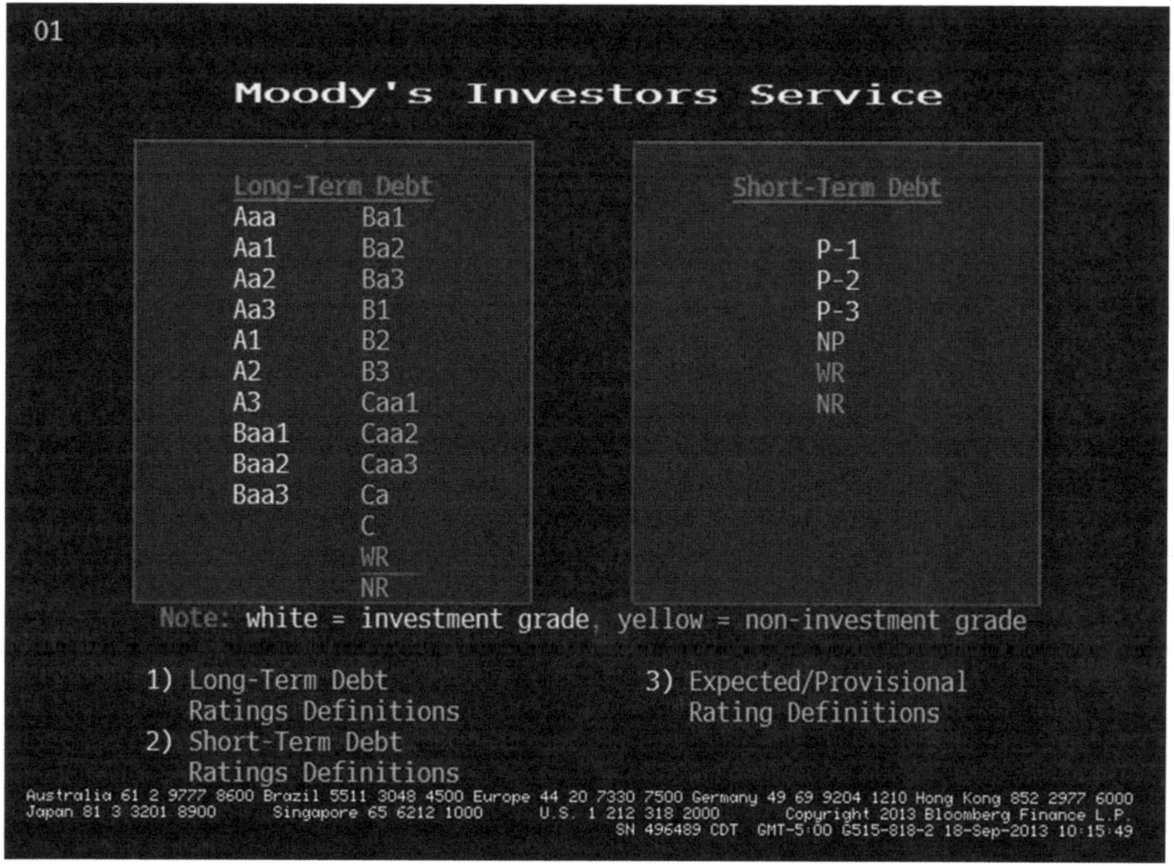

Figure 8.3 Bond Ratings
Source: © 2014 Bloomberg L.P. All rights reserved.

```
01
                        Moody's Investors Service
                        Long-Term Debt Ratings                        Page 1/3

Moody's long-term obligation ratings are opinions of the relative credit risk
of fixed-income obligations with an original maturity of one year or more.
They address the possibility that a financial obligation will not be honored
as promised.  Such ratings reflect both the likelihood of default and any
financial loss suffered in the event of default.

Aaa   Obligations rated Aaa are judged to be of the highest quality, with
      minimal risk.

Aa    Obligors rated Aa are judged to be of high quality and are subject to
      very low default risk.

A     Obligations rated A are considered upper-medium grade and are subject
      to low credit risk.

Baa   Obligations rated Baa are subject to moderate credit risk.  They are
      considered medium-grade and as such may possess certain speculative
      characteristics.


Australia 61 2 9777 8600 Brazil 5511 3048 4500 Europe 44 20 7330 7500 Germany 49 69 9204 1210 Hong Kong 852 2977 6000
Japan 81 3 3201 8900      Singapore 65 6212 1000      U.S. 1 212 318 2000      Copyright 2013 Bloomberg Finance L.P.
                                                      SN 496489 CDT  GMT-5:00 G515-818-2 18-Sep-2013 10:16:30
```

Figure 8.3 *(Continued)*

Page

Moody's Investors Service
Long-Term Debt Ratings   Page 2/3

Ba   Obligations rated Ba are judged to have speculative elements and are
     subject to substantial credit risk.

B   Obligations rated B are considered speculative and are subject to high
     credit risk.

Caa Obligations rated Caa are judged to be of poor standing and are subject
     to very high credit risk.

Ca   Obligations rated Ca are highly speculative and are likely in, or very
     near, default, with some prospect of recovery of principal and interest.

C   Obligations rated C are the lowest rated class of bonds and are
     typically in default, with little prospect for recovery of principal
     or interest.

WR   Withdrawn

NR   NR is assigned to an unrated issuer, obligation, and/or program

Australia 61 2 9777 8600 Brazil 5511 3048 4500 Europe 44 20 7330 7500 Germany 49 69 9204 1210 Hong Kong 852 2977 6000
Japan 81 3 3201 8900   Singapore 65 6212 1000   U.S. 1 212 318 2000   Copyright 2013 Bloomberg Finance L.P.
                                      SN 496489 CDT   GMT-5:00 G515-818-2 18-Sep-2013 10:17:12

Figure 8.3 *(Continued)*

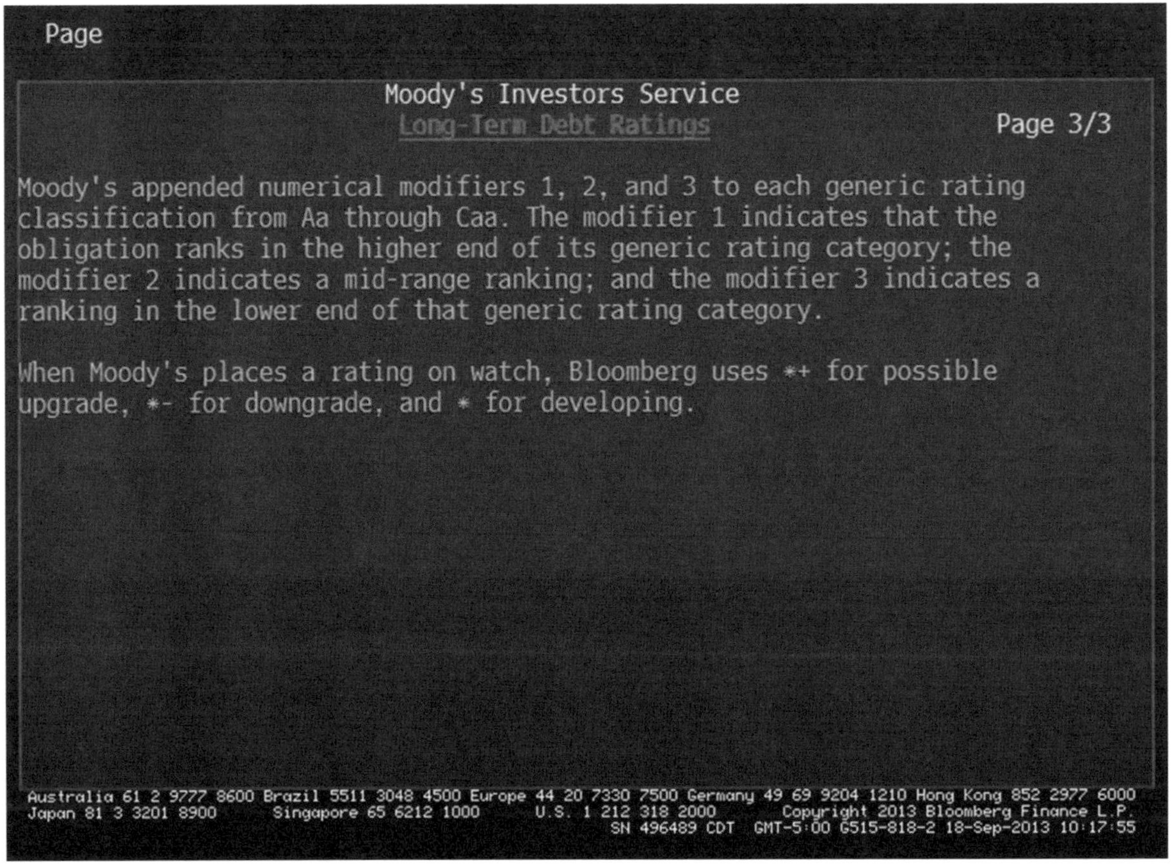

Page

Moody's Investors Service
Long-Term Debt Ratings
Page 3/3

Moody's appended numerical modifiers 1, 2, and 3 to each generic rating classification from Aa through Caa. The modifier 1 indicates that the obligation ranks in the higher end of its generic rating category; the modifier 2 indicates a mid-range ranking; and the modifier 3 indicates a ranking in the lower end of that generic rating category.

When Moody's places a rating on watch, Bloomberg uses *+ for possible upgrade, *- for downgrade, and * for developing.

Australia 61 2 9777 8600 Brazil 5511 3048 4500 Europe 44 20 7330 7500 Germany 49 69 9204 1210 Hong Kong 852 2977 6000
Japan 81 3 3201 8900   Singapore 65 6212 1000   U.S. 1 212 318 2000   Copyright 2013 Bloomberg Finance L.P.
SN 496489 CDT GMT-5:00 G515-818-2 18-Sep-2013 10:17:55

Figure 8.3 *(Continued)*

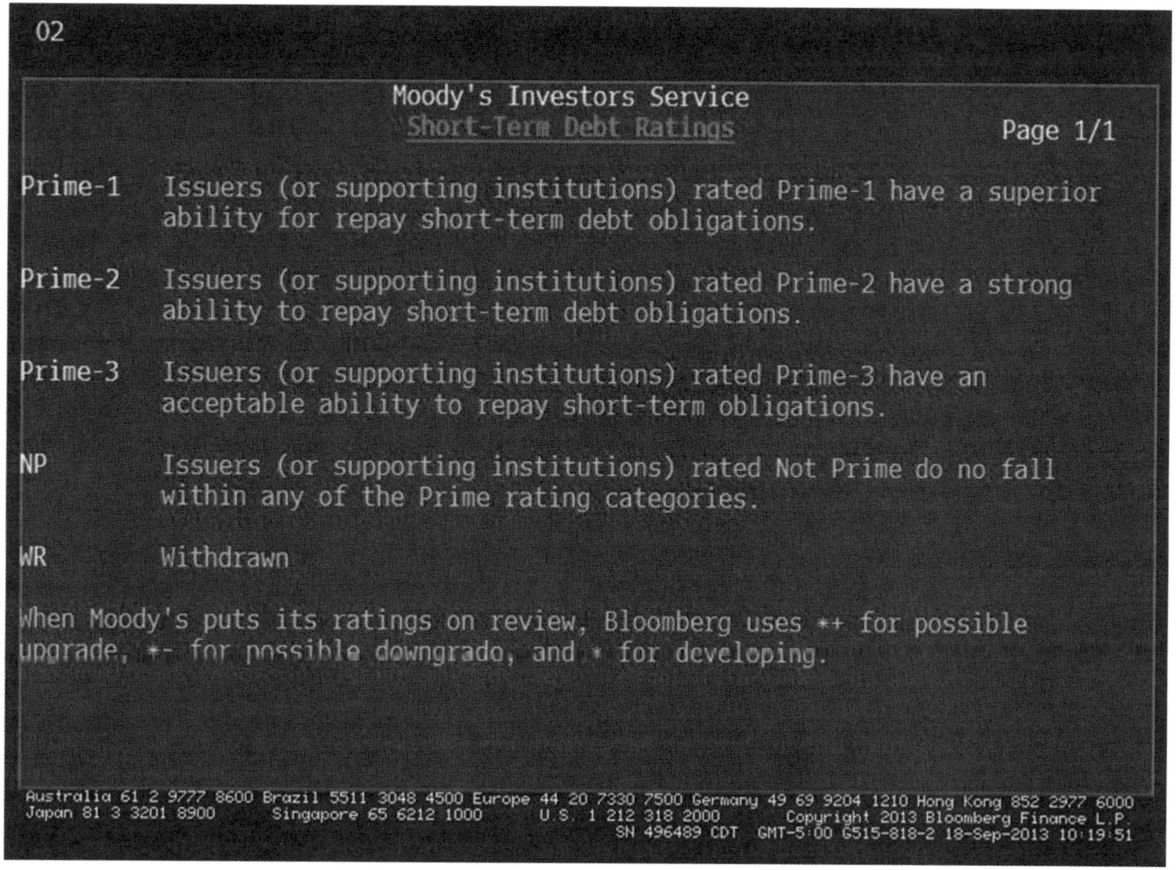

02

Moody's Investors Service
Short-Term Debt Ratings
Page 1/1

Prime-1   Issuers (or supporting institutions) rated Prime-1 have a superior ability for repay short-term debt obligations.

Prime-2   Issuers (or supporting institutions) rated Prime-2 have a strong ability to repay short-term debt obligations.

Prime-3   Issuers (or supporting institutions) rated Prime-3 have an acceptable ability to repay short-term obligations.

NP   Issuers (or supporting institutions) rated Not Prime do no fall within any of the Prime rating categories.

WR   Withdrawn

When Moody's puts its ratings on review, Bloomberg uses *+ for possible upgrade, *- for possible downgrade, and * for developing.

Australia 61 2 9777 8600 Brazil 5511 3048 4500 Europe 44 20 7330 7500 Germany 49 69 9204 1210 Hong Kong 852 2977 6000
Japan 81 3 3201 8900   Singapore 65 6212 1000   U.S. 1 212 318 2000   Copyright 2013 Bloomberg Finance L.P.
SN 496489 CDT   GMT-5:00 G515-818-2 18-Sep-2013 10:19:51

Figure 8.3 *(Continued)*

Figure 8.3 *(Continued)*

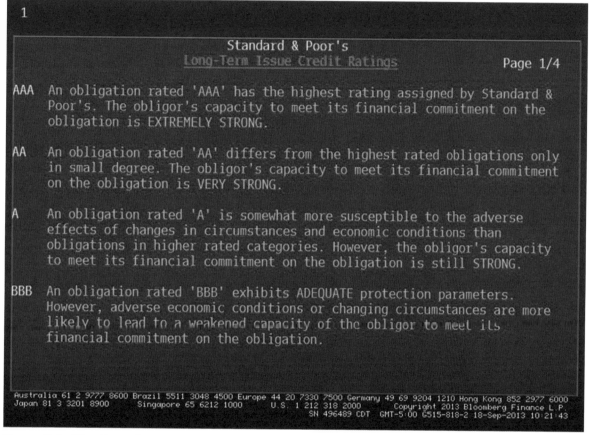

1

Standard & Poor's
Long-Term Issue Credit Ratings   Page 1/4

AAA An obligation rated 'AAA' has the highest rating assigned by Standard & Poor's. The obligor's capacity to meet its financial commitment on the obligation is EXTREMELY STRONG.

AA An obligation rated 'AA' differs from the highest rated obligations only in small degree. The obligor's capacity to meet its financial commitment on the obligation is VERY STRONG.

A An obligation rated 'A' is somewhat more susceptible to the adverse effects of changes in circumstances and economic conditions than obligations in higher rated categories. However, the obligor's capacity to meet its financial commitment on the obligation is still STRONG.

BBB An obligation rated 'BBB' exhibits ADEQUATE protection parameters. However, adverse economic conditions or changing circumstances are more likely to lead to a weakened capacity of the obligor to meet its financial commitment on the obligation.

Australia 61 2 9777 8600 Brazil 5511 3048 4500 Europe 44 20 7330 7500 Germany 49 69 9204 1210 Hong Kong 852 2977 6000
Japan 81 3 3201 8900   Singapore 65 6212 1000   U.S. 1 212 318 2000   Copyright 2013 Bloomberg Finance L.P.
                                             SN 496489 CDT GMT-5:00 G515-818-2 18-Sep-2013 10:21:43

Figure 8.3 *(Continued)*

```
Page

                         Standard & Poor's
                   Long-Term Issue Credit Ratings                    Page 2/4

Obligations rated 'BB', 'B', 'CCC', 'CC', and 'C' are regarded as having
significant speculative characteristics. 'BB' indicates the least degree of
speculation and 'C' the highest. While such obligations will likely have some
quality and protective characteristics, these may be outweighed by large
uncertainties or major exposures to adverse conditions.

BB    An obligation rated 'BB' is LESS VULNERABLE to nonpayment than other
      speculative issues. However, it faces major ongoing uncertainties or
      exposure to adverse business, financial, or economic conditions which
      could lead to the obligor's inadequate capacity to meet its financial
      commitment on the obligation.

B     An obligation rated 'B' is MORE VULNERABLE to nonpayment than
      obligations rated 'BB', but the obligor currently has the capacity to
      meet its financial commitment on the obligation. Adverse business,
      financial, or economic conditions will likely impair the obligor's
      capacity or willingness to meet its financial commitment on the
      obligation.


Australia 61 2 9777 8600 Brazil 5511 3048 4500 Europe 44 20 7330 7500 Germany 49 69 9204 1210 Hong Kong 852 2977 6000
Japan 81 3 3201 8900      Singapore 65 6212 1000      U.S. 1 212 318 2000      Copyright 2013 Bloomberg Finance L.P.
                                                          SN 496489 CDT  GMT-5:00 G515-818-2 18-Sep-2013 10:22:24
```

Figure 8.3 *(Continued)*

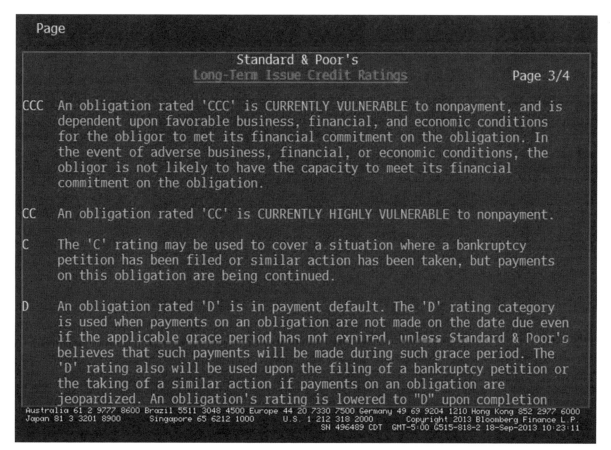

Page

Standard & Poor's
Long-Term Issue Credit Ratings   Page 3/4

CCC An obligation rated 'CCC' is CURRENTLY VULNERABLE to nonpayment, and is
     dependent upon favorable business, financial, and economic conditions
     for the obligor to met its financial commitment on the obligation. In
     the event of adverse business, financial, or economic conditions, the
     obligor is not likely to have the capacity to meet its financial
     commitment on the obligation.

CC   An obligation rated 'CC' is CURRENTLY HIGHLY VULNERABLE to nonpayment.

C   The 'C' rating may be used to cover a situation where a bankruptcy
     petition has been filed or similar action has been taken, but payments
     on this obligation are being continued.

D   An obligation rated 'D' is in payment default. The 'D' rating category
     is used when payments on an obligation are not made on the date due even
     if the applicable grace period has not expired, unless Standard & Poor's
     believes that such payments will be made during such grace period. The
     'D' rating also will be used upon the filing of a bankruptcy petition or
     the taking of a similar action if payments on an obligation are
     jeopardized. An obligation's rating is lowered to "D" upon completion

Australia 61 2 9777 8600 Brazil 5511 3048 4500 Europe 44 20 7330 7500 Germany 49 69 9204 1210 Hong Kong 852 2977 6000
Japan 81 3 3201 8900   Singapore 65 6212 1000   U.S. 1 212 318 2000   Copyright 2013 Bloomberg Finance L.P.
                                            SN 496489 CDT GMT-5:00 G515-818-2 18-Sep-2013 10:23:11

Figure 8.3 *(Continued)*

Page

Standard & Poor's
<u>Long-Term Issue Credit Ratings</u>   Page 4/4

of a distressed exchange offer, whereby some or all of the issue
is either repurchased for an amount of cash or replaced by other
instruments having a total value that is less than par.

Plus (+) or minus (-): The ratings from 'AA' to 'CCC' may be modified by the
addition of a plus or minus sign to show relative standing within the major
rating categories.

r   The "r" modifier was assigned to securities containing extraordinary
        risks, particularly market risks, that are not covered in the credit
        rating. The absence of an "r" modifier should not be taken as an
        indication that an obligation will not exhibit extraordinary
        non-credit related risks. Standard & Poor's discontinued the use of
        "r" modifier for most obligations in June 2000 and for the balance
        of obligations (mainly structured finance transactions) in November
        2002.

Australia 61 2 9777 8600 Brazil 5511 3048 4500 Europe 44 20 7330 7500 Germany 49 69 9204 1210 Hong Kong 852 2977 6000
Japan 81 3 3201 8900   Singapore 65 6212 1000   U.S. 1 212 318 2000   Copyright 2013 Bloomberg Finance L.P.
                                              SN 496489 CDT GMT-5:00 G515-818-2 18-Sep-2013 10:23:46

Figure 8.3 *(Continued)*

2

Standard & Poor's
Short-Term Issue Credit Ratings   Page 1/3

A-1 A short term obligation rated 'A-1' is rated in the highest category by
Standard & Poor's. The obligor's capacity to meet its financial
commitment on the obligation is strong. Within this category, certain
obligations are designated with a **plus sign (+)**. This indicates that the
obligor's capacity to meet its financial commitment on the obligation is
extremely strong.

A-2 A short-term obligation rated 'A-2' is somewhat more susceptible to the
adverse effects of changes in circumstances and economic conditions than
obligations in higher rating categories. However, the obligor's capacity
to meet its financial commitment on the obligation is satisfactory.

A-3 A short-term obligation rated 'A-3' exhibits adequate protection
parameters. However, adverse economic conditions or changing
circumstances are more likely to lead to a weakened capacity of the
obligor to meet its financial commitment on the obligation. A small
portion of speculative-grade credits, those with outstanding short-term
creditworthiness, may obtain an 'A-3' short-term rating (i.e., cross over
to investment grade for their short-term rating). These issuers should
have relatively low default risk over the near term, despite speculative
grade characteristics over the medium to long term.

Australia 61 2 9777 8600 Brazil 5511 3048 4500 Europe 44 20 7330 7500 Germany 49 69 9204 1210 Hong Kong 852 2977 6000
Japan 81 3 3201 8900   Singapore 65 6212 1000   U.S. 1 212 318 2000   Copyright 2013 Bloomberg Finance L.P.
SN 496489 CDT   GMT-5:00 G515-818-2 18-Sep-2013 10:24:19

Figure 8.3 *(Continued)*

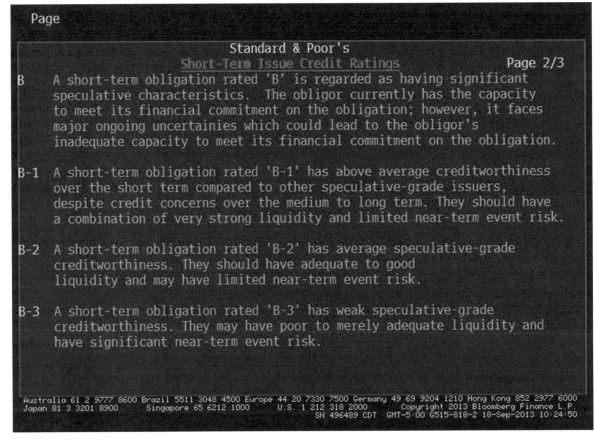

Figure 8.3 *(Continued)*

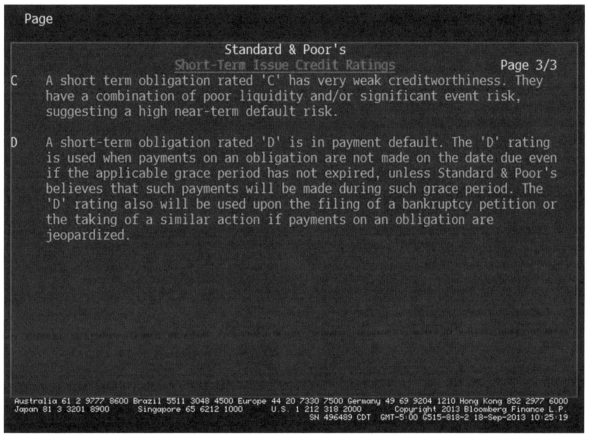

Figure 8.3 *(Continued)*

Ratings

Municipal bonds receive credit ratings similar to sovereign and corporate bonds in an effort to make investors aware of the levels of potential default. Their credit quality reflects the ability of the borrower to pay their loans.

Inflation

Inflation is considered one of the worst deterrents to bond performance. Inflation is a rise in the prices of a basket of goods and services over time. Inflation erodes the purchasing power of money. For a fixed-income investor that is expecting a specific amount of return from coupon payments semiannually, an increase in prices could erode the value of the fixed payments.

When inflation climbs, bond investors will generally reduce the amount they are willing to pay for a given bond, and demand more interest, which decreases the price of a bond.

Additionally, most central banks have a mandate of price stability. As inflation rises, central banks are apt to change monetary policy, increasing interest rates in an effort to slow down the climb of inflation. This increase in interest rates by central banks will usually have a negative effect on the value of all interest-rate products.

Strategies

Fixed income is sometimes viewed as a simple bond-trading strategy but there are many different strategies

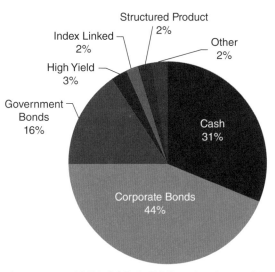

Figure 8.4 AUM £67.8 Billion by Asset Class in a Fixed-Income Portfolio
Source: SWIP, December 31, 2012.
[1] This figure and asset breakdown includes all assets managed by Fixed Income.

within fixed income. To illustrate the diversity of a fixed-income portfolio, please refer to the real example portfolio in Figure 8.4. SWIP is one of the largest fixed-income managers in Europe, and the firm shared a breakdown of a past fixed-income portfolio to give readers a sense of how investments are spread across multiple assets. As you can see, a fixed-income portfolio includes high yield bonds, government debt, corporate bonds, and other fixed-income products.

Now that you see the complexity even just within the fixed income market, we will cover some of the many fixed-income strategies used by hedge funds below.

Arbitrage

A popular fixed-income hedge fund strategy is arbitrage. Fixed-income arbitrage is similar to other arbitrage strategies in that it seeks to profit from pricing inefficiencies between fixed-income securities. This strategy gained mass attention in the end of the 1990s after Long-Term Capital Management L.P. collapsed, taking down the returns of many investment banks and other hedge funds trading in related securities. Long-Term Capital Management earned a high level of praise and an extraordinarily high level of assets under management for its fixed income arbitrage strategy.

The hedge fund, managed largely by academics and ex-Salomon Brothers traders, was highly successful in executing a fixed-income arbitrage strategy primarily focused on various government bonds. The fund would perform convergence trades when liquidity or other factors affected the present value of one bond compared to a similar bond trading at a different price. When this pricing discrepancy occurred, the Long-Term Capital Management fund would trade based on the theory that there were different prices between two similar securities. They would purchase the recently created off-the-run *bond* which would slip slightly in price when a new on-the-run *bond* would be generated from the treasury. Eventually, the prices of the two bonds would converge when maturity would occur.

When Long-Term Capital Management could identify mispriced securities and forecast the timing of this convergence with some degree of accuracy, the returns on executing this trade were eye-popping and especially so when magnified by leverage. Leverage, as we have discussed in this book, amplifies not only the potential returns but also the potential risks and losses for a strategy. Long-Term Capital Management learned this painful lesson when it suffered significant losses in 1998 as Russia defaulted on its government bonds and the firm faced margin calls that threatened to blow up the fund, only to be rescued by a group of private investors organized by the Federal Reserve. The problem that LTCM faced was when a liquidity crisis arose, investors flocked to on-the-run bonds, which pushed up the price of the bonds that LTCM was short.

This tale, masterfully told in Roger Lowenstein's *When Genius Failed*, thankfully did not end with a global financial meltdown but it serves as an important reminder of how hedge funds can control a significant portion of the fixed-income market and assume the risks and rewards of such a strategy. Long-Term Capital Management was one of the most prestigious hedge funds out there, relying on models and academic theories to manage risk and take on greater leverage, until it wasn't and its losses were far greater than the fund's brilliant partners ever predicted. We asked the head trader and portfolio manager at a New York-area fixed-income hedge fund for his take on the enduring

DEFINITION:
Off-the-Run

Refers to a security that is not the most recently issued. Off-the-run bonds generally trade at a discount.

DEFINITION:
On-the-Run

Refers to the most recently issued and most liquid security that has been issued. On-the-run bonds generally trade at a premium.

impact of Long-Term Capital Management's story. He reflected that, "it has left emotional scars on the Fixed Income Relative Value (FI-RV)/Arbitrage investment strategy. Most investors' first introduction to the FI-RV strategy is through the example of LTCM's demise. It is very difficult to overcome the negative connotation associated with LTCM, even though all of their FI-RV trades were winners (they just had flawed sizing/correlation/volatility profiles for each strategy)."

Arbitrage strategies exist with the capital structure of corporations and are evaluated by fixed-income hedge fund managers who concentrate on capital-structure arbitrage. This type of strategy looks for mispricing within a capital structure and will generate a market-neutral position, such as long senior bonds and short common stock, or long leveraged loans and short junior debt.

Spread Trading

Spread trading is a market-neutral strategy where an investor purchases one fixed-income security and simultaneously sells another debt security. Spreads can be categorized as calendar spreads, intersovereign spreads, and cross-market spreads.

Calendar Spreads

Calendar spreads take advantage of a widening or flattening of a yield curve. To transact a spread trade an investor would take a long position on one tenor of a yield curve and a short position on a longer tenor period of the yield curve (or the reverse).

When the short end of a yield curve steepens (widens) relative to the long end of the curve, investors perceive that interest rates will be declining and the short end will benefit more quickly than the long end. Alternatively, when the short end of a yield curve flattens relative to the long end, investors believe that rates are likely to increase, and therefore prices on the short end will decline at a quicker pace than the long end of the curve.

Intersovereign Spreads

Intersovereign spreads, which are often referred to as the interest rate differential within the currency markets, are the difference between one country's sovereign rates and another country's sovereign rates. Generally, investors look to transact these trades using similar tenors such as 2-year yields or 10-year yields. The spread is usually highly correlated to the movements in the spot-currency market and is a way for a fixed-income trader to speculate on the direction of a currency. The majority of the time, hedge fund managers who focus on global macro strategies will engage in this type of trading.

Cross-Market Spreads

A cross-market spread is a trade in which a portfolio manager purchases a fixed-income product in one market, say corporate bonds, and simultaneously sells a bond with a similar tenor in another market, such as U.S. treasuries. In this type of trade the investor wants to take advantage of a corporate bond spread that pays the investor to hold the pair. The investor is also looking for a market-neutral trade that will insulate the investor from general interest rate movements.

One of the most popular cross-market spreads is agency bonds versus U.S. treasuries. *Agency bonds* (also known as govies) are bonds that are collateralized by the housing markets and issued by pseudo-government agencies such as Fannie Mae and Freddie Mac. The agency markets prior to the financial crisis were once among the most sophisticated markets in the world. The collapse of the housing market in the United States that led to the financial crisis has undermined that business to a large extent.

There are a number of ways to take specific views using spread trading. For example some investors take two positions: one position is in short-term, low-risk bonds; the other position is in long-term, high-risk bonds. The former position has high liquidity and a lower coupon rate; the latter has a higher coupon rate to compensate the investor for the low liquidity due to the long-term maturities of the bonds. The positions are heavy on opposite sides of the fixed income spectrum, thus the barbell nickname for this strategy. The strategy is based on the aforementioned reversion-to-the-mean theory in that the investor expects that in the case of an extreme-but-temporary event, the long-term bonds will weather the storm because their maturity dates are sufficiently far off; the short-term bonds will likely be minimally affected by the event because they are highly liquid and safe. The strategy does not invest in intermediate-term bonds because these will likely be the most highly affected by extreme movements and less likely to recover than long-term bonds.

Preferred Stocks

There are a number of fixed-income strategies that center on preferred stock. Companies will issue preferred stock to raise capital as an alternative to bonds. Preferred stocks are bought and sold in a way that is very similar to common stocks, but they act more like bonds than stocks. Investors buy them for the steady dividends. Unlike common stocks, investors will not see capital appreciation and in most cases, the dividend never goes up either.

The term *preferred* means that a firm must pay the dividends due on its preferred shares before it pays any common stock dividends. Also, if a company goes bankrupt, preferred holders have priority over common-stock shareholders.

Options and Futures

Derivatives investment vehicles, such as futures and options, allow traders to actively initiate risk in underlying assets using the leverage provided by both futures and options. Futures on bonds or notes are the obligation to purchase (or sell) a specific bond or note on a specific date. An option is the right but not the obligation to purchase (or sell) a specific fixed income product on or before a certain date.

Futures markets on fixed-income products are liquid and provide access to numerous strategies including calendar spreads, intersovereign spreads, and cross-market spreads. In the United States, there are futures on 2-year notes, 5-year notes, 10-year notes, as well as 30-year notes.

Options on futures or cash products allow portfolio managers to take levered positions on the direction of fixed-income products, while using options to generate income or speculate on the direction of an underlying product.

For example, similar to a covered-calls option strategy, an investor can purchase a bond, and simultaneously sell a call option on the bond. The sale of the call generates premium, while the bond coupon earns yield. If the fixed-income market moves lower, the investor's loss on the price of the bond will be partially made up for by the premium received on the call. If the price of the bond moves higher, the bond might be called away from the investor at a higher price.

Swaps

A swap is an exchange of cash flows that is used as a financial instrument to speculate or hedge a financial fixed-income product. A swap has a fixed-price payer, who receives a floating price and benefits as the price of a fixed-income product rises. The opposite side of a swap is the floating-price payer who receives a fixed price.

The swap market is prevalent within the fixed-income market, and was initially used by corporate customers to hedge their interest-rate exposure.

Who Runs a Fixed-Income Hedge Fund?

The majority of fixed-income hedge fund managers started their careers at an investment bank, usually at a fixed-income, derivative-, or bond-trading desk. Typically, the trader will rise in the ranks to run that division at the investment bank or brokerage firm and eventually decide to strike out on their own in pursuit of bigger profit and greater autonomy.

In today's regulatory and financial environment, many investment banks are forced to reduce the size of their trading desks and even eliminate whole business units. The layoffs, reduced compensation, and other pressures on the traditional investment banking, fixed-income business have led many traders to join or launch their own hedge funds.

The financial incentives in managing a hedge fund are, of course, legendary, and the prestige of running a world-class hedge fund is well recognized; so it is no wonder that many talented fixed-income professionals have looked to execute a strategy similar to what they did at an investment bank. Now, instead of running a bank's proprietary trading account or trading for the bank's clients, the manager can run his own hedge fund the way he likes and enjoy the benefits including: collecting performance and management fees; trading on his own account; having the ability to hire his own team and control compensation; working on his own schedule without having to answer to any superiors; selecting the investors that he wants in the fund; the ability to trade with greater leverage and often in more exotic strategies, and, for the most part, to operate outside the strictures and oversight of regulators. The lures are obviously there, and these incentives help explain why the fixed-income strategy continues to expand.

A fixed-income hedge fund manager will likely have at least a strong working knowledge, if not full expertise, in a number of fixed-income products including: U.S. treasury securities; sovereign and municipal bonds; corporate bonds; asset- and mortgage-backed securities; and swaps, options and futures related to fixed-income securities. The manager and his team will then build strategies based on these securities; these will either be arbitrage or non-arbitrage strategies. An arbitrage strategy is one that takes advantage of large changes in prices and extreme volatility for a particular security; during these events, identical products may have very different prices, therefore creating a trading opportunity.

Why Invest in a Fixed Income Fund?

Now that we have learned some of the reasons why the fixed-income strategy has risen to prominence with hedge funds, we will now look at what has drawn investors to this strategy. For many investors, fixed-income securities are more familiar than merger arbitrage because most investors have either directly or indirectly purchased a fixed-income security. The idea of a bond is not foreign or dauntingly complicated; however, the way that hedge funds trade bonds and other fixed-income products is more complex, risky, and often more lucrative than the types of fixed-income allocations to which average investors are accustomed.

The objective for many fixed-income hedge funds is similar to the objective for ordinary fixed-income investors: steady income with low volatility. Hedge funds are not known for low risk and low volatility but many fixed-income arbitrage hedge funds seek to earn consistent returns through a variety of fixed-income investments. Most fixed-income hedge funds invest globally and will likely have a superior ability to take advantage of changes in interest rates, government issues, new fixed-income products, and other changes in the industry that an average individual investor may otherwise miss.

Industry Insight

For a granular look at the fixed-income hedge fund strategy we interviewed Derek Barnes, portfolio manager and head of trading at a $700M+ New York-area, fixed-income hedge fund.

Richard Wilson: Can you please briefly describe the type of fund you work and your role there?

Derek Barnes: Here is what I am responsible for at our fund:

Run all trading for $700M fixed-income, relative-value portfolio.

Execute all real-time global OTC and listed investment products.

Analyze specific risk of each strategy as well as systematic risk of entire portfolio.

Monitor counterparty risk and collateralization levels.

Coordinate with IT programmer to improve operational and trading infrastructure.

Spearheaded one of the first interest rate swaps to settle on LCH.Clearnet.

In addition to trading, responsible for actively managing 6 percent of fund's assets.

Mentor development of junior trader and portfolio manager.

Richard C. Wilson: Is there a typical background for a fixed-income manager? My understanding is that most FI managers come from bond-trading desks at the larger investment banks. Is this correct, or are there other common paths to working at a fixed income fund?

Derek Barnes: I would tend to agree that most FI managers come from sell-side rates trading positions at large investment banks. There is a perception that many managers have an inclination for mathematics; however, "old-fashioned" trading and people skills are not as coveted as they used to be.

Richard C. Wilson: How would you explain to someone unfamiliar with the strategy how a fixed-income hedge fund operates and executes the strategy?

Derek Barnes: My employer works very slowly because we are not frequent traders searching for a quick few ticks. We start with a quantitative analysis of every sovereign debt-related-rates product on earth and then overlay that data with our opinions, which are formed from things like reading the newspaper and remaining informed with current events. Ultimately the decision to invest or not invest in a particular strategy is a subjective and human one that belongs to the fund manager. Once a dislocation or inefficiency is found and a strategy is implemented, we are patient and we wait (oftentimes for years) for efficiency to return and monetize this strategy.

Richard C. Wilson: Can you give us examples of two specific fixed-income strategies and how they would be built in a portfolio in terms of the types and sizes of positions?

Derek Barnes: Sure, here are two such examples:

1. UK Quantitative Easing Bond Curve Trade: Bank of England in 2009 declared their intent to buy back 25 percent of all outstanding UK Gilts with maturities between 5 and 25 years. This caused yields to rise sharply three to four years out and five-year yields dropped sharply. We bought/received this three-to-four-year high rate, sold/paid the five-year low rate and bought/received long end. Once the BOE expanded its buyback to all maturities, this bond curve kink fixed itself and we monetized the trade.

   Sizing for this trade is best done with a focus on volatility of the butterfly and its historical correlation to the other strategies within the fund. Maintaining a basket of 10 to 20 negatively correlated strategies, with no one strategy contributing to more than 10 percent of the volatility profile of the fund overall, is best practice for managing risk.

2. Bonds versus Libor–Swap-Spread Trade: The yield difference between Libor-based assets and government-bond-based assets should theoretically be consistent over maturities if the credit profile of both the country and Libor are expected to remain constant. In mid-2004, Japanese bonds deliverable into the JGB 7-year bond future traded at Libor flat, and 30-year JGBs also traded at Libor flat. The market implied that JBG and Libor yields would be similar over the next 30 years; however, 18-year JGBs yielded about 20 basis points (bps) more than the corresponding Libor. In order to capture this anomaly we receive 1X 7-year Libor versus sell 1X 7-year JGB/pay 2X 20-year Libor versus buy 2X 20-year JGB/receive 1X 20-year Libor versus sell 1X 20 year JGB. Three years later this relationship became efficient again and the 20-year spread matched the 7-year and 30-year spreads.

Again, sizing for this trade is best done with a focus on volatility of the butterfly and its historical correlation to the other strategies within the fund. Maintaining a basket of 10 to 20 negatively correlated strategies, with no one strategy contributing to more than 10 percent

of the volatility profile of the fund overall is best practice for managing risk.

Richard C. Wilson: Do you believe Long-Term Capital Management has had an enduring impact on fixed-income hedge funds or is that firm viewed as a singular event atypical of this strategy?

Derek Barnes: Yes, it has left emotional scars on the Fixed Income Relative Value/Arbitrage investment strategy. Most investors' first introduction to the FI-RV strategy is through the example of LTCM's demise. It is very difficult to overcome the negative connotation associated with LTCM, even though all of their FI-RV trades were winners (they just had flawed sizing/correlation/volatility profiles for each strategy).

Richard C. Wilson: What types of risks does a fixed-income hedge fund management team have to take into account in a typical trade?

Derek Barnes;

a. Tail-risk options are sexy, but there are none that protect the FI investment business. They tend to always fight the previous battle and can't predict what catastrophe will come next.

b. Leverage is a four-letter word and it is easily manipulated and misunderstood by 99 percent of the world. Convincing investors and counterparties that volatility and correlations are the best measures of risk is a daunting challenge.

c. FI-RV investors need to be long-term investors with multi-year time horizons. Rare occasions of drawdowns are the best time to invest in this strategy, even though it is scary to see everyone else unwinding and running for cover.

Richard C. Wilson: How has fixed-income investing changed since the financial crisis, if at all?

Derek Barnes: It has changed dramatically. Bank prop-trading desks are shrinking and disappearing every day, which leaves more and more great FI-RV opportunities for hedge funds with long-term investment horizons.

Richard C. Wilson: What are some significant trends you are seeing in the fixed income strategy or the hedge fund industry as a whole?

Derek Barnes: Bank prop-trading desks are going the way of the dodo bird, and many FI-RV hedge funds that drifted away from their initial mandate (due to their impatience?) have underperformed.

Richard C. Wilson: What is a typical day for you and your management team? We want to give our readers a sense of what it's like to run a fixed-income hedge fund, so any and all details are welcome.

Derek Barnes: In the A.M., read news and research. Pay no attention to flows from the sell side because we don't care about intraday moves—we look at the big picture. Crunch numbers and back-test any ideas, discuss within the firm, etc. Maintain existing trades, and re-hedge when necessary. In the afternoon, prepare for possible trades to put on or take off tomorrow. Read more news and research and get a feel for where the world is today versus where it should be.

Richard C. Wilson: Is there anything else you'd like to add?

Derek Barnes: This is a dirty and rough business with sharks all around you. Unfortunately, nice guys tend to finish last, the squeaky wheel gets the oil, and you eat what you kill. Be careful out there, and don't do anything that will cause you to lose sleep at night. Watch your back!

We were fortunate to have Derek Barnes share his fixed-income portfolio management expertise with us. I hope this interview helped to shed some light on the fixed-income hedge fund strategy.

Conclusion

The fixed-income markets are a broad and liquid market allowing investors to allocate significant capital using a multitude of investment strategies. Many fixed-income strategies are non-correlated to the general direction of the fixed-income markets, as they pertain to specific products or sectors.

Beyond geographically broadening an investor's exposure to fixed-income investments, a fixed-income-focused hedge fund can adopt a range of unique strategies related to fixed-income securities that go beyond simple municipal, mortgage, or government bonds. Fixed-income funds will employ unique and often complex strategies within the fixed-income niche or related to a particular fixed-income product.

Test Yourself

Answer the following questions.

1. True or False: A fixed-income strategy entails investing in an asset class where the investor is entitled to a fixed amount on a preset schedule.
2. True or False: A fixed-income strategy always generates returns that are above the market average.
3. Spread trading is:
   A. A strategy where a combination of options, futures, and/or securities are bought with multiple strike prices and expiration dates.
   B. The investment banking practice of spreading investments across multiple sectors.
   C. When hedge funds invest solely in short positions.
4. True or False: Fixed-income arbitrage hedge funds seek to earn consistent returns through a variety of fixed-income investments.
5. A swap is:
   A. The process of trading securities for equity.
   B. An exchange of cash flows that is used as a financial instrument to speculate or hedge a financial fixed-income product.
   C. Asset-backed securities invested evenly throughout an investment period with the main object of capital preservation.
   D. Institutional financial products sold to the general public in exchange for a small equity position within a hedge fund.

6. True or False: Swaps were initially used by corporate customers to hedge their interest-rate exposure.
7. Which is an example of a fixed-income strategy? (Circle all that apply.)
   A. Short-selling government bonds
   B. UK quantitative easing bond curve trade
   C. Obtaining long positions in technology ETFs
   D. A bond versus Libor swap-spread trade
8. True or False: The reason for the higher yields on corporate bonds is the potential for default is generally lower than a country.
9. An example of evaluating monetary policy to predict a change in the fixed-income market would be:
   A. Purchasing bonds with a low interest yield before any Federal Board of Governors meeting.
   B. Noting that central banks will become much more accommodative when growth is robust and prices are rapidly moving higher.
   C. Understanding short-term interest rates are influenced by market participants, where long-term rates generally affect bank deposit rates such as the prime rate.
   D. Noting that central banks will be accommodative in times when growth is slow and prices are stable, and will lower interest rates to increase growth and employment.

Answers can be found in Appendix B.

CHAPTER 9

Convertible-Arbitrage Strategy

The convertible-arbitrage strategy thesis is similar to long/short equity or capital-structure arbitrages where the portfolio manager is looking to benefit from the pricing of a company's convertible bond relative to its common stock.

What is a Convertible Bond?

A convertible bond is a hybrid fixed-income security that has a bond component that pays a coupon, along with an equity component that contains optionality that is linked to a conversion feature. The option portion of the convertible bond allows the holder to exchange the convertible bond for common shares at a set conversion price, which is similar to a strike price for an option.

Buying the convertible bond places the investor in a position to hold the bond, or to convert it to stock if he anticipates that the stock's price will rise.

Convertible bonds offer investors equity-like return with the protection of a coupon against adverse downside movements. The value of the bond component is influenced by interest rates, credit quality, and the maturity date, while the equity option's value is influenced by the underlying stock's price, implied volatility, and dividends.

Corporations view convertible bonds as an inexpensive way to handle financing, as the bond's coupon is often much lower than straight debt. Coupons are lower and achieve a higher value by the optionality associated with turning the bond into a stock. While the convertible bond market is liquid within the United States, there are also significant convertible markets in Europe and Japan.

Convertible bonds are often issued because the issuer is negatively viewed in the credit markets or simply lacks an established credit rating because it is a new corporation. Generally there is a higher perceived risk of convertible borrows by lenders because convertible bonds suggest a lower credit rating and greater risk of default.

Some investors do not invest in convertible bonds, either because of risk-management restrictions or personal aversion to the sector. This reduces the liquidity in the convertible bonds market, compared to other bond markets.

Strategies

A popular convertible-arbitrage strategy is static trading. The aim is to simultaneously purchase a corporation's convertible bonds and sell short the same corporation's common stock.

The idea behind convertible arbitrage is that a company's convertible bonds are sometimes priced inefficiently relative to the company's stock. Convertible arbitrage attempts to profit from this pricing error.

The logic of this trade is that if the corporation's stock price falls then the hedge fund will profit from the depreciating price of the stock it sold short. In addition to the gains from the short sale, the hedge fund will earn income from the coupon on the convertible bonds it still holds, and the bonds' price will typically depreciate less than the stock price due to the income component of the security.

In this strategy, the hedge fund is long the corporation's credit but short the corporation's stock because the fund holds the corporation's debt but is betting against the stock's current market value. The trade is a spread trade where the portfolio manager is looking for a convergence between the implied price of the common stock from the convertible bond and the actual common stock price.

In the same example, if the corporation's stock price increases, the short will obviously lose money but the expectation is that the loss will be partly offset by the income from the bond, along with an increase in the price of the bond. Although it is likely the loss from the stock short will be greater than the gains on the convertible bond, this is not the ideal circumstance.

The scenarios that create opportunities within a convertible-bond strategy are that a new issue convertible bond undervalues the embedded equity-call option value; or long-only convertible bond investors undervalue the embedded call option.

Types of Arbitrage Techniques

Carry trades typically involve a high hedge ratio that could approach 100 percent, and they trade like a synthetic put on the stock. Theoretically, a long call position, which has a short that is more than the delta of the call, trades like a put position where the investor gains if the underlying security moves lower. Managers who use convertible arbitrage and focus on carry techniques like to use low-premium bonds. The cash flow created by the coupon, combined with a market-neutral hedge ratio, are the key return drivers of the strategy.

This type of static trading yields include the bond's interest coupon plus the short sale rebate less borrowing costs of the short stock position, along with payable dividends from the short position (when a manager is short a stock he is liable for any dividends that are paid).

DEFINITION:
Static Trading

A type of trading when simultaneous and opposing positions are obtained in a company, government, or security.

DEFINITION:
Carry Trades

A strategy where a long position is obtained in a security, like a stock or bond, simultaneously with a short position on the asset underlying the security, like a future.

Returns are also generated from buying undervalued bonds and/or from effectively trading the hedge ratio. High levels of leverage can allow a manager to produce robust returns after locking in specific cash flows.

A short-sale rebate is a portion of the interest in a T-bill account earned by a hedge fund from shorting a security. Once a stock is returned to the lender the T-bill interest is then rebated to the hedge fund.

Gamma trading is an approach that strives to constantly alter the hedge ratio based on the embedded option's implied volatility. Gamma, which will be described in more detail later in this chapter, is the change in delta relative to the share price of the stock. Volatility traders usually trade convertible bonds in the hybrid stage, where they manage residual risks to accept or hedge in an effort to generate profits.

These bonds have a high-default probability and the embedded option is out-of-the-money. This means that the price at which an investor can convert to stock is well above the current level.

The return profile in credit trading focuses on the capital-structure arbitrage between the senior convertible bond and the junior common stock. The returns are more directional and depend on the manager's assessment of the issuer's enterprise value.

Convertible-Arbitrage Risks

Convertible arbitrage, like most strategies, has risks that are proportional to the reward. One of the key areas of risk stems from the convertibility function of the convertible bond. Most convertible bonds require a specified amount of time to be held prior to the optionality of converting the bond into a stock is activated. This open period needs careful evaluation to determine in advance if market conditions will coincide with the time frame in which conversion to a stock is permitted.

Risks associated with a convertible-arbitrage strategy stem from the ways in which the portfolio manager determines they will attempt to generate income. Some of the risks associated with a convertible arbitrage strategy are optionality risks, call risks, interest rates risks, and default risk. Once managers select a convertible bond that is appropriate for their given strategy, a hedge ratio must be determined. The hedge in this strategy is the amount of shares of the common stock that will be shorted to neutralize directional market risk. With the right hedge ratio, the convertible arbitrage position can be profitable regardless of whether the stock rises or declines.

For a delta-neutral strategy, the hedge ratio is set so that the position is market neutral initially. This strategy profits from the cash flow generated from selecting an undervalued convertible bond and any rebalancing of the hedge ratio if the underlying stock price moves significantly. The rebalancing is known as *delta hedging* and is similar to hedging an option.

Delta Hedging

The delta of a convertible bond is the risk associated with outright directional movement of the underlying stock. The delta is mitigated by using an offsetting

DEFINITION:
Gamma Trading

A strategy where trades are placed based off the gamma of an asset. Gamma refers to the change in the price of a derivative in relation to the price of the actual asset. In other words, gamma refers to the convexity of the asset.

DEFINITION:
Credit Trading

A trading approach that generally focuses on distressed convertible bonds and the conversion to junior common stock.

short-sale position in the underlying stock, which changes as the price of the underlying stock changes. The option value of the convertible bond is the source of change of the delta of the option. The delta of an option is the sensitivity of an option price relative to changes in the price of the underlying shares.

Delta hedging is the process of setting or keeping the delta of a portfolio as close to zero as possible. In practice, maintaining a zero delta is very complex because there are risks associated with actively hedging large movements in the underlying asset price.

Delta hedging establishes the required hedge and may be accomplished by buying or selling an amount of the underlying asset that corresponds to the delta of the portfolio. By adjusting the amount bought or sold on new positions, the portfolio delta can be made to sum to zero, and the portfolio is then delta neutral.

For example, let's assume that a portfolio manager purchases a convertible bond where the conversion price is 20 percent out-of-the-money (higher than the current price). In theory, the delta of the option is approximately 20 percent, which means that for every share that the manager can convert at a higher price, the current underlying delta is 20 percent of that number. If the price of the stock increases, the value of the option will increase from the directional move but only by 20 percent of the number of convertible shares.

To hedge the delta of an option in the example above, a trader would sell an amount of shares equal to the delta of the option. In this case, the trader would sell 20 percent of the shares that can be converted into common stock.

The delta of the option will change as soon as the price of the underlying shares change. If the price of the stock increases, the delta of the option would change and this in turn would change the amount of the delta that was hedged. In the example an increase to the level of the conversion rate would increase the delta to approximately 50 percent. To hedge the delta a portfolio manager could consider short selling more shares. The delta of an option moves as the underlying share, which is referred to as the gamma of the option. Gamma is a derivative of delta, and is the rate of change of the delta.

An option-pricing model that uses many of the inputs associated with the convertible bond will assist a portfolio manager with the appropriate hedge needed to keep the position delta neutral.

One of the risks associated with delta hedging within a convertible-bond strategy is the availability of a stock loan. A stock loan is a loan that is granted in order for an investor to short sale a stock. The lender loans the stock to an investor at a specific interest rate, and will receive the stock back from the investor when the short sale is terminated.

Conversion Price Risks and Benefits

The level of the conversion price represents a risk similar to the risks associated with strike map risk. As the price of a stock approaches the conversion price of a convertible bond, the gamma of the option increases.

A portfolio manager needs to understand that the delta of the convertible bond will increase at a quick pace as the stock price approaches and passes the conversion price. This scenario is true whether the markets are moving higher toward the conversion price or the share price is moving lower toward the conversion price.

Higher levels of gamma mean that the volume of delta hedging will increase in and around the conversion price of the convertible bond.

An at-the-money strategy requires a short sale of approximately 50 percent of the delta of the number of shares that can be converted by the convertible bond. If the share price rises, the loss from a short position in the stock could be less than the gain from the convertible bond's price appreciation. This is the case because the gamma associated with the conversion feature theoretically makes the owner of the bond longer underlying shares as the share price rises. Unless the delta is hedged instantaneously, the bond price should outperform. On the other hand, if the share price falls, the gains from shorting the stock could exceed the loss on the convertible bond. The price of the convertible bond cannot fall below the bond floor. This is the lowest value that convertible bonds can fall to, given the present value of the remaining future cash flows and principal repayment.

Deep in-the-money convertible bonds are attractive for their income advantage. These are usually highly leveraged trades, as the proceeds from selling the underlying stock short can be used to buy more convertibles because of the high delta.

Deep out-of-the-money or "busted" convertible bonds can be attractive as a fixed-income play. These convertibles have very low deltas and changes to the underlying share price and are often mispriced. However, these convertibles can be attractive because the investor receives the upside of a significant rise in the share price similar to a leap option. Additionally, the yield on the bond is often equivalent to that of a straight bond without a conversion factor.

Time Decay

Convertible bonds have a maturity date and many also have call dates. A call date is the date when the issuer of the bond has the right to recall the bond. Whether the bond has a call date or just a maturity date, the option to convert the bond to a stock will be terminated when the bond matures.

Part of the valuation of a convertible bond is the time to maturity and how long the owner of the bond has the right to convert that bond into a stock. Longer periods of time to maturity are directly correlated to the value of the convertible bond.

The owner of a convertible bond can hedge his or her time decay in an effort to increase the value of the convertible bond. In essence, a convertible bond is similar to owning a bond and owning the right to purchase a stock at a specific strike price. By selling the right (which is the optionality associated with the convertible bond), the owner enhanced the income generated from the bond. This would only make sense if the bond price was undervalued, and the bond owner is selling the optionality for more than it was purchased.

Convertible bonds are often purchased at premium prices to par, so call risk generally guarantees a loss on the position as the bond will be called at par.

Interest-Rate Risks

Convertible bonds are corporate bonds and therefore have exposure to corporate-interest rates. Corporate-interest rate exposure can be broken down into interest-rate risk that is defined by sovereign risk, and a spread relative to corporate risk that is driven by the demand for risk and credit quality.

Sovereign-Interest Rates

Sovereign-interest rates are the yields where a country can borrow capital. There are a number of factors that go into determining sovereign-borrowing yields. Yields are generally driven by market sentiment, and the economic backdrop of a specific country. Short-term yields are generally driven by a target yield directed from the country's central bank and the view of market participants with regard to any changes to the central bank's interest rate policy. Yields beyond two years to maturity are generally driven by market sentiment.

As an economy begins to expand, interest rates usually increase as market participants begin to anticipate that the central bank will raise rates to moderate the economy and reduce the risk of inflation. As an economy contracts, interest rates usually fall as market participants begin to anticipate that the central bank will reduce interest rates to spur growth.

Corporate Yields

A corporation issues bonds to raise money in order to expand its business. Corporate-credit spreads are earned in exchange for default risk through the mechanism of credit-default swaps, which give exposure to the credit spread associated with a specific company. Corporate interest rates generally trade as a spread to sovereign-interest rates.

Credit risk is considered the extra yield paid to the lender to compensate investors for taking default risk. The coupon of a bond is usually fixed upon issuance and is adjusted by the market price of the bond falling and the yield rising to the appropriate credit spread.

Credit is also a function of liquidity. Most corporate bonds are traded in the secondary market, making it difficult to always get a continuous price with a relatively tight bid/off spread. This particular risk could become more severe in developing markets as well as corporations with lower credit quality.

Since hedge funds are thought to hold a significant percentage of the outstanding convertible bonds in the United States, there is a potential lack of liquidity in down markets. The beta of a convertible bond is likely higher given everyone will move to the exit door at the same time.

Inflation is another risk that erodes future fixed-cash flows. Inflation increases prices of a standard basket of goods and services. Anticipation of inflation, or higher inflation, may depress the prices of bonds. Higher levels of inflation will reduce the demand for fixed-income products as investors look for assets that will retain their value in a rising price environment.

Who Manages Convertible Arbitrage Hedge Funds?

Convertible arbitrage hedge funds are managed by investment professionals with deep experience in the bond and options market. In order to analyze and accurately evaluate the issuers, convertible-arbitrage managers must be adept at fundamental analysis of corporations. Due to the frequent crossover in convertible-arbitrage strategies, managers must be highly competent and comfortable in both analyzing and trading debt and equity securities.

Convertible-bond managers also need to have a robust knowledge of the option markets and be comfortable analyzing and trading risks associated with options. Understanding the option-valuation process is key in a manager's ability to trade the gamma and delta of a convertible bond.

The Benefits of a Convertible-Arbitrage Strategy

Investors are often attracted to convertible-arbitrage funds for a number of reasons, including the market neutrality of the strategy and the exposure and flexibility of investing in debt securities with an equity option. In general, most convertible-arbitrage managers are not exposed to either the bond market or the equity market, but instead use the combination of both to take spread risk, which employs optionality to generate returns above corporate debt.

Conclusion

The convertible-arbitrage strategy has produced attractive returns over the past couple of decades. Returns using this strategy are uncorrelated to stock and bond strategies and can perform well in many different market environments.

The principal risk is the manager's ability to find mispriced, undervalued securities rather than beta relative to the equity or bond markets. Managing a market-neutral strategy is difficult and requires knowledge of a company's fundamentals, the global macro environment corporate bond spreads, and option trading. Although the strategy generates robust risk-adjusted returns, the importance of the manager cannot be underestimated. Investors looking for a strategy that is uncorrelated to the equity and bond markets are likely to find a strong alternative in convertible arbitrage.

To download several videos related to the focus of this chapter and to watch over 125 total video modules and expert audio interviews, please activate your free account here: http://HedgeFundGroup.org/Access.

Test Yourself

Answer the following questions.

1. Static trading is:
   A. A trading strategy where a position is obtained and then held for a given period.
   B. A type of trading when simultaneous opposing positions are obtained.
   C. Identical to arbitrage trading.
   D. A type of trading when simultaneous agreeing positions are obtained.

2. True or False: Beta hedging is a strategy where at least two positions are taken with the goal of keeping the beta, or the sensitivity to change in the value of a derivate based on the change in an underlying asset, to zero.

3. True or False: An at-the-money strategy requires a short sale of 100 percent of the delta of the number of shares that can be converted by the convertible bond.

4. True or False: Sovereign interest rates are the yields at which a country can borrow capital.

5. A carry trade is:
   A. A strategy where a hedge fund goes long in a security and short in a related derivative.
   B. A strategy where a hedge fund goes short in a security and long in a related derivative.
   C. A strategy where a hedge fund cashes in trades that have carried over from the previous quarter.
   D. A strategy where a hedge fund reinvests in trades that have carried over from the previous quarter.

Answers can be found in Appendix B.

CHAPTER 10

Quantitative and Algorithmic Trading Strategies

Quantitative trading is an investment strategy that relies on mathematical formulas and price action to recognize trading opportunities. These types of strategies can be as simple as analyzing the "dogs of the Dow," which look for the 10 worst-performing Dow stocks from the prior year, to statistical arbitrage, which looks at covariance matrices to determine the best-performing portfolio.

Algorithmic trading strategies are systematic strategies that can use quantitative investment approaches to generate investment returns. The two concepts are similar with quantitative strategies focusing on the research end of the investment process and algorithms evaluating the execution end of the investment methodology.

This chapter will define quantitative and algorithmic trading strategies and discuss how hedge funds use these strategies to generate consistent returns. It will then focus on specific strategies that are used and the basis for employing quantitative or algorithmic investment strategies.

Quantitative Trading

Quantitative trading strategies are employed by many hedge funds as the strategy removes much of the human element from investment decisions. Quantitative strategies remove much of the discretion from the risk-management process, which decreases emotions involved in the trading process such as fear and greed.

A quantitative trading strategy uses computer software programs programmed by geniuses and highly intelligent employees to identify price patterns and specific trading behavior. Market trends can be uncovered based on the price action of a security and the distribution of volume. Securities trade in a cyclical pattern that can be recognized by sophisticated computer software.

For example, by analyzing price action, a quantitative analyst can find market environments wherein assets are demonstrating trending behavior relative to consolidative behavior. Once patterns are detected that foreshadow this type of behavior, a program can initiate trades or manage risk in a way that will profit from such a market environment.

Quantitative-trading strategies differ from qualitative strategies as quantitative strategies use specific mathematical criteria to determine relative value as opposed to subjective criteria. The goal behind a quantitative strategy is to uncover investment opportunities in undervalued securities, in addition to identifying assets that are dear.

Quantitative-investment techniques are also used to analyze and manage risk exposures in a portfolio. Specific types of price action that might be unnoticeable to the naked eye can be evaluated by a mathematical formula, and potentially avoid substantial losses that might occur in a discretionary strategy. By relying on mathematical formulas, an investment adviser might be better able to identify imbalances or vulnerabilities in a portfolio.

Psychology

Quantitative investing is largely driven by research and computer software, but there is a human element

that is required. For a quantitative program to begin, a portfolio manager has to initiate the program and, although theoretically the manager is not involved in making the day-to-day trading decisions, he or she is responsible for turning off the program if it begins to generate substantial drawdowns.

The psychology of managing the risk associated with large drawdowns in quantitative strategies is critical to the long-term success of a trading program. An example of such an issue occurred during the financial crisis when quantitative hedge funds such as Renaissance Technologies experienced a huge drawdown during the latter half of 2007 (Burton, 2008). If the managers of many of the large quantitative funds shut down after a few months of negative returns, they would have never been able to rebound and generate the successful returns that followed.

Algorithmic Trading

Algorithmic trading, which is also known as *algo* trading, automated trading, black-box trading, or system trading, is the use of electronic platforms for initiating and managing trading positions. Algorithms execute computerized trading instructions that include a price level, the notional value of the asset to be placed within a trading order, along with specific exit instructions that generally do not require any human intervention.

Algorithmic trading is done by hedge fund traders as it helps manage market impact and risk. Market makers on the sell side use algo trading to provide liquidity to the market, generating and executing orders automatically.

High-Frequency Trading

High-frequency trading is the most pervasive category of algorithmic trading. High-frequency trading strategies utilize computers that make methodical trading decisions to initiate positions based on information that is received electronically. The speed of this decision is based on information that is computed before a human is able to make the decision and therefore can profit from information arbitrage.

The structure of the capital markets has been altered by high-frequency trading, which has created fast markets along with market melt-ups and meltdowns. Increasing computing power and the ability to quickly move information across lines has created an inequality that has led to continued investment in high-frequency trading. High-frequency trading has grown significantly, as you can see in Figure 10.1, despite concerns raised by regulators and other investors.

Positions taken by hedge funds that engage in high-frequency trading may be held for only seconds, or fractions of a second, with the computer trading in and out of positions thousands of times a day. Investment concerns engaged in high-frequency trading rely heavily on their computer reliability and the processing speed of their trades.

The benefits and the costs of high-frequency trading form a debate that continues to generate interest from regulators and liquidity providers. High-frequency trading may cause new risks to the financial system. High-frequency trading has been found to have contributed to volatility in the May 6, 2010, Flash Crash (see Figure 10.2), which saw the Dow Industrial average decline nearly 1,000 points within a 15-minute period. High-frequency liquidity providers were found to have withdrawn from the market, creating a vacuum of liquidity.

Pattern Recognition

One of the benefits of quantitative trading is the ability of a computer to monitor market-price action that would normally go unrecognized. Quantitative analysts back-test price patterns to determine if they foreshadow future price directions; most back-tested, quantitative systems that attempt to determine future price action are either trend-following or mean-reversion strategies.

Patterns

Support and resistance levels along with trend lines form the basis of trading patterns that have been used throughout history to predict future market movements. The concept is based on the theory that history, along with human psychology, repeats itself, and that a specific grouping of market movements will foreshadow a market direction. Quantitative

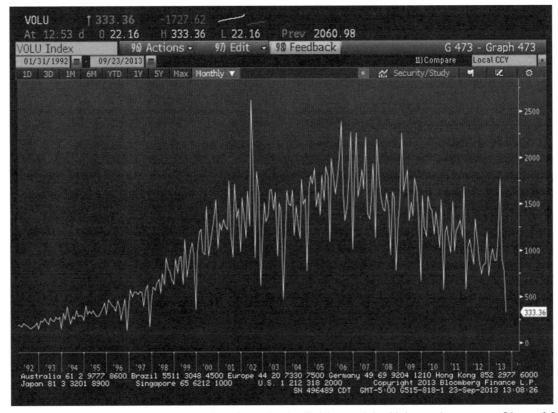

Figure 10.1 High-Frequency Trading Growth, As Evidenced by Volume Increases Since 1992
Source: © 2014 Bloomberg L.P. All rights reserved.

strategies attempt to recognize both continuation and reversal patterns in an attempt to determine the next market movement.

Continuation patterns express a pause within market sentiment that eventually refreshes. Reversal patterns reflect market consolidation prior to a reversal of sentiment and market-price action. There are a number of interesting reversal and continuation patterns. Two of the most popularly used are the head-and-shoulder pattern, and the flag pattern.

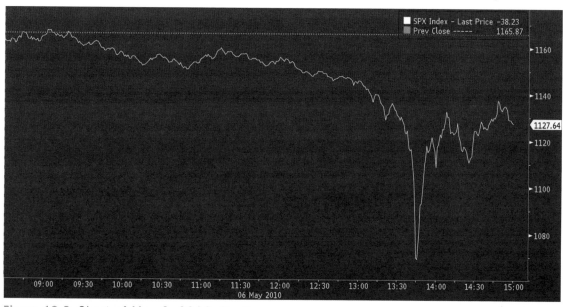

Figure 10.2 Chart of May 6, 2010, Decline
Source: © 2014 Bloomberg L.P. All rights reserved.

Head and Shoulder

The head-and-shoulders pattern is a reversal pattern, and it is most often seen at the end of an uptrend. The reverse head-and-shoulder pattern usually signifies the end of a downturn. The beginning of the reversal of an uptrend will likely coincide with market consolidation. The left shoulder of the pattern coincides with the largest market volume seen within the pattern. Forces of supply in the form of selling generate resistance, creating an intermediate top.

The intermediate top is met with market enthusiasm, which pushes prices to a new high, which is again met with selling. The first intermediate high is considered the left shoulder, while the new high is looked at as the head of the pattern (see Figures 10.3A and 10.3B for examples of this pattern).

Volume that coincides with the head is generally less than volume experienced during the left shoulder. After moving lower and hitting support, which forms the neckline, buyers return and

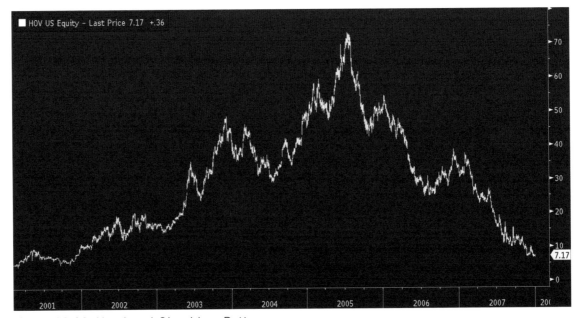

Figure 10.3A Head-and-Shoulders Pattern
Source: © 2014 Bloomberg L.P. All rights reserved.

ultimately push through to a new intermediate high, which fails to break resistance created by the head. The right shoulder generally experiences the least market volume associated with the head-and-shoulder pattern. The failure to breach the upside creates downward pressure, testing the neckline. Support of the market is a trend line that creates the neckline. The head-and-shoulder pattern is complete when the market breaks the neckline.

Volume generally increases dramatically when the neckline is broken.

Flags

Flags are continuation patterns that signal a consolidation prior to a resumption of the current trend. Flags are generally observed after large market advances, and the pole of the flag is generally a break out. A security will usually continue to move in the direction of the flag.

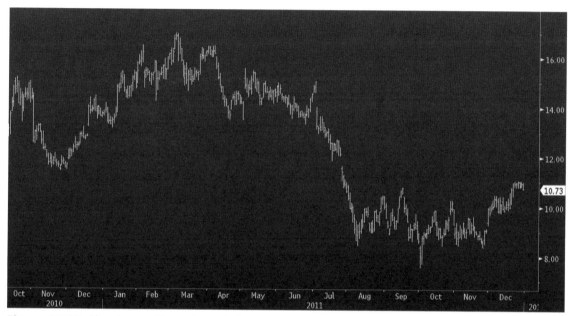

Figure 10.3B Head-and-Shoulders Pattern

Trading Strategies

The following are explanations of a number of different trading strategies employed by quantitative hedge funds. These trades can be highly complex—quant funds draw talent from the Ivy Leagues and there is rarely a simple investment made by these sophisticated traders—so we will not be able to cover all the ins and outs of each trade, but this chapter will give you a good, fundamental understanding of these strategies.

Pair Trading

The most common form of pair trading exists within the equity markets as a quantitative analyst can find stocks that operate in similar businesses such as Dell and Hewlett Packard.

A market-neutral strategy is one in which the investor is attempting to garner returns without assuming outright directional risk. A pair trade accomplishes this objective by assuming relative-value risk.

> **DEFINITION:**
> **Pair Trading**
>
> A market-neutral quantitative trading strategy where the objective is a relative value of one asset versus another.

For example, a pair trade is initiated when an investor purchases one stock and simultaneously sells short the same notional value of another stock. If an investor purchases $1,000 of Dell, they would simultaneously sell short $1,000 of Hewlett Packard.

Pair trades are most effective when the two stocks that are used are highly correlated and co-integrated.

When assets share the same business and operational models, their stock prices are generally correlated and usually have a similar market beta.

Pair trading attempts to avoid swings in the direction of a market and attempts to benefit from capturing the beta of the market. Pair traders are interested in situations where highly correlated stocks temporarily diverge in price, only to snap back at a later date.

Pair-Trade Analysis

One of the best ways to analyze two stocks is to evaluate the movements of the ratio of price between the two assets. The ratio is calculated by dividing one stock price by another stock price. The ratio of two highly correlated stock prices reflects a robust gauge of the return profile of each stock and can be monitored and back-tested.

Mean-Reversion Techniques

Mean-reversion techniques are one of the most common ways for analysts to trade stock or asset pairs. One of the most recognized ways to handle a mean revision of a stock price ratio is to use a Bollinger-band technique. Bollinger bands, first introduced by John Bollinger, measure a specific standard deviation beyond a defined moving average to determine if a stock price ratio has stretched beyond a certain interval.

For example, one of the default measures for many Bollinger band strategies is determining if an asset price has moved beyond 2 standard deviations of a 20-day moving average. An analyst would use a similar default for a stock-pair ratio and analyze whether a ratio has moved beyond 2 standard deviations from a 20-day moving average of a ratio. This type of analysis can be calculated by an analyst using a spreadsheet, as well as a number of software products that calculate different studies on pair ratios.

A Bollinger-band method would look to purchase one stock and simultaneously sell short another stock when the ratio of the two stocks reached the Bollinger low of the ratio (2 standard deviations below the 20-day moving average), and potential take profit when the ratio reverted back to the 20-day moving average of the ratio. The reverse trade would take place when the ratio reached the Bollinger high (2 standard deviations above the 20-day moving average) of the ratio price.

The length of time of the ratio divergence and then the following ratio convergence can be estimated, by back-testing a ratio-trading strategy that allows specific types of strategies to be created. The default of 2 standard deviations and a 20-day moving average would need to be analyzed per trading pair to find the optimal quantitative-trading strategy.

Pair Returns

The ratio generated by a pair of assets is generally less volatile than the outright movements of individual assets, and therefore the returns produced by a pair-trading strategy are considered smoother than the returns of individual assets.

A pair-trading strategy that follows a mean-reversion strategy allows investors to capture gains without a large move in the direction of an individual asset. A pair-trading, market-neutral strategy allows the investor to capture profits in sideways markets when a pair is moving but the benchmark is consolidating.

A correlation analysis is also important when attempting to find pairs that will generate robust returns. The key for an analyst is to find pairs that are co-integrated with the same path and stochastic motion that diverge in returns and drift back to normal over time. Many times a breakdown in correlation will follow earnings releases or other issues that hurt an individual stock price. It is important for an analyst to realize that stock prices change for a reason and a divergence can last for a long period of time.

Risks of Pair Trading

Although investors who trade relative-value pairs do not face directional risk, spread risk needs to be monitored in a similar manner. Portfolio managers who generate quantitative pair-trading systems need to evaluate the risks associated with pair trading and have optimal stop levels to help monitor drawdowns. It is easy to become drawn into believing that a pair

will always converge, but markets have a way of remaining illogical longer than an investor can remain solvent. Exiting a pair transaction can be based on a percent profit-and-loss calculation or a relative-ratio calculation.

Statistical Arbitrage

Statistical arbitrage is a concept that is defined by the ability to evaluate mispriced assets and to benefit from their future expected value. This type of trading strategy is not a true arbitrage as it does not guarantee a specific profit. Statistical-arbitrage-trading strategies are based on short-term mean reversion and encompass numerous securities using powerful quantitative and algorithmic methodologies.

Statistical arbitrage requires extensive data mining and automated trading systems to produce returns. The underlying root of statistical arbitrage is similar to pair trading, but expands on the strategy by using hundreds or thousands of stocks that are pooled together.

The mathematics of a statistical arbitrage trading strategy is a variance–covariance methodology. Stocks are ranked as good-return stocks down the ladder in an effort to benefit from future good or bad returns. After the stocks are ranked, the stocks with good scores are purchased while the stocks with bad scores are sold short. The next phase of the statistical-arbitrage process is to reduce the risk associated with the process. During this period, the stocks are offset to reduce outright market risk.

Statistical-Arbitrage Risks

Statistical arbitrage in theory works over a long period of time. During short periods, there can be adverse stock losses as markets randomly move in a stochastic nature. As mentioned prior, if an investor does not possess the liquidity to work through periods of losses, this strategy will eventually create a default. Markets have a way of finding the path of most pain, and convergence will only occur once this process is completed.

As the financial crisis began to unfold in late 2007, numerous hedge funds that participate in statistical-arbitrage strategies experienced extreme losses as stocks continued a divergent path. As liquidations continued to generate an unwinding of positions, hedge funds with weak hands were unable to continue to hold their positions, creating a snowball effect that generated significant losses. Because the funds were closed quickly, there was undue pressure on the other stock prices, causing adverse returns.

Portfolio Optimization

The goal of portfolio theory is to allocate investment in an optimal way in order to generate the most efficient risk-adjusted returns. Mean variance optimization is a quantitative investment methodology that allows investors to make asset allocations by considering the trade-off between risk and return.

In conventional mean-variance optimization the goal will be to maximize the expected return given a specific level of risk. Portfolio optimization was developed by Harry Markowitz. An American economist and professor of finance at the University of California San Diego, Markowitz is best known for his work on modern portfolio theory and how risk, asset allocation, return, and diversification affect a portfolio. Markowitz's work on portfolio optimization has led to different portfolio-trading strategies that attempt to generate robust returns from quantitative analysis, theoretical back testing, and forward testing.

The majority of back-testing procedures evaluate the profitability of trading strategies based on returns calculated from historical data. Many portfolio managers use back-testing to prove that a strategy has worked in the past. This method of back-testing is uncertain, as there are a number of issues related to using historical data that can be refined by using data simulations.

An assumption that is often used when back-testing historical data is that past events can predict future outcomes. This assumption could be considered flawed because trading environments are constantly changing. Testing using historical data is driven by past events and fails to incorporate the randomness of future price action.

Simulation

In an effort to devise a solution associated with the pitfalls of backtesting using historical data, quantitative analysts have employed an optimization technology that uses simulation to create a time series.

A simulation creates a time series from a probability distribution, which may exist over a future investment period and can be back-tested to determine if the strategy has merit.

The simulation is statistically rigorous and applies mathematical formulas to generate a data series. The simulations are based on probability, which can be viewed as a coin toss. For example, it is unlikely that you will toss a coin 10 times and find heads in all 10 results. The tosses are called independent events, which means that the prior results have no effect on future outcomes.

Asset markets move within a random nature over short periods of time. The prices of securities within the capital markets can follow random paths that are mimicked by simulations. The strategies back-tested using mathematical formulas demonstrate a strong probability of success on many diverse portfolios of securities. By back-testing on simulations of data, analysts mimic potential future price action and avoid analyzing historical data.

Capital-Structure Arbitrage

Capital-structure arbitrage is a strategy used by quantitative analysts at many hedge funds. The strategy is geared toward taking advantage of mispricing within a company's capital structure. For example, a portfolio manager could purchase subordinate bonds, while simultaneously shorting senior bonds. Another example would be to purchase common stock of a company and short the credit-default swaps of the same company.

A portfolio manager is evaluating the price structure of the same company and looking for relative value with different securities on the same company.

Capital-structure arbitrage is similar to statistical arbitrage, but it is not a real arbitrage in that a profit does not exist immediately from entering the trade. In theory this type of trade is less risky than an outright trade, as it forms the basis of a market-neutral strategy.

Volatility Arbitrage

The option market provides numerous opportunities for quantitative analysts to take advantage of mispricing as it relates to implied volatility. Implied volatility is one of the inputs used to price an option. It can be defined as the market's view of how much a security will move over a specific period of time on an annualized basis. Implied volatility is quoted in percentage terms. For example, an implied volatility of 25 percent would mean that traders expect the underlying security to move by 25 percent during the course of a year.

The implied volatility of a stock will change with the strike price of an option. The strike price is the price at which the buyer of a call option has the right but not the obligation to purchase the underlying stock on or before the expiration date. As the strike price moves away from the underlying price, the implied volatility will change. Changes to implied volatility as the strike price moves out-of-the-money is referred to as the *skew* of the option-term structure. This change of implied volatility of skew is based on the supply and demand of specific options and can create implied volatility arbitrage situations.

Momentum

Quantitative-momentum-trading strategies define periods when asset markets are moving in a specific direction and are likely to continue to generate further momentum in that direction. One of the most popular momentum strategies is the moving average convergence divergence index created by Gerald Appel.

The moving average convergence divergence index works in two ways. The first is to identify periods of accelerating momentum (both positive and negative momentum) and periods of divergence, when a market is decelerating while the underlying price action is continuing to drift in a diverging direction.

A MACD buy signal is created when the spread (which is defined as a short-term moving average minus a long-term moving average) crosses above a short-term moving average of the spread. The default used by Appel is the 12-day moving average, the 26-day moving average, and the 9-day moving average of the spread. A MACD sell signal occurs when the spread crosses below the 9-day moving average of the spread.

The MACD can also be viewed as a histogram that reflects the index level along with the spread moving average. When the index moves above the zero-index level, a buy signal is created, while a sell signal is generated when the spread moves below the zero-index level.

A MACD-bullish divergence occurs when a security forms a lower low (confirming a downtrend) while the MACD makes a higher low, generating a divergence between price action and the MACD. A MACD-bearish divergence occurs when price action forms a higher high, confirming an upward trend, and the MACD creates a lower high, generating a divergence.

The MACD indicator is quantitative as it relies solely on price action to determine specific opportunities that exist within the capital markets. The moving average convergence divergence index is unique because it brings together momentum analysis along with divergence analysis. This unique blend of trend and momentum can be applied to daily, weekly, or monthly charts. Quantitative analysts will look for a number of time horizons to optimize momentum on a specific security. When an analyst is looking for less sensitivity they may consider lengthening the moving averages. A less sensitive MACD will still oscillate above/below zero, but the centerline crossovers and signal-line crossovers will be less frequent.

The MACD line is calculated using the actual difference between two moving averages. This means MACD values are dependent on the price of the underlying security. This means that the comparison of MACD is not valuable as the analysis will depend on the underlying price of a security.

Industry Insight

We spoke with Josh Parker, Managing Partner of the Gargoyle Group, to share his insights gleaned from running quantitative-driven hedge funds.

Richard Wilson: Can you please briefly describe the type of fund you work and your role there?

Josh Parker: I am the President and CEO of Gargoyle Asset Management L.L.C. and Gargoyle Investment Advisor L.L.C. We have three product lines, all of which center on the fact that short index call options are the best way to hedge an equity portfolio. Our two hedge funds invest 100 percent of their respective assets in a portfolio of quantitatively-selected U.S.-listed stocks. To hedge the market risk, one hedge fund endeavors to maintain an options portfolio that is equivalent to 50 percent short "the market," and the other endeavors to maintain an options portfolio that is equivalent to 100 percent short "the market."

Richard Wilson: Is there a traditional path through academics, internships or career that is common among quantitative fund managers? I imagine a background in mathematics, statistics, and financial modeling are essentials.

Josh Parker: Yes, and none of the principals of the Gargoyle Group travelled that route. I, for one, am a lawyer by training and practiced law for over 20 years. The connection is through the game of bridge. I and one of my partners are national champions. All of the partners and several of the key employees, directly or indirectly, were brought to the floor because my mentor, Mike Becker, a former world champion and member of the Bridge Hall of Fame, believed that the skills that make good bridge players make good option traders. Over the course of a half dozen years in the mid-1980s, Mike trained over 100 bridge players to become successful option market-makers on the floor of the American Stock Exchange. That was how I, Gargoyle's other partners, and several of Gargoyle's top employees became involved in options trading.

Richard Wilson: Wow, that's a really interesting path to options trading.

How would you explain to someone unfamiliar with the strategy how a quantitative hedge fund works?

Josh Parker: While oversimplifying the answer, there are two pure strategies—qualitative and quantitative. A qualitative method depends on an analyst's ability to evaluate the balance sheet, etc. of each prospective company. The quantitative method, on the other hand, believes that unemotional, formula-based stock selection is superior. Put in "good" inputs and out pops "good" outputs. Most managers are neither 100 percent qualitative nor 100 percent quantitative.

Richard Wilson: Do you consider your hedge fund trading low-frequency or high-frequency?

Josh Parker: In the world of hedge funds, I would say we are low-frequency compared to the frequency with which most hedge funds trade either stocks or options.

Richard Wilson: Do you see a connection between the rise of large quantitative hedge funds like Renaissance Technologies and the increasing role of high-frequency trading?

Josh Parker: Yes. I see two trends. First, success begets imitators, and no one has been more successful than Renaissance. Renaissance, however, did not start as a high-frequency shop as we use the term today. The way pure multi-strategy quant funds have been competing is by looking at ever smaller time slices.

Richard Wilson: I think the public perception of quant funds is a bunch of computers spitting out numbers and executing trades with very little human element. Why is that perception wrong?

Josh Parker: I think your question assumes a certain definition of "quant fund." If by "quant fund" you mean the high-frequency, every-millisecond-counts trading of Renaissance, Citadel, and others, then the perception is not wrong. I believe quant fund is broader than that. To me, a quant fund is any fund that is principally governed by the law of large numbers and/or relies on dispassionate, number-driven investing. Our funds fit within the second definition but not the first.

Richard Wilson: That's a fair distinction. What are some of the benefits you see in a well-managed quantitative hedge fund? Is it diversification, low correlation, high returns?

Josh Parker: Trading is an extension of one's human nature. As humans, we let our emotions get the better of us even when/as we know we are reacting emotionally. A well-managed quant fund takes emotion out of the equation, which permits a manager to select his goals and allow the system to achieve those goals dispassionately.

Richard Wilson: Can quantitative hedge funds exist in the new age of transparency post-Madoff and post-financial crisis? How do you protect your "secret sauce" while still allowing investors and regulators to understand the risks and trades in the strategy?

Josh Parker: Yes. First, transparency does NOT mean handing over the secret sauce. Everyone knows the main ingredients of Coca-Cola . . . but no one knows the exact formula. The same can be true of quant funds. Second, I have always felt that I could hand over our formulas and strategies to someone and s/he would never be able to stay with it. Because it was not developed by him/her, s/he would not have the confidence to stick with the strategy through thick or thin.

Richard Wilson: What are the biggest risks associated with quantitative hedge funds? Are there any standard guards against these risks like an investment committee, chief risk officer, or board of advisors?

Josh Parker: With our hedge fund, there is minimal risk beyond the risks associated with stocks and options because we have humans at the controls. Pure black-box operations always run the risk that something unexpected happens (doesn't it always?) for which the computer was not properly programmed . . . and you get a Flash Crash.

Richard Wilson: Is it a challenge explaining the intricacies of a quantitative strategy to someone who is not mathematically-inclined or maybe doesn't relate to the strategy?

Josh Parker: No. Over many years we have refined our explanation so that, depending on a prospect's level of sophistication, we have a good explanation that s/he will understand.

Richard Wilson: How is your team structured? Is there a portfolio management team and chief investment officer that work on the strategy and trading and another side that handles the other aspects like programming, investor relations, operations, IT, etc.?

Josh Parker: In the beginning, there were two of us. I designed the strategy and he critiqued and improved it as well as did most of the execution. Now, we have a different person/department for each function, including functions that we did not have when we started—IT, marketing, and sales.

Richard Wilson: What advice can you offer to someone who is just launching a quantitative hedge fund?

Josh Parker: Patience. This is not a "build-it-and-they-will-come" business. Post-2008 and post-Madoff investors want a long track record and institutional infrastructure, which takes time and money, respectively.

Richard Wilson: I know they're not exactly comparable, but why do you think that a fund like Renaissance Technologies has been so consistently successful while Long-Term Capital Management failed so fantastically? They both had incredibly smart portfolio managers and principals but only one remains. Are there lessons in either narrative for today's hedge funds?

Josh Parker: This is a fascinating question. I read *When Genius Fails* and a couple of other books on the (Long-Term Capital Management) LTCM debacle. From what I read, all of LTCM's strategies were convergence strategies. The Nobel Laureates relied too heavily on history and did not adequately diversify . . . even though they thought having convergence strategies in dozens of different markets was diversification. Mind you, they were "right" in the sense that if they could have held the positions, they would have eventually made a killing. What they forgot/never knew was what John Maynard Keynes purportedly said: "You have to be able to stay solvent longer than the market can remain irrational." In that, LTCM failed ignominiously. As for Renaissance, what it does is so secretive, one can only speculate. I assume they are truly diversified and have an appreciation of risk/leverage that was missing at LTCM.

Richard Wilson: Are there any business management or operations challenges that you face?

Josh Parker: One challenge we often find among hedge funds is that you can have a brilliant portfolio manager but if you don't have the staff and structure to adequately service your employees and investor needs then you run into trouble. Our biggest problem today is not infrastructure but asset gathering. The vast percentage of the inflows goes to funds/investment managers with more than $5 billion in AUM. With a little less than $1 billion but the infrastructure to support many multiples of that, we have the costs of the biggest managers without the assets.

Richard Wilson: What is a typical day for you and your management team? We want to give our readers a sense of what it's like to run a quantitative hedge fund so any and all details are welcome.

Josh Parker: Incredibly boring. It is a job. A job that we love, but the goal is not to make it exciting but to maximize our clients' risk-adjusted rates of returns. We conduct research every day. We monitor the stock markets every minute of every day. We trade only when required by our discipline to maintain a somewhat constant market hedge.

I hope this interview gave readers a better sense of what it takes to run a quantitative hedge fund.

Conclusion

Quantitative and algorithmic trading involves the use of technology to find opportunities within the capital markets to generate returns using mathematical formulas. This approach mitigates the human element but still requires a portfolio manager to push the start button. There are a multitude of strategies that can be used to generate quantitative returns, many of which focus on market-neutral strategies.

Technology is a critical part of quantitative and algorithmic trading, as it not only drives the research needed to test the strategies but also is required to generate returns for strategies that profit on lightning-fast information. Although most of the strategies used in quantitative trading are robust, these strategies have risk, which needs to be quantified in order for a portfolio manager to generate the most efficient risk-adjusted returns.

Test Yourself

Answer the following questions.

1. Quantitative strategies entail:
   A. Removing the human element from trading.
   B. Using computer programs and algorithms to trade.
   C. Analyzing price actions.
   D. All of the above.

2. True or False: Quantitative-momentum-trading strategies define periods when asset markets are moving in a specific direction and are likely to continue to generate further momentum in that direction.

3. True or False: The majority of back-testing procedures evaluate the profitability of trading strategies based on returns calculated from historical data.

4. True or False: The MACD indicator is quantitative because it doesn't rely on price action to determine specific opportunities that exist within the capital markets.

5. Capital-structure arbitrage:
   A. Contends that when markets are moving in a specific direction, they will continue to do so if they have substantial momentum.
   B. Aims to take advantage of mispricing in a capital structure.
   C. Involves going long in an asset while going short in a derivative of that asset.
   D. Is a strategy a hedge fund employs where capital is injected into a firm to restructure management.

Answers can be found in Appendix B.

CHAPTER 11

Managed Futures

Managed futures are a type of alternative investment that incorporates a number of hedge fund trading strategies using futures as investment vehicles. Managed futures are considered an alternative investment relative to mainstream investments such as stocks and bonds, and help round out a portfolio as they generate investment returns that are generally uncorrelated to mainstream investments. Futures contracts provide tremendous flexibility for investment managers, allowing both long and short positions that open up a broad range of strategies to enhance returns, since performance can be strong during both increasing and decreasing market conditions.

The managed-futures business has increased substantially throughout the years. According to the Chicago Mercantile Exchange, which is the largest U.S. clearing organization of regulated futures, managed futures have grown from approximately $20 billion in 1990 to more than $325 billion at the end of 2011. As you can see in Figure 11.1, the CME total order volume continues to grow today.

This chapter on managed futures broadly defines the business and touches on the benefits from this investment approach. There will be a brief discussion of futures as an investment vehicle, along with how leverage and margin affect investment returns. The chapter concludes with a number of different investment strategies used within the managed-futures industry.

Defining Managed Futures

Managed futures use regulated futures contracts as the investment vehicle to generate returns for a hedge fund manager. Futures contracts are tradable investment vehicles that are entered into by two parties and follow a specific underlying asset that is delivered

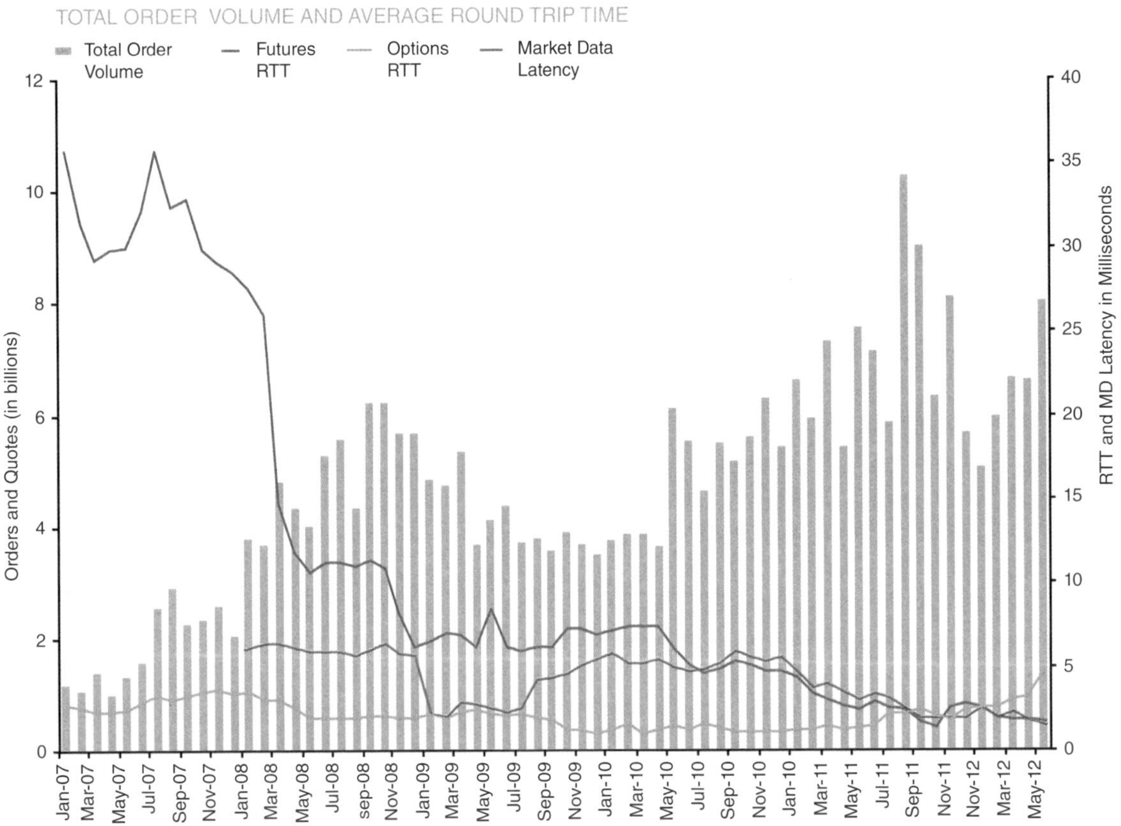

Figure 11.1 Chicago Mercantile Exchange Total Order Volume—January 2007 to May 2012
Source: Chicago Mercantile Exchange.

at a specific date in the future. For example, the global petroleum market uses benchmarks such as West Texas Intermediate crude oil and Brent North Sea Crude Oil that are actively traded with futures contracts.

Futures Contracts

Many futures contracts are physically delivered instruments that reflect the underlying price of an asset on the delivery date. Investors who trade physically delivered futures contracts usually exit their position or roll their positions to a deferred contract prior to the delivery date to avoid accepting delivery of an asset. As one can imagine it is a lot easier to accept delivery and sell U.S. Treasury bills compared to corn or soybean oil. It might be hard to imagine trading futures contracts because the underlying assets are so diverse and common, but we have included a very simplified diagram in Figure 11.2 to show how the buyer will purchase a futures contract from a seller using a clearinghouse, such as the Chicago Mercantile Exchange.

Futures contracts that are not physically delivered are referred to as financially settled contracts. The settlement process for a financial contract differs from physically delivered contracts in that the profit or loss associated with the transaction changes hands on the settlement date. For example, if an investor purchased financially settled WTI crude oil, they would either pay the difference between the purchase price and the settlement price on the last trading day or receive that amount if their trade settled in-the-money. Financially settled contracts, similar to physically delivered contracts, can be actively traded throughout their life cycle.

Each futures contract that is cleared by a major exchange, such as the Chicago Mercantile Exchange or the Intercontinental Exchange, has specific contract details that make it unique. In addition to describing the time and dates that the contract actively trades, the contract specifications describe the size of each contract to assist a trader in the

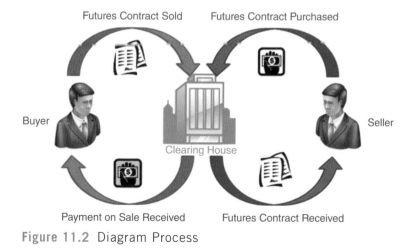

Figure 11.2 Diagram Process

process of determining the notional value of each contract traded. For example, as you can see in Figure 11.3, one contract of WTI NYMEX crude oil delivers 1,000 barrels of crude oil. At a price of $90 per barrel, the notional value of each contract is $90,000 dollars.

The contract specifications also describe the currency that a contract is traded in, along with the value

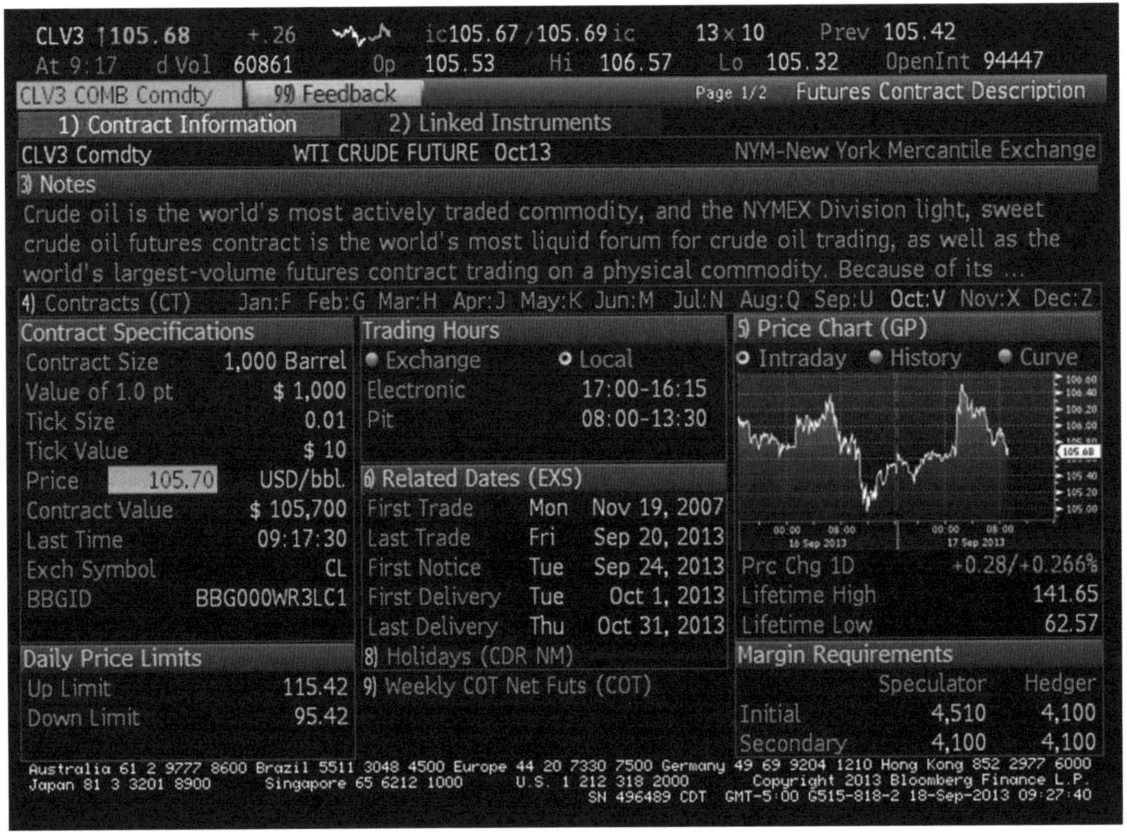

Figure 11.3 Contract Details
Source: © 2014 Bloomberg L.P. All rights reserved.

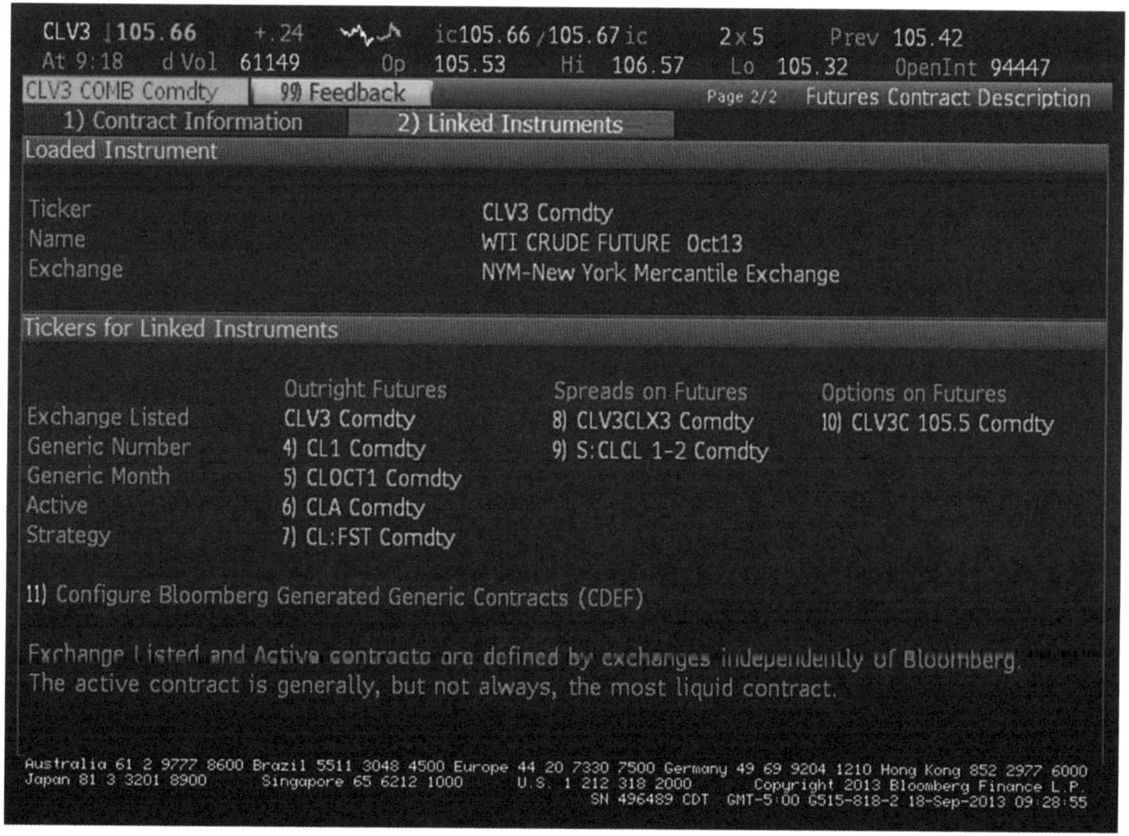

```
CLV3 ⌐105.66    +.24   ⌐⌐⌐⌐    ic105.66/105.67 ic    2 x 5    Prev  105.42
At 9:18   d Vol 61149     Op   105.53    Hi   106.57    Lo   105.32    OpenInt  94447
CLV3 COMB Comdty      99) Feedback                   Page 2/2   Futures Contract Description
    1) Contract Information        2) Linked Instruments
Loaded Instrument

Ticker                        CLV3 Comdty
Name                          WTI CRUDE FUTURE  Oct13
Exchange                      NYM-New York Mercantile Exchange

Tickers for Linked Instruments

                    Outright Futures     Spreads on Futures      Options on Futures
Exchange Listed     CLV3 Comdty          8) CLV3CLX3 Comdty      10) CLV3C 105.5 Comdty
Generic Number      4) CL1 Comdty        9) S:CLCL 1-2 Comdty
Generic Month       5) CLOCT1 Comdty
Active              6) CLA Comdty
Strategy            7) CL:FST Comdty

11) Configure Bloomberg Generated Generic Contracts (CDEF)

Exchange Listed and Active contracts are defined by exchanges independently of Bloomberg.
The active contract is generally, but not always, the most liquid contract.

Australia 61 2 9777 8600 Brazil 5511 3048 4500 Europe 44 20 7330 7500 Germany 49 69 9204 1210 Hong Kong 852 2977 6000
Japan 81 3 3201 8900    Singapore 65 6212 1000    U.S. 1 212 318 2000    Copyright 2013 Bloomberg Finance L.P.
                                             SN 496489 CDT  GMT-5:00 G515-818-2 18-Sep-2013 09:28:55
```

Figure 11.3 *(Continued)*

of each tick size (each tick is the smallest unit measure of movement) in currency value. The specification document describes whether a contract is physically or financially settled, along with the period of settlement, the months of listed contracts, how settlement will take place, and any specific grades or qualities that need to be delivered for physically delivered contracts.

The specifications describe the regulation, which reflects the number of contracts that can be held by either hedge funds or commercial entity given their importance to certain industries. While currency positions will rarely effect changes within the vast FOREX markets, a large position held by a hedge fund can influence the price movements of a smaller market such as rice. In detail the contract specifications show the maximum daily fluctuation that can legally occur for a specific contract, which clearly needs to be evaluated by futures traders. Please see Figure 11.3 for an example of a futures contract.

Limit Movements

One of the key issues associated with futures trading is there are specific limits to the amount a contract can move on any individual trading day. When a contract reaches its limit up (or down), trade will be halted unless the price moves in the opposite direction. For example, if an S&P 500 index futures contract is limit down for a trading session, no trades can take place when the price is lower than the limit. Only trades where the price is higher than the limit price can take place for the balance of that trading session. It is very important that futures traders understand this mechanism, as traders who are caught in the wrong direction will not be able to liquate their positions during that trading session. If your risk management is based on your ability to exit a position when a specific level is reached, it is imperative that you understand the nuances associated with specific types of futures contracts limits.

Benefits of Managed Futures

Asset allocation is an important diversification tool, as the process of adding uncorrelated strategies assists in reducing portfolio risk.

Managed futures is an asset class that generates diversification because the investment vehicles provide access to a broad range of global markets such as equities indices, bonds, currencies, and commodities. Additionally, managed-futures-trading strategies can perform well during times when other asset classes underperform. For example, when inflation is rising and interest rates start to climb, commodities futures generally outperform while stocks and bonds decline in value. During the 1990 Gulf War, while stock prices were declining, managed futures positions in oil and gold showed robust gains. You can see in Figure 11.4, the S&P 500 Index relation to oil prices in the 1990's. As you can see in this overlay, oil price volatility appears to have had a significant impact on the S&P 500.

Some of the most widely recognized work on the efficient frontier performed by Nobel-prize-winner Harry Markowitz shows that a diversified portfolio, which holds a basket of investment vehicles that are uncorrelated, will reflect the best risk-adjusted returns over a long period of time. See Figure 11.5 for a diagram of the basic efficient-frontier curve.

Managed-futures strategies also provide access to risk exposure that is global in nature, allowing hedge fund managers to tap markets that could be in a

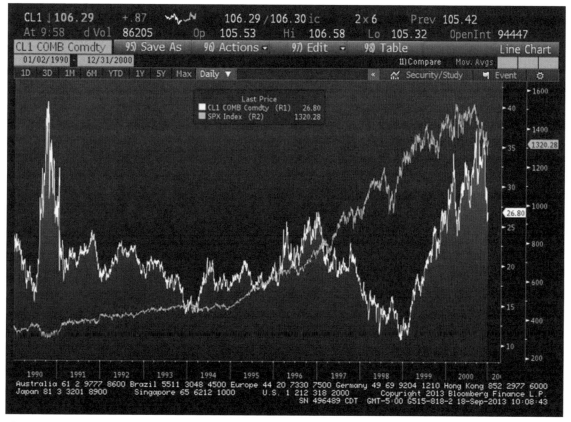

Figure 11.4 S&P 500 Index and Oil Prices in the 1990s
Source: © 2014 Bloomberg L.P. All rights reserved.

different stage of their economic cycle, relative to an investor's domestic market.

Managed futures generally provide robust liquidity and allow hedge fund managers to avoid significant drawdowns. Because managed futures investors can take long or short positions they can avoid long-only strategies that decline in value during adverse market conditions.

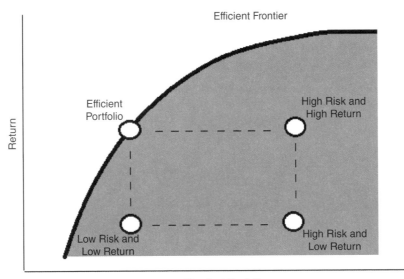

Figure 11.5 Efficient Frontier Diagram

Margin

Margin is an amount of capital used by a clearinghouse to calculate how much an investor should post to their brokerage account per position to protect the broker/clearinghouse from adverse movement on a specific security. Many clearinghouses globally use SPAN risk array (The Standard Portfolio Analysis of Risk system), a methodology that calculates performance and bond requirements by analyzing different potential market scenarios based on the positions held and the historical volatility of those instruments.

The SPAN-risk system was developed by Chicago Mercantile Exchange and is seen as the standard for portfolio-risk assessment. According to the CME, currently 50 registered exchanges and regulatory agencies throughout the world use the methodology to track risk and determine margin requirements.

This type of methodology includes numerous inputs to determine the initial margin bond required that allows an investor to control higher levels of capital, which generates a level of leverage. For example, the Chicago Mercantile Exchange (at the time this chapter was composed) required investors to post $4,950 dollars for every contract of WTI NYMEX crude oil. At a price of $90 dollars per barrel, and a notional value per contract of $90,000 ($90 * 1,000 barrels), the leverage available to investors is slightly more than 18:1 ($90,000/$4,950 = 18.18). In essence, $4,950 of capital allows an investor to control $90,000 of notional value of crude oil. Initial margin requirements constantly change, and most exchanges will provide brokers a number of weeks to inform their clients of future changes.

SPAN-risk calculation analyses risk by calculating the worst-case scenario for a security over a specific length of time. This calculation is similar to a value-at-risk calculation and is computed by calculating gains and losses that the security would provide under different market conditions.

Most clearinghouses also employ a second level of margin that is referred to as *maintenance margin*. This second level of margin requires an investor to post capital equal to the losses within a portfolio usually on a dollar-for-dollar basis. If the capital within an account falls below the acceptable level, the broker (who is a member of the clearing exchange) will issue a margin call.

When a margin call occurs, a broker will prompt an investor to either provide additional capital to the account or unwind their positions. If capital is not provided and the investor does not unwind the position, the broker will unwind the position for their client, which sometimes occurs during adverse market conditions.

How Leverage Affects Returns

Leverage within the futures industry is a built-in part of the contract specifications. Each clearinghouse within the futures industry provides a specific leverage ratio that allows investors to control a specific notional quantity based on capital posted as initial margin.

Leverage can have a substantial effect on the returns of a portfolio. As mentioned earlier, leverage can enhance returns but cuts two ways. For example, each NYMEX gasoline contract requires an investor to post $5,500 dollars to control (at the time this chapter was written) approximately $130,000 of gasoline per contract. A one-cent move in the price of NYMEX Reformulated Gasoline would produce a gain/loss of $420 dollar or approximately 7 percent ($420/$5,500 = 7.6 percent). The actual percent move of 1 cent (.01/$3.2) for wholesale gasoline is minor when compared to the leveraged return. The leverage associated with a gasoline futures contract can obviously enhance the gains but also produce some significant losses.

Performance

Managed futures, as an aggregate alternative investment class, have experienced robust returns during the past three decades relative to other benchmarks, such as stocks and bonds. The BarclayHedge CTA index has seen *9.5 percent* average annual returns over the past three decades from 1982 through 2012. In comparison, the Standard & Poor's 500 index provided an annual average return of 9.6 percent during the same time period, so CTA funds have kept up with the steady growth of the U.S. stock market (Barclay Hedge).

For perspective on what the public equities market returned over the years, Figure 11.6 shows that $1 invested in the S&P 500 (a common hedge fund

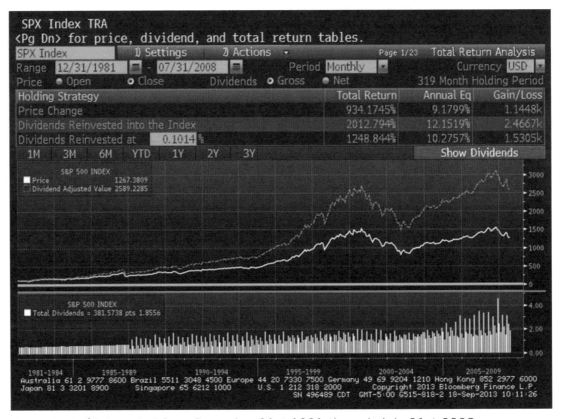

Figure 11.6 $1 Invested from December 31st 1981 through July 31st 2008
Source: © 2014 Bloomberg L.P. All rights reserved.

performance benchmark) in 1982 would be worth approximately $1,267 mid-way through 2008 and a dividend-adjusted value of $2,589.

Participants

The managed-futures-trading business attracts numerous participants that are categorized by regulators, which helps investors understand the different types of people who are managing money in this alternative-asset business. Fund managers include commodity trading advisors (CTAs), futures commission merchants (FCMs), commodity pool operators (CPOs), and trading managers.

Commodity trading advisors are businesses that initial transactions and manager risk. According to the Nation Futures Association (NFA), which is a regulatory body, there are nearly 2,000 CTAs registered with the NFA.

Futures commission merchants are brokers who provide access to futures exchanges for CTAs and individuals, clear and execute trades, and provide administrative tools and investment performance to investors.

Commodity pool operators assemble private or public pools of capital that invest within the futures markets. Most pool operators invest directly through commodity trading advisors. According to the NFA there are more than 1,000 registered pool operators.

Trading managers are individuals who assist in the process of finding reputable commodity trading advisors that meet the risk-to-reward profile of investors.

Many of these managers have intricate tools that can help analyze the historical track record of an advisor and find those that are non-correlated to stock- or bond-market performance.

Analyzing Risk

Risk is a key component to every investment activity. Determining the risk-adjusted returns or the risk relative to other investment activity is a crucial exercise to undertake prior to risking capital. The Commodity Futures Trading Commission (CFTC), the regulatory body that oversees the futures industry, requires that each customer who participates in futures-related business that manages capital receive risk-disclosure statements. Every investor should analyze an investment-manager's track record—although past performance is not indicative of future returns, it does provide a guideline of how a manager generates returns.

One of the key metrics that an investor should analyze is the manager's worst drawdown from peak to trough. Additionally, managers usually provide a metric of return volatility, such as the Sharpe Ratio, which is the average return over the standard deviation of returns.

Fees

Management fees within the alternative-asset world and specifically within managed futures are generally higher than those within the equity markets.

Generally, total management fees include a flat fee for managing capital along with an incentive fee based on the returns to the investor. The incentive fee is based on performance and is net of all expenses and the management fee. For example, on a $10,000 trading account that has returns of 20 percent, a management fee of 2 percent, and administrative expenses of 1 percent, the investor would receive $11,243 at the end of the year or a return to the investor of $1,243 net of fees.

The performance fee is net of all transaction costs and brokerage commissions. Most managers only pay themselves a performance fee if the account is above its high-water mark. This means if the account loses money in its first year and then rebounds to a profit, the incentive fee is based purely on profits above the initial account value. For example, if an account starts at $10,000, loses $1,000 in the first year and then makes $2,000 in the second year, the incentive fee is based on the account value $11,000 minus the initial account value $10,000.

Regulation

The National Futures Association (NFA) describes their organization as a self-regulatory body for the U.S. futures industry. Their mandate is to safeguard market integrity, protect investors, and help their members meet their regulatory responsibilities.

According to the NFA, membership is mandatory for those managing managed futures, which assures that everyone conducting business with the public on the U.S. futures exchanges adheres to the same high standards of professional conduct. NFA is an independent regulatory organization with no ties to any specific marketplace.

The Commodity Futures Trading Commission (CFTC) is a regulatory body overseen by the Congress created in 1974. The agency is independent and has a mandate to regulate commodity futures and option markets in the United States. The mandate has recently been expanded by the Dodd-Frank Wall Street Reform and Consumer Protection Act.

According to the CFTC's website (www.cftc.gov/About/MissionResponsibilities/index.htm), the agency's goal is to assure the economic utility of the futures markets by encouraging their competitiveness and efficiency; protecting market participants against fraud, manipulation, and abusive trading practices; and by ensuring the financial integrity of the clearing process.

Both the CFTC and the NFA have many utilities that can be used by investors to monitor and evaluate managed-futures managers. This includes analyzing any issues or complaints about a manager that would allow an investor to determine if the risk associated with a manager is worth the potential reward.

Trading Strategies

Managed futures provide a wide breadth of trading strategies that are used by trading managers to generate returns. One of the key benefits to a manager is

DEFINITION:
High-Water Mark

The highest value a fund has achieved. The high-water mark is a common term included in hedge fund limited partnership agreements, helping to ensure that investors receive a healthy return.

KEY POINT

Under the leadership of Chairman Gary Gensler, the CFTC expanded to match the dramatic growth of the derivatives and commodity trading markets.

their ability to control large amounts of notional value of capital based on the leverage that is provided by futures contracts.

Investment strategies range from technical-analysis strategies to long–short strategies. Each strategy used by a managed-futures trading advisor is based on a specific risk-to-reward profile that needs to be analyzed carefully by a prospective investor.

Spread Trading

Spread-trading strategies are defined by the simultaneous purchase of one futures contract and the sale of another futures contract. These types of relative-value trades take advantage of inefficiencies within the futures markets and a trader's ability to spot arbitrage situations. An example of this type of trade would be the purchase of a 10-year treasury future and the simultaneous sale of a 5-year treasury future. This trade is referred to as an interest rate flattening curve, where the reverse (purchase of a 5-year and sale of a 10-year treasury) is called an interest rate curve steepener.

Futures contracts provide investment managers with the opportunity to trade spreads on a global basis where they can take positions in Japanese markets versus positions in German markets. The global nature of managed futures allows managers to search globally for arbitrage opportunities.

Within the commodity space, futures provide spread trades that reflect commercial operations. For example, a long gasoline short crude oil position, known in the industry as the *gasoline crack*, reflects the refining margins produced by the oil refining process. A similar process is reflected with soy beans, where a trader can purchase soy bean oil and sell soy beans to reflect a portion of the soybean crush.

Many traders in the commodity space will also capitalize on storage plays, where a trader takes physical delivery of a commodity such as heating oil, and sells a futures contract to take advantage of the term structure of a futures curve. For example, if a contango exists in the futures market, where deferred prices are higher than spot prices (the settlement price on a commodity contract at its spot date), a trader can purchase the physical heating oil and simultaneously sell a deferred futures contract if the storage rates of holding heating oil are less than the profit created by the contango.

Arbitrage Strategies

Within the liquid foreign-exchange market, many managed-futures traders try to take advantage of discrepancies between cash value of a currency pair relative to futures values of a currency pair. A futures contract is made up of the spot currency and a forward curve. This product is traded in the FOREX forward market, while simultaneously trading in the futures market. There are times when the cash market has a different value than the futures market which is quickly arbitraged out by traders who are constantly watching this phenomenon.

There are also arbitrage opportunities that exist when analyzing a currency cross relative to two currency pairs. For example, there will be instances when a long position in the cross-currency pair EUR/GBP has a different value than a long position EUR/USD and a short position in GBP/USD. Futures traders will constantly monitor these values looking for an opportunity to arbitrage the currency pairs.

Trend Following

Trend following is a type of technical analysis that attempts to identify a trend. A trend occurs when price action moves in one direction over the course of a specific period of time. One of the best indicators of a trend is a moving average. A moving average is the average of a specific number of prices that changes with time. For example, a 10-day moving average is the average of the past 10 days; on the eleventh day, the first day is dropped from the calculation of the average. If a moving average is climbing, the trend of the market is generally climbing; when a moving average is falling, the trend is usually declining.

Investment managers will use trend-following strategies as an adjunct to discretionary-trading methodologies, as well as systematic back-tested trading strategies. One of the most popular discretionary-trading strategies is to use a moving-average-crossover strategy. This type of strategy defines a trend when a short-term moving average moves above/below a long-term moving average. When this occurs,

the trader initiates a position in the direction of the trend.

Back-testing

Many investment managers use a systematic approach and use back-testing to formulate a robust trading system. Back-testing a trading strategy entails determining if the investment strategy generates profits over a specific period of time. The process evaluates the profitability of a trading strategy based on historical data. Many portfolio managers use back-testing to prove a strategy they have created works, but fail to evaluate a number of issues that are inherent in evaluating historical returns. Back-testing can be a way to develop a successful trading strategy but there are a number of pitfalls, which include fitting a curve and weak risk-adjusted returns.

One of the key assumptions when evaluating a specific trading strategy is determining if the strategy will work in the future. A strategy that has too many criteria can work when evaluating historical data, but will fail to work when the trading environment changes. For example, a strategy that works when a market is trending might fail if the market consolidates for a number of years. Criteria that is fit to a specific period (known as fitting the curve) will likely have a difficult time producing robust results when forward tested on live data.

Another factor that is imperative to evaluate is slippage, which is the difference between estimated transaction costs and the amount actually paid for a specific security. There will be a number of instances when a trader does not transact at the exact price generated by the strategy, which needs to be incorporated into the profit-and-loss calculations. Additionally, commissions also need to be considered, as they also have an effect on the total profit-and-loss generated by the back-tested strategy.

Futures themselves can create certain problems, as each contract has a specific maturity date that needs to be incorporated into a back-tested system. Many investment managers use continuation contracts that reflect a specific calculation of a rollover into a new futures contract when evaluating historical back-tested returns.

Prior to back-testing, an investor would determine if the strategy was defined in a way to fit the investor's risk-to-reward profile. For example, conservative investors should try to avoid a strategy in which the returns are extremely volatile. Testing should also take place over various time frames, to avoid results that only work over a small sample period. Investors should understand the historical results on a trading strategy are not a guarantee that a strategy will work in the future.

Industry Insight

To bring all of this together we interviewed Drew Day, Co-Founder of MicroQuant, a CTA and financial technology firm, and a Principal at Lexington Asset Management, a quantitative commodity-trading advisor

and pool operator, which employs a sophisticated trading strategy known as a long-volatility strategy.

Richard C. Wilson: Can you please briefly describe the type of fund you work and your role there?

Drew Day: I am a Director & Principal for Lexington Asset Management, a quantitative commodity-trading advisor and pool operator based in Raleigh, North Carolina, and the Cayman Islands. At Lexington, we employ a sophisticated trading strategy known as a long-volatility strategy. As a director and principal, I am responsible for the strategic direction of the firm's primary focus areas including: trading and research, marketing and sales, and operations and compliance.

Richard C. Wilson: Is there a typical background for a CTA or managed-futures fund manager?

Drew Day: Most CTA/managed-futures fund managers have a strong background in quantitative finance, engineering, and prefer technical analysis. The latest trend is for CTA/MF fund managers to have experience in developing trading technology. The managers that have the ability to develop workable trading technology will have a significant advantage over the competition.

Richard C. Wilson: How would you explain to someone unfamiliar with the strategy how most managed futures and CTA funds execute their strategy?

Drew Day: For those new to the managed-futures industry, they may want to think of managers falling in two primary categories, which include quantitative managers and discretionary managers. The majority of the assets in managed futures are being controlled by quantitative managers, who generate buy-and-sell decisions in the markets based on rule-based computerized trading systems. With modern technology and the development of the Internet, quantitative managers can route orders directly to brokers and exchanges. Many CTAs favor quantitative models over discretionary approaches because they offer consistence in their approach as they are unaffected by human emotions. Discretionary managers base their trading decisions on fundamental and or technical analysis of the markets. These traders are a minority in the managed-futures industry and tend to generate track records that are uncorrelated to industry benchmarks.

Richard C. Wilson: What are some of the strategies within managed futures and CTA funds that you believe are most popular or that you are most familiar with?

Drew Day: The most common approach to trading the markets in the futures industry is the trend-following approach. Many managers believe that there is a propensity for futures markets to experience meaningful price trends over time and they seek to exploit these trends by holding positions in the direction of the major trend. When trends are not present, trend-following approaches can experience drawdowns, a term that relates to losing portfolio equity from peak levels. Other strategies that have become more popular in recent years include short-term trading strategies, which are designed to hold trades for several hours or several days. These approaches tend to avoid the portfolio volatility associated with trend-following strategies and are therefore desirable when markets are in choppy, sideways stages. Many managers have adopted both trend-following and short-term approaches in order to generate more attractive reward-to-risk ratios.

Richard C. Wilson: Can you give us an example of two additional managed-futures strategies and how they would be built in a portfolio in terms of the types and sizes of positions?

Drew Day: Additional strategies that can be considered by CTAs include pattern-recognition strategies and arbitrage strategies. As a component of an overall portfolio, the weighting of these strategies depends on their correlation to the overall portfolio. The weighting of an arbitrage strategy would depend in large part on the markets over the manager.

Richard C. Wilson: What are some significant trends you are seeing in the managed futures or CTA fund strategy or the hedge fund industry as a whole?

Drew Day: In recent years we have witnessed a migration away from traditional trend-following approaches. This has been a result of market conditions that will most likely reverse once markets return to their trending norms. We are also witnessing managers take advantage of offshore master-feeder structures, with the leading domiciles being the Cayman Islands and British Virgin Islands.

Richard C. Wilson: What is a typical day for you and your management team? We want to give our readers a sense of what it's like to run a managed-futures-related hedge fund, so any and all details are welcome.

Drew Day: The CTA/MF business is one of the most competitive businesses in the world. However, it is also one of the most rewarding. In my personal opinion, CTA/MF's strategies, when managed properly, provide the best risk-management solutions to investment portfolios. If you plan on managing a CTA/MF Fund, you will need to focus on three primary areas: (1) Trading and Research, (2) Marketing and Sales, and (3) Compliance and Operations.

From the trading end of the business, the first thing that most traders do, even before brushing their teeth, is to check on what the markets did overnight. Most markets now trade 24 hours a day, so a lot can happen overnight.

The next thing the trading-desk manager or portfolio manager will do is to check with the night desk to gather any trading information, or fills on orders. Smaller CTAs will usually combine the position of portfolio manager and trading-desk manager into a single position. Larger CTAs will have entire departments to monitor trade execution and portfolio performance.

Once a trading desk manager understands what the markets have done overnight, then he or she begins to check to make sure that all of the strategies have the correct positions. It is not uncommon to have a broker misplace a contract here and there, and it is the job of the trading-desk manager to hunt down these missing trades. The rest of the day involves monitoring the trading strategies to insure that they are being traded correctly. If markets are slow, a trading-desk manager might test a new idea or do a little research. Larger managers will have an entire department of researchers dedicated to building new, better, or different approaches to trading in the markets.

From the operational end of the business, there is a myriad of behind-the-scenes responsibilities to focus on at any point in time. Because most CTAs start small, this can become a potential problem. The regulatory requirements of the NFA and CFTC are constantly changing, and it can be time consuming to stay abreast of such changes to ensure that your firm is in compliance. For those with offshore master-feeder structures, the managers must also familiarize themselves with the compliance and reporting deadlines for the offshore domicile. Depending on the type of structure you use, you will need to become familiar with the quarterly and annual reporting requirements of the NFA and CFTC.

We also spoke with Tony Gannon, co-founder and CEO of Abbey Capital, where he also heads up the investment committee. We wanted to learn from Tony's perspective running several multi-manager funds with allocations to managed futures, FX, and global macro managers.

Richard C. Wilson: Can you please briefly describe the Abbey Capital and your role there?

Tony Gannon: Abbey Capital manages a number of funds, most of which are multi-manager funds with allocations to managed futures, FX, and global macro managers. As former FX and futures traders, we believe this provides an edge in the selection of managers in this area, and the construction of multi-manager portfolios, which may generate strong risk-adjusted returns. All managers have the ability to be long or short, and typically trade in a range of FX and futures markets. We aggregate all of these managers in a portfolio to create a highly diversified fund that tends to have a low long-term correlation to bonds and equities. This is an attractive diversifier for traditional portfolios consisting of long-only exposure to bonds and equities. In relation to my role, I am the co-founder and CEO of Abbey Capital and head up the Investment Committee.

Richard C. Wilson: What is the typical background for a CTA or Managed Futures fund manager?

Tony Gannon: Managers come from a variety of backgrounds. The most typical backgrounds we see are 1) quantitative analysts and traders who had previously worked at one of the large CTAs or hedge funds, who now want to establish their own firm, (2) traders who started market making or trading on the floor of one of the commodity or futures exchanges and have evolved from there, and (3) former proprietary traders from investment banks. However, the industry is very diverse, and it is not uncommon to meet managers with backgrounds in academia, engineering, or physical science.

Richard C. Wilson: How would you explain to someone unfamiliar with the strategy how most managed futures and CTA funds execute their strategies?

Tony Gannon: Managed futures traders and CTAs can take long or short positions in the markets they trade and can use multiple time frames (from intra-day through to long-term) depending on the nature of the program. They typically trade futures contracts on regulated markets by executing through a futures broker, and trade foreign exchange markets by executing with banks trading in the interbank FX market.

CTAs can be broadly classified into two trading categories: systematic and discretionary. Systematic traders use computerized signals and algorithms to identify trends or price patterns in markets. Systematic CTAs aim to remove human emotion, and often rely on predetermined stop-loss orders to limit losses and let profits run. Systematic strategies typically involve no discretion and, in the majority of cases, trading execution is automated.

Discretionary strategies are based on fundamental judgments and analysis. Discretionary

CTAs tend to use fundamental data to assess markets, and often base the timing of trades on technical analysis. Some Discretionary CTAs may use systematic models that are driven by economic and fundamental factors as inputs in their investment process. Discretionary managers typically execute by giving market or limit orders to their brokers.

Richard C. Wilson: What are some of the strategies within managed futures and CTA funds that you believe are most popular or that you are most familiar with?

Tony Gannon: Systematic strategies dominate the industry, managing $260 billion at the end of 2011 (BarclayHedge). The most popular systematic strategy is trend following. Trend followers do not try to predict future price moves, but instead examine the likelihood of persistence in an existing market trend. Systematic trading strategies overcome many of the behavioral biases that afflict discretionary traders and investors.

A subset of systematic CTAs focuses on short-term price moves; they typically look at the one to five day period. These strategies aim to quickly adapt to market conditions, generating returns during periods when longer-term, trend-following CTAs often see a lack of defined trends. The combinations of positions and timeframes held by short-term strategies can result in low correlations between them and also with trend-following CTAs. This characteristic makes short-term trend

followers an attractive adjunct to a broader managed futures strategy.

Richard C. Wilson: Can you give us an example of two additional managed futures strategies and how they would be built in a portfolio in terms of the types and sizes of positions?

Tony Gannon: Global macro is another strategy that is often executed primarily via futures and FX markets. Global macro managers can be systematic or discretionary and can differ from trend followers in the inputs they use; trend followers typically rely on price data whereas systematic and discretionary macro managers often use economic- and market-based data as inputs in their investment process. An allocation to global macro can be beneficial in a multi manager managed futures portfolio, because at various points in time macro managers may be able to identify a potential change in a trend before there is evidence of a trend change in the price. Equally they can exit a position before there is a change in the trend, providing a different return stream profile than trend-followers. At Abbey Capital, we use a core-satellite approach, allocating a core allocation to trend following, diversified with allocations to satellite strategies such as global macro and counter-trend.

Another futures strategy that we identify as a satellite strategy is value-based trading. This strategy generally involves a systematic approach and seeks to exploit value differentials between markets and lead-lag relationships between markets. Like global macro, this type of trading can produce positions and returns streams that are uncorrelated to trend following, particularly at turning points in trends, and can provide valuable diversification in a multi-manager CTA portfolio.

Richard C. Wilson: How has managed futures investing changed since the financial crisis, if at all?

Tony Gannon: Managed futures performed very strongly through the financial crisis, and many investors really took note of the benefits that managed futures may provide in a portfolio during severe equity bear markets. In the three years after the crisis, performance in the industry has not been as strong since many markets have not exhibited as much trending behavior. This may have been related to the frequent market interventions from government officials and central banks through the period and certainly the lower levels of volatility in many markets. The frequent risk-on risk-off pattern made trading difficult for certain strategies. In 2013 we have seen evidence of a diminishing effect from risk-on risk-off as a driver of markets. We also have noted lower levels of correlation across markets. Currency markets have seen heightened levels of volatility and strong trends have emerged in the Japanese Yen for example. We see these as positive indicators for the industry.

Since the crisis we have seen the emphasis on operational due diligence and counter-party risk assessment increase. These are core elements of the investment process—both for Abbey Capital as an allocator and for investors in the funds we manage. We expect to see, and need to be able to show, strong risk processes and the ability to respond quickly to market changes and events. Fund structure is also increasingly important as investors seek to reduce contagion risk.

Richard C. Wilson: What are some significant trends you are seeing in the managed futures or CTA fund strategy or the hedge fund industry as a whole?

Tony Gannon: We have seen growing interest in managed futures from institutional investors in the last number of years, which has been reflected in the growth of assets under management in the industry. Although this has slowed somewhat in the last 18 months it does appear that there is a structural trend toward greater allocations to alternative investments from institutional investors. Trading in futures is not suitable for all investors, given its speculative nature and the high level of risk involved, however as an asset class that can deliver uncorrelated returns and high levels of liquidity and transparency, we believe managed futures will continue to attract inflows as part of this structural trend.

The trend toward more regulation of the alternative investment industry in both the United States and Europe is presenting a challenge for the industry in terms of transparency and investor protection. This may help bring hedge funds and managed futures to a wider audience but will provide an additional burden on managers and allocators to meet the new standards.

Richard C. Wilson: What is a typical day for you and your management team? We want to give our readers a sense of what it's like to run a managed-futures-related hedge fund, so any and all details are welcome.

Tony Gannon: A typical day at Abbey Capital starts with a review of the overnight moves in the FX and futures markets and a review of portfolio and manager performance. Our research team monitors a range of risk measures and reports on any risk, portfolio or manager issues to the investment committee for review. We have an ongoing dialogue with our managers, giving us a clear understanding of what is driving their performance and of any business or portfolio issues. At a business level, our management team is responsible for each of the diverse areas of our business from business development and client services to compliance and finance and back office.

It was nice having Tony Gannon of Abbey Capital and Drew Day of Lexington Asset Management share their experiences in the managed-futures sector.

Conclusion

Managed futures are considered one of the most liquid alternative investment asset classes that can be used by investors to diversify a portfolio. Futures provide access to global markets that open up numerous trading strategies for use in different market conditions. Trading strategies used in the managed-futures business are generally uncorrelated to stocks and bonds and can perform well during many market environments.

The managed-futures business has increased substantially throughout the past three decades and should continue to gain traction as futures derivatives expand globally.

To download several videos related to the focus of this chapter and to watch over 125 total video modules and expert audio interviews, please activate your free account here: http://HedgeFundGroup.org/Access.

Test Yourself

Answer the following questions.

1. The highest value a fund has achieved is referred to as:
   A. The peak.
   B. The high-water mark.
   C. The trough.
   D. The defined growth pattern.

2. True or False: The overall value of the managed-futures market has decreased substantially over the past two decades due to regulation in the Social Security Act.

3. True or False: Unlike stocks in general, leverage does not have any substantial effect on returns when speaking specifically about managed futures.

4. Efficient frontier theory states:
   A. Frontier markets, although risky, are incredibly efficient and produce great returns.
   B. Allocation of capital into one sector or firm is the most efficient way to organize a portfolio.
   C. Holding a basket of assets that are uncorrelated will produce the best returns.
   D. The only way to produce an efficient portfolio for an investor is to stay one step ahead of the industry insight.

5. True or False: The Sharpe ratio is used to determine the violability within a portfolio.

Answers can be found in Appendix B.

CHAPTER 12

Credit- and Asset-Based Lending

Over the past few decades hedge fund strategies have broadened significantly and diversification has generated demand for asset-based and credit-based-lending strategies. Prior to the 2008 financial crisis, asset and credit lending had fully infiltrated the ranks of hedge funds, as the competitive nature of the lending sector had pushed lenders to the far reaches of the credit spectrum.

Asset-based lending is the funding of projects or operations secured by an asset. The collateral posted by the borrower is an asset that will be confiscated if the borrower defaults on the loan. A home mortgage is one of the best examples of an asset-based loan. In this example, a bank or hedge fund will lend money backed by the house as collateral for the loan.

Other examples include lending to a corporation based on assets that might not be used to collateralize other loans. These loans come into play when borrowing capital cannot be accomplished by normal routes of fund raising such as selling bonds or borrowing on an unsecured basis. Typically, these asset-backed loans use inventory, accounts receivable, machinery and equipment, real estate, or reserves.

Many times a corporation will need access to immediate capital for project financing needs or mergers and acquisitions. Despite the collateral posted for this type of loan, they are generally accompanied by higher interest rates, and can be very lucrative to the lender. When an organization has the infrastructure to monetize the collateral, asset-based lending can prove to be an extremely lucrative investment strategy.

Corporate clients on many levels are involved in asset-based lending. At the Fortune 500 level, national and regional banks, along with investment banks, are vying for asset-based lending businesses. At the hedge fund level, capital usually reaches further out on the credit spectrum, which further enhances the potential gains.

DEFINITION:
Asset and Credit Lending

Where an asset is offered as collateral for a loan; in other words, upon default of the loan the asset is seized by the lender.

Smart Investor Tip

Overcollateralization leads to more profits from defaulting because the lending party could potentially gain control of assets worth 1.5x to 3x the value of the loan made. For example, a real estate firm gets a $5M development loan and guarantees it with $7.75M worth of developed properties and then defaults on their payments.

Asset-based loans are geared toward providing working capital or cash flow for short periods of time to meet financing needs of corporations. Companies that generally do not have access to the capital markets use asset-based lending to assist in their financing needs. Asset-based lending goes well beyond loans based on the assets pledged as collateral. The process involves determining the appropriate credit to charge a lender based on their cash flow and credit history. The collateral assists in reducing the interest rate that the borrower would pay on an unsecured loan.

Distressed Debt

Distressed debts are the loans that are priced well below par, offering investors robust rates based on the ability of the borrower to repay their loan. The term refers to the debt of companies that have defaulted or have a significant chance of filing for bankruptcy at some time in the future.

The attractiveness of distressed debt is the risk relative to the reward. Distressed debt pays its investors a significant premium in terms of the coupon associated with the bonds a company has issued. If a distressed company avoids bankruptcy or emerges from bankruptcy, the owners of the bonds could stand to generate significant profits.

Distress debt backed by collateral does not necessarily make the asset secure. The value of the collateral can move independently of the company's ability to fund their debt, which would push the debt into distressed

conditions. For example, mortgage-backed securities during the U.S. subprime crisis are a perfect example of debt that was backed by collateral that become distressed as the collateral became less valuable.

Distressed-Debt Transactions

There are many forms available to investors to initiate risk within the distressed-debt environment. The two main vehicles for risk assumption to distressed debt are the bond market or a distressed firm itself.

- The bond markets are the most liquid capital market that provides access to risk on distressed debt. Bonds can be acquired easily as access is restricted to many mutual funds due to regulations concerning their holdings. Most mutual funds are restricted from holding debt of firms that have defaulted. Due to these rules, a large supply of debt is available shortly after a firm defaults.
- Restructuring debt directly with the distressed firm is another option that provides direct access to the distressed-debt market. The process involves working with the company to extend credit on behalf of the fund. This credit is usually in the form of bonds but can also be a revolving credit line. If a small portion of a portfolio is direct debt and the debt is shared by other hedge funds, the risk could be considered diversified.

Within the world of private equity and distressed debt hedge funds, managers will take on an activist

DEFINITION:
Distressed Debt

A government, corporate, or bank security that is in default, under bankruptcy, or nearing default.

role in which they become directly involved with the management and finances of the firm and provide direction based on similar experiences. Hedge funds can also restructure the debt and alter the payments of existing debt, which can provide the company with financial flexibility, freeing up cash flow to correct other problems.

There are significant advantages associated with owning the debt of a distressed company over the equity. Debt is more senior in the capital structure and therefore takes precedence over equity when retrieving assets in the case of liquidation.

Distressed debt is an instrument that can generate outsized returns but has characteristics of a venture-capital product. If a company emerges successfully from bankruptcy, its bonds could triple in value, moving from 10 cents on the dollar to 40 cents on the dollar. If this return is based on 1 percent of the hedge fund's capital, the return to the hedge fund is approximately 3 percent before fees. If the company remains in bankruptcy, the loss is 100 percent of the capital or a loss of 1 percent. This risk-to-reward ratio is very attractive on a small pool of capital but can be considered too binary for an entire hedge fund.

The basic goal of a distressed-debt purchaser is to purchase bonds of companies that are undervalued given the stress the company's earnings are facing. This could be because management has underperformed or the company has experienced malfeasance by an officer or employee. In any event, if an investor believes that the assets of the firm are worth more than the current valuation of the company, a distress situation is available and can be capitalized on with bond purchases.

Evaluating Asset-Based Loans

Asset-based loans (ABLs) are generally focused on a few metrics, which include the credit quality of the company looking for a loan and the collateral. With a standard bank facility a borrower has a pre-set credit limit that typically is reviewed annually by a credit officer. With an ABL loan the borrowing is tied to the asset base of your firm or collateral. For a company, the loan is tied to receivables, inventory, equipment, and real estate.

The term structure of ABL loans is usually multi-year while the credit facility at a bank is usually reviewed every year and based on historical financial performance. Asset-based lending focuses on monitoring a company's assets at the start of the loan and periodically during the tenor of the loan. While a conventional lender focuses on operating ratios and loan covenants, ABL loans concentrate on the quality of the collateral.

A covenant is the language in the loan that describes the specific financial ratios a company must keep from defaulting on a loan. If covenants are too vigorous a lender is put in a position where they will likely take possession of the collateral, which is a strategy that many hedge funds use when constructing opportunities.

Advance Rate

Advance Rate determines the value of collateral in the asset-based lending market, which differs from firm to firm. While hedge funds are more apt to find creative ways to define risk, traditional lenders are generally more conservative.

Receivables are a common asset to collateralize. A generalized way the finance industry determines the advance rate on receivables is to subtract a multiple of the dilution rate plus a factor. In determining the advance rate, a lender will look at factors including receivables.

An example of how a wine-asset-based lender handles this process is to lend capital against 60 percent of the wine stored in a verified cellar. For example, a hedge fund that will lend capital against the value of prominent wines will value the wine based on their expertise and use a basic dilution formula to calculate the advanced rate. If the dilution rate is 20 percent, and the multiple is $2X$, then the advanced rate for the wine lender is $1 - 2$ (.20 percent) is 60 percent.

This estimated value could be reduced further by X percent to achieve a value at which the hedge fund will lend capital. By reducing the estimated value and only lending against a portion of the collateral while holding all the collateral, the hedge fund ABL lender is producing an asset to lend against that is unlikely to fall below the reduced value of the collateral. In the case presented, a $100,000 wine portfolio would need to fall more than 41 percent for the collateral to become less than the outstanding loan.

Situations can arise when collateral falls well below advanced-rate levels. During the 2008 financial crisis collateralized debt and mortgage obligations moved to near zero values when the housing markets collapsed.

Hedge Fund History

Asset-based lending can trace its genesis to commercial finance companies that operated as lone entities outside of other institutions. Hedge fund involvement in the asset-based lending environment saw a rapid increase in assets under management, geometrically growing from 1 billion in 2004 to approximately 16 billion in 2010, according to Bloomberg (see Figure 12.1).

The growth in asset-backed lending as a hedge fund strategy grew in part with the growth of alternative investments that strive to produce returns that are uncorrelated to equity and fixed-income returns. Institutional demand has been the biggest driver of this trend as returns within the equity spaces were underwhelming during the first decade of the new century. ABL was also less crowded as an investment space than traditional hedge fund strategies, including global macro and long/short equity.

As you can see in Figure 12.2, asset-based hedge funds have produced robust returns that produce uncorrelated returns when compared to the S&P 500 as a benchmark. ABL funds did not hold a large portion of the mortgage-related toxic debt held by large

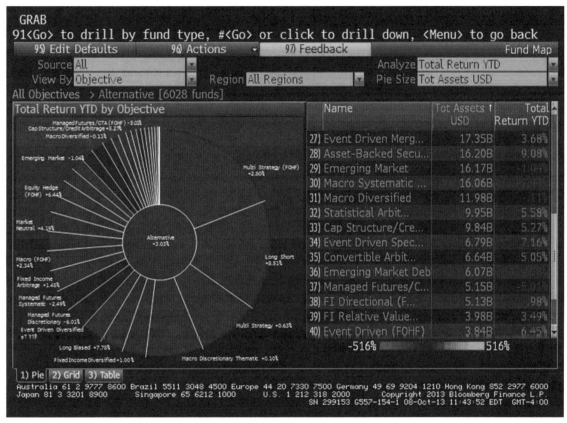

Figure 12.1 Asset-Based Lending Growth 2004 to 2010
Source: © 2014 Bloomberg L.P. All rights reserved.

financial institutions during the financial crisis. By keeping their dry powder, many ABL funds were able to take advantage of the troubles in a large asset base and capitalized on their ability to purchase debt at historically low prices.

Hedge funds in the ABL space have increased competition and have been able to take advantage of traditional lenders who have changed their credit standards. ABL hedge funds and traditional asset-based lenders often work on joint ventures in deals.

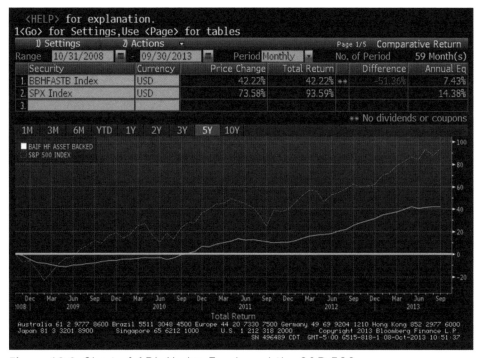

Figure 12.2 Chart of ABL Hedge Funds and the S&P 500
Source: © 2014 Bloomberg L.P. All rights reserved.

By taking on the more risky portions of a deal, the hedge fund–traditional fund combination can broaden the base of the loan package.

The financial crisis that began in 2008 nearly pushed the ABL strategy to extinction. In 2013 the industry looks to be on the mend. A recent report released by the Commercial Finance Association shows asset-based lenders increased their total credit commitments to U.S. businesses by 2 percent during the fourth quarter of 2012 and by 6.7 percent over the past year.

The CFA's Asset-Based Lending Index showed credit utilization rates hit their lowest level during the financial crisis at 34.6 percent during the fourth quarter of 2009. Since that time, credit utilization steadily climbed to 41.8 percent in the second quarter of 2012 (Commercial Finance Association, 2013).

Second Lien

Innovation within the hedge fund industry has led to the development of many types of investment vehicles, which is certainly the case within ABL funds. Asset-based hedge funds are well-known for their desire to move out the credit curve, with the comfort that they have the operational knowledge of how to monetize an asset that is used for collateral.

ABL funds will move beyond accounts receivable, inventory, and other typical types of collateral in an effort to secure asset-based loans. Hedge funds will collateralize probable and proven reserves of commodities such as oil and natural gas, receivables backed by claims involving litigation outcomes, real estate, and intellectual property.

Hedge funds in the ABL space use innovative financing techniques to accomplish a goal that might be unattainable using standard formula-based approaches. The second lien, which incorporates the mezzanine space, requires hedge fund style techniques and has priority in the capital structure over unsecured lenders and equity investors. Second-lien debt is second to first-lien loans made by other secured lenders on the same collateral.

In the early 2000s, the second-lien loan market was transformed by ABL funds by broadening the scope of general financing needs, which included dividend payments and leveraged buyouts. Volume increased substantially over the latter half of the first decade as borrowers found second-lien loans attractive because of their flexibility and their ease to acquire prior to the 2008 financial crisis.

The lower cost of capital for second-lien lenders was their priority in the capital structure over mezzanine lenders and unsecured lenders with enhanced rights in bankruptcy. Second-lien loan issuance has flat-lined since the financial crisis, while unsecured mezzanine finance has grown in attractiveness.

The most important issue asset-based hedge funds consistently face is the ability to preserve interest in the pledged collateral. The legal issues faced by second lenders are the inter-creditor agreements that must make the payouts in the case of a default or bankruptcy. Bondholders that are senior to second lenders will attempt rights that are free and clear from control of second lenders. This pertains to control of common collateral and issues related to the borrower.

With an obvious conflict of interest between first- and second-lien lenders, legal matters arising from the control of collateral will sometimes occur. Inter-creditor agreements typically do not halt payments to second-lien lenders. These agreements are subject to a substantial amount of legal uncertainty in part because of the lack of a consistent regulatory body that oversees these agreements.

Risks

ABL-fund investing has considerable risks, which include the risk of depreciation of the collateral. One of the headwinds that hedge fund managers face is

> **DEFINITION:**
>
> **Lien**
>
> A legal term used to describe the granting of a security interest based on a property to secure payment of debt.

that the tenor for an average loan is approximately five years, which is longer than most investors expect to have restrictions on their capital. Many ABL funds were caught in positions in which the collateral they were holding during the financial crisis fell well below the value of the loan, creating losing positions that needed to be liquidated.

Conflicts of Interest

Asset-based hedge fund lenders can create conflicts of interest since they have the ability to take positions with derivative instruments that may be inversely correlated to the performance of the borrowers. Theoretically, an asset-backed lender could hedge their lending position with equity or credit-default swaps on a borrower. Hedge funds remain attractive to borrowers as the flexibility, ability to quickly deploy capital, and willingness to take risks make the industry unique.

How an ABL Strategy Works

Hedge funds with robust track records generally attract capital and deal flow, but there is still a need for an intermediary to assist in the process. An active broker market surrounds the asset-backed lending process where intermediaries are contacted to line up potential funding. Intermediaries are generally helpful with introductions, but a final agreement outlining specific requirements between a borrower and lender is consummated directly between the two parties.

In the world of derivatives, the International Swaps Dealers Association agreement is helpful in defining specific criteria that need to be met for an agreement, while the universe of asset-back lending has customized agreements between two parties.

Once a hedge fund expresses interest in a project, the hedge fund needs to counter the borrowing request laid out by the borrower. The first step is to determine the value of the collateral that will be pledged for capital.

Types of Collateral Analysis

Most lenders have a field examination that visits the borrower's operation to better understand their businesses. Examinations assist the borrower as they help value the maximum amount of liquidity that can be supported by the collateral from an independent valuation.

A field examination is geared toward verifying the collateral and confirming financial information, which helps the lender evaluate the borrower's business. Generally the borrower is responsible for the costs associated with a field examination.

Another type of confirmation is an accounts-receivable verification. Verifying accounts receivable is the process of confirming a borrower's receivables directly with the borrower's customers.

Field Examination Example

Energy businesses enjoy asset-based lending facilities. One of the most popular uses of collateral is energy, which has a specific value if it can be developed properly. Many times a small-to-medium sized oil developer will come to an asset-back lender looking for capital to develop a well that has probable reserves. A hedge fund manager would have to have their own inspectors and engineers determine the value of the probable reserves, which would then be discounted by the hedge fund to determine the capital to be allocated against the reserve given the risk that it cannot be developed.

For example, assume a well has estimated reserves of 1 million barrels of oil. A hedge fund might be willing to lend capital against 50 percent of the reserves against a pledge by the borrower against the entire reserve. If the hedge fund manager believes the reports from his engineer that there is a strong likelihood of developing all 1 million barrels of oil, then lending against 50 percent of the probable reserves might be prudent.

The next step in the process is the cost associated with developing the oil. An asset-based lender would need to determine this cost as part of the interest rate that he will charge a borrower in case the borrower defaults on the loan and the hedge fund manager is on the hook to develop the oil himself.

The lender will also need to determine the credit worthiness of the borrower and the ability of the borrower to pay back the loan. In some cases, the lender might want to see the borrower default as the value of the asset pledged far outweighs the capital risked in the loan.

A hedge fund in an energy-development project also faces the market risk associated with the product that is being developed. For example, crude oil prices fluctuate on a daily basis, and the loan that is issued is predicated on the borrower receiving a specific price of the crude oil that is developed.

Hedging

In the instance of energy development, a borrower might be forced to hedge their future cash flows in an effort to secure the loan. By locking in cash flows, the lender is mitigating the market risk associated with the loan. With this hedge comes the risk that the oil is not developed, and there is no gain to offset a potential loss from the crude oil hedge. The hedge fund would need to believe that they could take control of the collateral and monetize it to provide an offset to their hedge prior to requiring a hedge on market risk.

For a hedge fund to be able to produce this type of product, they would have to have a credit background where they understood the risks associated with developing crude oil from probable reserves. They would also need to have the expertise to understand the jargon of an oil engineer, and the financial wherewithal to be able to transact a crude oil hedge within the derivative or physical oil markets.

In many cases, such as real estate or liability claims, it is difficult to hedge an investor's exposure mark to market movements of the collateral. In these cases, an asset-based lender will need to provide enough of a cushion to reduce any negative slippage that occurs from mark-to-market movements in the collateral.

Smart Investor Tip

Many asset-backed lenders who are hedge fund managers have financial institution or banking experience, and have come across similar deals in their careers. A manager's ability to understand market, operation, and credit risk is key to successfully running ALB risks.

An example of how a wine-asset-based lender handles this process is to lend capital against 35 percent of the wine stored in a verified cellar, and to add an additional haircut of approximately 10 percent. For example, a hedge fund that will lend capital against the value of prominent wines will value the wine based on their expertise, and they subtract 10 percent of the value to come up with a haircut value.

This estimated value will be further reduced by 65 percent to achieve a value that the hedge fund will lend capital against. By reducing the estimated value and only lending against a portion of the collateral while holding all the collateral, the hedge fund ABL lender is producing an asset to lend against that is unlikely to fall below the reduced value of the collateral. In the case presented, a $100,000 wine portfolio would need to fall more than 69 percent for the collateral to become less than the outstanding loan.

Closing an Asset-Based Loan Deal

Asset-based loans require specific knowledge of an industry and experience in closing ABL deals to insure a smooth transaction. Most companies do not use internal counsel to represent them in an ABL transaction. Most internal counsels are jack-of-all-trades types and do not possess specific, technical knowledge that is imperative in order to represent the legal interests of an ABL.

To ensure you have appropriate representation, a hedge fund needs to interview a number of recommended legal firms. Managers or originators should inquire about the firm's specific experience in asset-based lending.

Industry Insight

To add an industry perspective of what is going on in the credit hedge fund space we reached out to Louis Gargour, CIO of LNG Capital, a European-based credit hedge fund.

Richard C. Wilson: Is there a typical background for a credit fund manager?

Louis Gargour: I would imagine that many professionals working in asset-backed lending and credit funds come from a banking background, credit analyst backgrounds, prop trading, and, in some cases, classics and other nonrelated industries—but years of training are required.

Richard C. Wilson: How would you explain to someone unfamiliar with the strategy how a credit fund works? Can you explain specifically asset-backed lending and how that strategy is executed by a hedge fund?

Louis Gargour: The typical definition of credit is the obligation to pay back a sum of money in the future, and during the period of time you have lent the money you are paid interest with the principal typically paid at the end of the loan period. A good simple example of asset-backed lending is a mortgage. The bank will lend you money but if you do not continue paying they take back the security, i.e., take over ownership of the house, therefore the loan is backed by an asset. Other strategies can include credit card receivables, i.e., the asset is the receivable by the credit card company and you invest in the fact that you have first claim on receivables from the payments made by credit card holders. One of the first asset-backed securities was an Italian toll road where the bond was going to be paid back from revenues of everyone that used the toll road. In this particular example the asset is a toll road, and the cash flow from operations went to pay interest and principal over time.

Richard C. Wilson: What are some of the different credit strategies out there? Do hedge funds specialize in a particular area or niche?

Louis Gargour: Investors typically consider credit as a single strategy, however this is misleading as there are a wide array of credit strategies ranging from buying bonds and holding them, to arbitrage strategies that exploit inefficiencies and take advantage of any changes in different securities. For the purposes of this article we can categorize different strategies as being either low volatility, medium volatility, or high volatility. Additionally, we can categorize them as being non-directional such as relative value, or directional such as distressed-event driven, and high yield. The lowest volatility, safest strategies center what I would categorize as market-neutral, relative-value strategies. In these market-neutral investments, two securities

are held and the investor is compensated if their relationship changes. These strategies tend to have low or no correlation to the underlying market, sect world trends, and other external beta drivers. The strategies generally speaking are deemed to create alpha. Moving up the risk spectrum the strategy focuses on a buy-and-hold of investment grade and government bonds. As we move toward lower-rated securities and to emerging markets we begin to have higher levels of volatility; higher returns; more risk; and the need for hedging and hedge fund techniques, such as short and long positions, individual position hedging, portfolio hedging, leverage, significant risk oversight, stop losses, and probability analysis of fat tails.

Richard C. Wilson: Can you give us examples of two specific credit strategies and how they would be built in a portfolio in terms of the types and sizes of positions? Is credit and ABL usually part of a larger portfolio of strategies or a single strategy with different credit investments?

Louis Gargour: The examples I like to use of two very different strategies are relative value and distressed. In relative value you buy one security and sell another, typically either a pair in a sector, i.e., buy Aston Martin and sell Peugeot or two parts of the same company's capital structure; for example you buy senior secured bonds and sell subordinate unsecured bonds. Relative value strategies can be a very large portion of portfolios as they tend to have low volatility, are market neutral, sector neutral, and, in some cases, name or company neutral. For that reason they can become a very large part of a portfolio as the risks are not that of the market but of discrepancies and differences between two sets of securities.

The second, very different, strategy that might coexist in a portfolio is distressed, whereby the breakup value of the company is determined and you look to buy securities with a very low cash price with the expectation of a massive uplift as a result of the company being sold, broken up, or receiving bailout or emergency financing from another company. This strategy needs to be a smaller proportion of the portfolio, as it is very binary in its outcome and can result in significant price movements leading to massive gains and losses, while another was exhibiting higher volatility. The tendency for this asset class is for market influences to also be reflected in the underlying valuation of these distressed securities as risk appetite, general propensity for risk, and alternative returns and other asset classes all drive the price of these securities.

The two strategies are very different in the sense that relative value typically has a very low beta and very high alpha component, i.e., the returns do not depend on market forces or general macroeconomics but depend on the convergence or divergence of two separate companies. Whereas the distressed investment typically relies very specifically on the outcome of one company and

outcome, it can be binary and is influenced by the general market trends, macroeconomic expectations, and the availability of capital credit, as well as people's risk appetite.

Richard C. Wilson: What are the largest opportunities you see in the credit market for a hedge fund to capitalize on? Is it real estate, corporations? What are the big areas?

Louis Gargour: The largest opportunities have to do with the peripheral dislocation caused by investor concerns in 2011 and 2012. This has created a corporate bond landscape, which in Italy, Spain, Portugal, Greece, and Cyprus creates significant opportunities for well-run companies to be much cheaper than they ought to be given their ratings, cash flows, leverage, and other financial criteria. I'm going to say very little about the specifics of our investments, however we have significantly outperformed our peers for the past two years as a result of our ability to analyze and invest in this area.

Richard C. Wilson: The tightening of credit after the fall of Lehman Brothers and ensuing financial crisis created an opening for hedge funds to lend money when banks and other traditional sources would not. How will credit hedge funds be affected if/when credit loosens to pre-crisis levels? Will there still be a role for hedge fund lenders?

Louis Gargour: I believe that hedge fund direct lending opportunities exist for lending to smaller companies that cannot borrow directly from banks.

Hedge fund managers are very good at credit analysis, security package analysis, and in modeling cash flows as businesses grow. Determining what the security package is (asset), lending against a security package that gives investors confidence that they will be repaid, or that the assets they will claim if they are not repaid are more valuable than the loans is the principal skill set in direct lending. Banks don't really want to focus on smaller companies. Therefore, the opportunity set exists not because the skill set of hedge funds are different than banks, but simply because the opportunity is too small or irrelevant for banks. However, I believe that as money stays cheap, the banks will begin to be interested again, move down the size scale, and begin to dis-intermediate hedge funds in the next two to four years.

Richard C. Wilson: How do you evaluate a loan? Do you rely simply on traditional lending practices and due diligence or are there additional measures you take to guard against default and mitigate risk to the fund and its investors?

Louis Gargour: The macroeconomic evaluation of pressures in that industry and in that sector affecting that company need to be scrutinized, as well as looking at the specifics of the company's leverage, cash flows, capital expenditures, operating expenditures, and a variety of other factors.

Richard C. Wilson: Do you invest in emerging markets and, if so, how do you lower the risk of lending to a party so far away?

Louis Gargour: We do not typically invest in emerging markets. It is a whole separate subset of skills that has less to do with credit skills than to do with sovereign and macroeconomic skills. It is part of my professional experience but not currently one of the strategies we pursue at LNG Capital.

Richard C. Wilson: Are there any business management or operations challenges that you face?

Louis Gargour: We often find that hedge funds have to quickly learn to manage a small business in addition to all the rigors of investing. The pressures generally affecting a hedge fund are that they have to be quite reactive to changes in the market both in sentiment and opportunity. Oftentimes the mix of strategies has to be dynamically changed and allocations to different sub-strategies need to be done in real time in order to take advantage of the opportunity set.

Richard C. Wilson: What are some significant trends you are seeing in the credit strategy or the hedge fund industry as a whole?

Louis Gargour: Trends are all very positive. We are seeing a plethora of new issuers offering exceedingly good value in sectors and industries where we want to focus our investments. We are seeing bank lending increased, therefore the flow of capital to hedge funds and other investors, which has created more demand for good investment opportunities. And finally the most important trend we are seeing is the emergence of Europe from a deep recession into the growth phase of the economic cycle. The dislocations caused by sovereign bailouts and perceived euro breakup have created an extremely interesting thing for investors, and I strongly suggest readers of this material do their homework on Europe.

Richard C. Wilson: What is a typical day for you and your management team?

We want to give our readers a sense of what it's like to run a credit hedge fund, so any and all details are welcome.

Louis Gargour: My typical day begins at 6 A.M. I go to the gym; I read the Financial Times, Wall Street Journal, before arriving in the office at around 7:45. I then begin to read news services until about 8:30, then we have our morning meeting with analysts and other members of the team. At 9, I begin speaking with the street, other fund managers, banks, and a variety of other information sources to better assess the market opportunities; spend the rest of the day analyzing companies, looking at opportunities, speaking with other members of staff, reanalyze companies, and making decisions on whether or not to invest. Throughout the day there is a reevaluation of concentrations in the portfolio sector, exposure rating, exposure country, exposure in order to fine tune and better understand the risks inherent in portfolio. I typically get home at 6:30, spend time with my three children—reading to them, having fun, maybe going to the pool. I'm usually in bed by 10 P.M., and read for half an hour.

Richard C. Wilson: Is there anything else you'd like to add?

Louis Gargour: Working for oneself in the hedge fund industry is a profoundly rewarding and intellectually challenging experience.

In addition to interviewing Louis Gargour, we were also able to interview Melissa Weiler, Senior Portfolio Manager of Crescent Capital Group LP.

Richard C. Wilson: Can you explain what type of investment strategy your firm runs in the credit space?

Melissa Weiler: Our fund targets the most attractive sub-sectors of the below-investment-grade credit market at a given point in the credit cycle. We utilize a dynamic asset-allocation process to take advantage of the evolving opportunity set. When market conditions warrant, we utilize leverage and shorts to help us achieve our investment objective.

Richard C. Wilson: Do you see a strong future for credit hedge funds?

Melissa Weiler: The short answer is yes. New providers of credit have continued to proliferate as memories of 2008 to 2009 fade. There will always be a role for hedge fund lenders in my opinion. However, pricing has compressed significantly in the current environment due to heightened competition and may not meet certain hedge funds' performance objectives.

Richard C. Wilson: How do you evaluate a loan? Do you rely simply on traditional lending practices and due diligence or are there additional measures you take to guard against default and mitigate risk to the fund and its investors?

Melissa Weiler: Our analysts undertake a rigorous investment-review process and, whenever possible, are active participants in structuring a given loan to guard against default and mitigate risk. In the current environment, the ability to influence structure is usually limited to smaller, less liquid loans.

Richard C. Wilson: Can you share with our readers what it is like to help run a credit hedge fund portfolio?

Melissa Weiler: The beauty of this business is that no two days are ever the same. Having said that, from a time-allocation perspective, my mornings are typically spent evaluating market developments and new issue investment opportunities, often with a very fast turnaround time. Afternoons are typically spent meeting with analysts and traders,

formulating portfolio strategy, analyzing position reports, etc.

I appreciated the interviews with Melissa Weiler of Crescent Capital Group and Louis Gargour of LNG Capital as they offered a real account of what it is like to manage a credit hedge fund.

Conclusion

In the wake of the financial crisis, the asset-backed lending strategy has flourished as banks have somewhat priced themselves out of the market for small and medium-sized borrowers. Continued creativity by hedge fund managers has allowed funds to take on securities risks at unsecured rates. Managers that have the expertise to take collateral on loans that have defaulted are in an excellent position to generate robust returns for their investors.

▶ To download several videos related to the focus of this chapter and to watch over 125 total video modules and expert audio interviews, please activate your free account here: http://HedgeFundGroup.org/Access.

Test Yourself

Answer the following questions.

1. Distress debt is:
   A. Debt that is traded on OTC exchanges.
   B. A government, corporate, or bank security that is already in default, under bankruptcy, or nearing default.
   C. A loan that has a rating of two stars or less by one of the three major rating agencies.
   D. Stocks with a market value that is lower than the original priced paid.

2. True or False: The borrower is responsible for the costs of a field examination.

3. True or False: A lien is a legal term used to describe when a security interest has been sold.

4. The advance rate is:
   A. The maximum percentage of the calculated collateral that a hedge fund will make available to the borrower as a loan.
   B. The minimum percentage of the calculated collateral that a hedge fund will make available to the borrower as a loan.
   C. The rate that is available to institutional banks prior to market fluctuation.
   D. The rate that is available to hedge funds from institutional banks prior to market fluctuation.

5. True or False: Asset-based lending is where an asset is offered up as collateral for a loan.

6. A typical definition of credit is:
   A. An asset that has been exchanged for another asset.
   B. Capital contributed by an institutional investor.
   C. A distressed loan.
   D. The obligation to pay back a sum of money in the future.

7. True or False: Theoretically, an asset-backed lender could hedge their lending position with equity or credit-default swaps on a borrower.

Answers can be found in Appendix B.

CHAPTER 13

Multi-Strategy Hedge Funds

A multi-strategy hedge fund utilizes multiple investment strategies simultaneously in order to add a layer of diversification and capture opportunities across multiple different investment products. Multi-strategy hedge funds allocate investor capital across a number of different hedge fund strategies in order to generate returns while reducing single-strategy exposure and often minimizing other risks like sector or industry risks.

The goal of a multi-strategy hedge fund is to produce robust risk-adjusted returns in all market conditions across many asset classes. Generally, multi-strategy hedge funds generate returns that are uncorrelated to standard benchmarks as well as the hedge fund community as a whole. The benefits of a multi-strategy fund include smoothed returns relative to single-strategy hedge funds. Strategies embraced in a multi-strategy fund include, global macro, long/short equity, credit, asset-backed lending, and merger arbitrage.

History of Multi-Strategy Funds

The development of the multi-strategy fund follows the path of the efficient frontier and the idea that a diversified portfolio will produce the best risk-adjusted returns. Although single-strategy funds can produce results that are robust for a short period, the volatility associated with the strategy also produces significant risks.

Multi-strategy funds also solve some of the issues related to capacity. Once managers reach the maximum capital that they could allocate to a strategy and meet the fund's investment goals, then the managers are often forced into other strategies in order to expand the assets under management of the hedge fund.

This search for capacity can be the impetus for the launch of new funds with different strategies. In some cases, managers add other investment talent to expand strategy capacity, and in other cases managers

DEFINITION:
Multi-Strategy Hedge Fund

A strategy where investments are placed both long and short in varying sectors of an economy as to ensure smooth returns regardless of economic conditions.

develop strategies internally. In this way, many of today's multi-strategy hedge funds were formed to expand beyond a single strategy.

Benefits

Multi-strategy funds provide benefits to investors in multiple ways. Diversification, which is the smoothing of the returns by allocating resources to many strategies, creates efficient risk-adjusted returns. Additionally, the ability to reallocate capital provides the multi-strategy manager with the flexibility to shift capital to the best-performing strategies. When opportunities arise for low-risk, high-reward investment opportunities, a manager can redistribute capital to enhance the hedge fund's gains.

Risks

The diversification of investment strategies will dilute the returns of a single hedge fund strategy that performs at maximum capacity. For example, a global macro fund that returns 25 percent over a year will be diluted by a merger arbitrage strategy that returns 10 percent. The main risk is significant underperformance during periods when riskier assets are performing at peak levels as well as allocation risks that bring down returns relative to peers.

Asset-allocation risk comes from the process of allocating capital to different types of instruments. Fund managers use this type of system to create a portfolio that will meet their assumed expectations of returns. Expectations assume specific types of assumptions which generate the risk. Asset allocation can be a process that is quantitative or qualitative. Quantitative asset allocation is a methodology where historical returns are evaluated and matrixes of the best-performing strategies are used relative to the worst-performing strategies.

Allocations to strategies are based on a manager's expected returns and the volatility of returns mandated by the hedge fund. The higher the risk associated with strategy, the higher the expected return. The goal is to create a basket of strategies that are generally uncorrelated to each other in an effort to generate returns in all types of market environments.

In addition, asset allocation is important because it has a major impact on whether you will meet your financial goal. Although investors in a multi-strategy firm might not expect to receive returns equivalent to a single strategy, investors do expect returns that justify paying a 2 percent management fee and a 20 percent incentive fee. A strategy mix that is too conservative will make it very difficult to meet your financial goals, and therefore disappoint investors. If a portfolio, on the other hand, is too risky the returns may reflect a track record that is too volatile.

One of the most important risks that most multi-strategy firms avoid is the risk of ruin. Market conditions can easily influence the survival rate of hedge funds, as recently observed during the 2008 financial crisis. Slews of single-strategy mezzanine-lending hedge funds were wiped off the map along with giant funds of funds. When others are wiped out, such as single-strategy funds, multi-strategy funds can swoop in and quickly benefit from others' losses.

A diversified multi-strategy hedge fund should create diversification on multiple levels, which include specific strategies along with asset categories. A situation can easily arise where the theories behind specific strategies overlap, generating risk in a specific sector that is identical. For example, an options trader could create a synthetic position in a stock or commodity that is the same risk as a strategy that is trading the stock on an outright basis.

Rebalancing a fund within a multi-strategy structure entails measuring historical performances based on past allocations. This concept can only be accomplished if hedge fund managers keep a historical record of past allocations. The allocation needs to be matched up with P&L performance, which will allow multi-fund managers to determine the best period of risk-adjusted performances. To determine the best risk-adjusted historical returns, a manager needs to examine allocations, and compare them to returns and the volatility of returns. High periods of profitability that create spikes in the return performance of a multi-strategy manager will be viewed with a bias, unless a manager used a concept similar to the Sortino ratio.

This risk-adjusted return analysis eliminates upward deviations from its calculation of its return matrix, and only focuses on downward deviations. This formula eliminates penalizing a manager for volatility of positive returns.

Although multi-strategy funds provide the diversification of a fund of funds, an investor is still using a large chunk of capital to generate returns on a single hedge fund shop. Lack of risk control within that single firm could have severe negative consequences for the investor.

Benchmarks

As competition in the multi-strategy hedge fund space developed, *bogeys* (performance benchmarks) were created to monitor the performance of multi-strategy funds. The IQ Hedge Multi-Strategy Tracker ETF (NYSE: QAI) was the first hedge-fund-style ETF and is the industry's largest alternative exchange-traded fund. The QAI was introduced in 2009 and marked a turning point in the environment. For the first time, investors and their advisors were able to have access to a hedge-fund-like strategy in an ETF. The benefits of lower costs than the 2 percent management and 20 percent incentive fee, along with liquidity, allowed non-accredited investors access to the multi-strategy fund sector.

QAI attempts to track the returns of the IQ Hedge Multi-Strategy Index. The index attempts to replicate the risk-adjusted return of hedge funds using various hedge fund investment styles, including long/short equity, market neutral, fixed income arbitrage, merger arbitrage, global macro, and emerging markets.

DEFINITION:
Rebalancing

The process of selling or purchasing assets within a portfolio to return the asset allocation to the initial desired level.

The introduction of an ETF-based alternative-investment strategy has given investment advisors a benchmark to measure prospective hedge funds in many alternative investment spaces. Since the launch of the QAI multi-strategy fund, the trust has accumulated 350 million in assets.[1]

Fees

Multi-strategy funds typically charge a management fee that can range from 0 to 4 percent and an incentive fee of 0 to 50 percent. They generally do not charge two layers of fees which, as you will learn in the funds of funds chapter, is a criticism directed at funds of funds.

Some multi-strategy funds offer a netting feature, which means that the performance of all underlying funds will be netted before calculating the excess performance fee.

Liquidity

Multi-strategy funds have the capability of offering daily liquidity, but most multi-strategy hedge funds offer liquidity quarterly, or annually. Multi-strategy funds are generally held in a limited liability hedge fund structure. Multi-strategy funds typically have a mix of liquid and less-liquid investments, which gives them the flexibility to provide liquidity using more liquid assets.

Not all funds in the multi-strategy space have the same liquidity profile. Some invest primarily in liquid securities and therefore may not have a lockup. A lockup is a period of time where the investor cannot remove capital from the fund. Some less-liquid strategies might require investors to hold capital within a fund for years.

Strategies

A multi-strategy fund offers access to a number of investment strategies including long/short equity, macro, credit/asset-based lending, and merger arbitrage. Each strategy offers specific market conditions that benefits investors. The goal of each strategy is to produce the best possible risk-adjusted returns despite market conditions. With that goal in mind, some of these strategies work best in specific types of market conditions.

Global Macro

A trending market is a condition when specific financial securities move in one direction that perpetuates over a specific period of time. Global macro hedge fund strategies generally perform extremely well when financial securities trend, as they can use leverage to enhance returns and potentially generate significant returns when markets are trending.

---

[1] www.indexiq.com/etfs/etfsiqh/etfsiqhmultistrat.html.

The benefit of a global macro strategy is that portfolio managers are searching for trends in many different types of financial products that are traded around the world. While there might be substantial periods of time when U.S. equity markets are consolidating, Japanese markets might be trending, representing opportunities for global macro traders.

Generally, global macro traders use leverage to enhance speculation and generate robust returns. Global macro trading can create volatility within its returns that is greater than the volatility of other hedge fund strategies. A trendless market that employs leverage can generate significant losses.

Global macro strategies usually view risks based on a calculation that is similar to a value at risk calculation. A portfolio manager in this sector would determine the most they could lose given a specific standard deviation of returns and report that to risk control.

Global macro funds generally stick to liquid assets that allow a manager to reflect a view of a specific economy or macro event. In general, the financial instruments used in this type of strategy are currencies, interest rate derivatives, stock indexes, and commodities.

Currencies

Currency strategies generally focus on the relative strength of one currency versus another. A currency is usually quoted as an exchange rate in the form of a currency pair. A currency pair is one country's currency relative to another country's currency.

Currency traders follow trends within the global economic environment as well as monetary policy. One major advantage of a strategy that is focused on currencies is the leverage that is employed within the currency markets. It is not uncommon for a currency trader to find leverage that is 200 to 1, which allows a manager to enhance his returns, while taking significant risks.

Interest-Rate Trading

Portfolio managers who actively trade interest rates within the context of a global macro strategy usually invest in sovereign debt instruments. This includes U.S. Treasury instruments, Japanese debt instruments, and European debt instruments.

Stock-Index Trading

Equity index investment managers use equity indexes to speculate on the direction of global bourses with a view toward growth or contraction. In general, index strategies are directional, but some managers trade spreads.

Long/Short Equity

A long/short strategy is an investing strategy that is used by hedge funds, where the portfolio manager concentrates on initiating and managing market-neutral positions. To accomplish this goal an investment manager will take long positions in stocks and simultaneously initiate short positions in different stocks. The goal is to match the notional value of the long positions with the notional value of short positions, but there will be instances where a manager is net long or net short.

Why Invest in a Multi-Strategy Fund?

Hedge funds, especially those that control more than $1 billion in assets under management, will typically require a minimum allocation of $1 million, along with an assessment of the investor to determine if they meet the required criteria as an accredited investor.

Allocating $1 million to an alternative investment such as a single hedge fund strategy is daunting relative to transparent, regulated, traditional investments or even a fund of hedge funds. A multi-strategy hedge fund that invests across multiple strategies could be the answer for many investors. The manager has greater flexibility in constructing a portfolio and adapting to changing market environments.

Investors understand the value of diversification of their investments and the benefits of a strong multi-strategy fund, including the costs of the fund.

Multi-Strategy Compared to Fund of Funds

Multi-strategy funds are often compared to a fund of hedge funds; the chart in Table 13.1 outlines the differences and similarities of a fund of hedge funds and multi-strategy funds. Unlike a fund of hedge funds, which adopts a strategy of allocating capital to specific types of hedge funds, a multi-strategy

Table 13.1 Fund of Funds versus Multi-Strategy

Characteristic	Multi-Strategy	Fund of Funds
Manages Capital for Outside Investors	✓	✓
Two Layers of Fees		✓
Makes Allocations to Other Hedge Funds		✓
Portfolio Management Team	✓	✓
Limited to Accredited Investors	✓	✓
Below-Average Minimum Investments		✓
Offers Investors Exposure to Multiple Strategies	✓	✓
Considered Both a GP and an LP (Allocator)		✓
Offers Reduced Exposure to Single Manager Collapse		✓
Considered a Single Manager Hedge Fund	✓	

fund does not charge an additional layer of management fees.

While a multi-strategy fund may rely on a single manager executing multiple investment strategies, the manager is not simply average at a lot of strategies; rather, most multi-strategy hedge fund managers have achieved exceptional proficiency in numerous strategies and will rely on a team of experts in each strategy.

Often, the manager will have a background in a particular strategy, fixed income, for example, but for various reasons (perhaps a need to boost the fund's capacity, or to take advantage of multiple opportunities) the manager will incorporate new strategies over time. Still, there is legitimate concern over whether the managers of each sub-strategy are truly best-of-breed in their respective strategies.

Within this context the fund of funds must rely on a hedge fund manager to stick to their general mandate to allow the fund of funds to generate a diversified breadth of returns. The multi-strategy fund has much greater control over the investment process and can allocate capital to the strategies that have the most efficient risk-adjusted returns.

Conclusion

There is a tradeoff that comes with greater diversification within a hedge fund methodology. Generally, multi-strategy hedge funds will not produce exceptionally strong returns over other single hedge fund strategies. If a single strategy, such as global macro, produces stellar returns one year, it does not necessarily translate to similarly stellar gains for a multi-strategy hedge fund that invests in global macro as one of its strategies. Since a multi-strategy hedge fund invests across multiple strategies simultaneously the returns are aggregated accordingly from the various strategies. The returns for the fund will include more than the best-performing strategies, so if fixed income, for example, suffers a bad year in the same year the global macro strategy performs well, then the overall returns for the multi-strategy will be a reflection of that strategy's diversity.

Most multi-strategy funds undertake a metamorphosis from a single-strategy fund as the hedge fund manager looks to increase the capacity the fund can offer. Investors are generally willing to give a successful, single-fund manager an opportunity to show that he or she can enhance a fund with different strategies and manage other portfolio managers who engage in diversified strategies.

Once a fund grows beyond a single strategy, risk management and asset allocation become the most important aspects of the funds' performance. A hedge fund manager who oversees a number of portfolio managers needs to understand the risk associated with each investment strategy and has to have a robust understanding of asset allocation and when to move capital to a winning strategy. The role of the manager takes on a role similar to a statistical-arbitrage strategy, where a system evaluates the best risk-adjusted returns and quickly allocates capital to the strategies that will likely perform the best in the future.

> To download several videos related to the focus of this chapter and to watch over 125 total video modules and expert audio interviews, please activate your free account here: http://HedgeFundGroup.org/Access.

Test Yourself

Answer the following questions.

1. One reason multi-strategy firms developed is:
   A. To expand the capacity of the firm.
   B. To become more leveraged in an individual sector of the economy.
   C. To produce returns that are far superior to single-strategy funds.

2. True or False: Because of the trend of globalization, multi-strategy funds are in direct contradiction of efficient frontier theory.

3. True or False: A multi-strategy differs from a fund of hedge funds in that it offers an additional round of fees due to diversification.

4. What are two reasons to invest in a multi-strategy hedge fund?
   A. Efficient frontier theory
   B. Laser-like focus and expertise on a single industry
   C. Diversification
   D. Multi-strategy funds produce much higher returns than other strategies every year

5. A multi-strategy fund can utilize which strategy?
   A. Currencies
   B. Interest rate
   C. Global macro
   D. All of the above

Answers can be found in Appendix B.

CHAPTER 14

Fund of Hedge Funds

A fund of hedge funds is a significant source of capital for single-manager hedge funds; the fund of funds structure provides a necessary, diversified, and democratizing platform by which investors can allocate capital to the hedge fund space. For some investors, the fund-of-funds structure is the only way to responsibly invest in hedge funds because the investor may lack the time, resources, or knowledge to actively manage a portfolio of hedge fund investments. Similarly, an investor may not want to put all their eggs in one hedge fund's basket, thus risking the chance that that hedge fund or, more broadly, the strategy, may suffer losses. Of course, there are disadvantages to the model, as you will learn in this chapter, and the fund-of-funds industry has generally faced a good deal of criticism over the years. Still, many investors, even large institutional investors, like pensions and endowments, choose to invest exclusively through a fund of funds for various reasons, and funds of funds remain an important investor group.

What Is a Fund of Hedge Funds?

A fund of hedge funds is a fund vehicle that allows investors to invest in multiple hedge funds, rather than a single-fund manager. These funds of funds are actively managed, so instead of a portfolio of different assets like equities and bonds, the management team manages a portfolio of different hedge fund managers. There are a number of advantages and disadvantages to a fund of hedge funds, along with different styles and strategies that need to be evaluated by prospective investors.

Fund Structure

In a typical fund of hedge funds, the management team will form a limited partnership and invite investors (limited partners) to pool their capital in the investment fund. Once the fund is formed and limited partners

> **DEFINITION:**
> **Actively Managed**
>
> A situation where a firm or firm manager manages a portfolio with the objective to beat or exceed industry benchmarks or indexes.

invest, the general partner will then actively manage that capital and invest it according to the fund's objective—in most cases, to protect and hopefully grow the fund's capital under management by investing in different hedge fund managers. The main goal of a fund of funds is to achieve returns via their asset-allocation skills.

The essential draw to a fund of hedge funds for investors is the potential to gain diversified exposure to the hedge fund industry without having to research and manage each individual hedge fund allocation. In the fund-of-hedge-funds model, the strategy is to generate efficient risk-adjusted returns by allocating capital to the most efficient hedge fund managers.

Funds of hedge funds are typically formed as limited partnerships but can sometimes be structured as a limited liability company. Funds are often offered as either an onshore or offshore funds.

The offshore fund has tax advantages for non-U.S. investors. The investors allocate money to the fund of hedge funds, and the manager in turn invests that capital in various hedge funds. To do so, the hedge fund manager should have an adequate level of knowledge and sophistication in the hedge fund asset class. There is no guarantee of a high rate of return with hedge funds; usually investors look for non-correlated returns to general equity or bond markets. Figure 14.1 illustrates the basic structure of a fund of hedge funds.

Fund-of-Funds Operations

So, what exactly does the management team do? The function of the management team is to oversee its portfolio (the money invested in the selected hedge

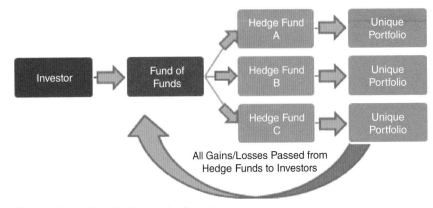

Figure 14.1 Fund of Funds Structure

funds) on behalf of its clients (the investors). A typical team is similar to other investment funds but with more experienced management executives, senior analysts, and less experienced associates and analysts. The fund will need experienced investment professionals to research, perform due diligence, and select hedge funds.

The research and due-diligence duties are particularly important because failure to perform adequate due diligence on the funds can have severe consequences. For example, investors who lost money from Bernard Madoff's now-notorious Ponzi scheme have criticized and even sued the fund managers that recommended or allocated to the fund for failure to perform adequate due diligence. This is certainly an extreme example of poor due diligence but it highlights the importance of proper and thorough due diligence.

The due diligence process is not only used to detect fraud or compliance issues, it is a way to sort potential hedge funds and determine what is most likely to produce alpha. During the research and due diligence phase, the management team looks at each fund manager's marketing materials, track record, and other relevant documents to understand and analyze the strategy; then the investment team decides whether it should be included in the portfolio.

The fund of hedge funds' ability to perform sufficient due diligence and research is considered a significant advantage of the fund of funds model. Less sophisticated investors or simply investors who lack

the time to sufficiently examine each fund will pay a premium (the fees paid to the fund of funds management company) in order to outsource the creation, evaluation, and active management of the portfolio. For example, a fund of funds analyst will carefully analyze how profits were made to insure that the fund did not make all of its money during a year in one area.

Once the money is allocated to hedge funds, the team will then monitor and evaluate the performance of each fund and weigh each manager's performance against benchmarks and peers, as well as other metrics, to actively decide whether the allocation is a good fit for the overall portfolio.

The fund of funds management team may find through a quarterly report, for example, that a manager is underperforming relative to the Dow Jones Credit Suisse Core Hedge Fund Index (a non-strategy-specific hedge fund performance benchmark) and submit a redemption notice to the fund. However, hedge funds offer limited liquidity, meaning that it is often difficult to redeem your money from the fund quickly. Hedge funds may allow redemptions on monthly, quarterly, or even just on an annual basis.

Liquidity

This is one of the biggest investor complaints against the hedge fund industry: that it's tough to get your money out if performance takes a dive or if the investor wants to redeem for other reasons. This should thus be considered a risk to investing in hedge funds and funds of hedge funds as well. Except in rare exceptions, there is no secondary market where an investor can sell interest in the fund of funds to other investors, so the investor must redeem from the fund of funds directly.

The fund's ability to actively manage and balance its portfolio is a key benefit to the fund-of-funds model. Investors often lack the time, skill, or sophistication to invest directly in hedge funds and take comfort in the idea that they can entrust their money to a team of experienced hedge fund industry professionals who will monitor and adjust the investments. These investors may not otherwise have felt comfortable investing in the hedge fund sector; thus, the fund-of-hedge-funds structure enables investors to gain access to hedge funds without the burdens associated with this type of investing.

Strategies

There are two distinct strategies employed within the fund-of-funds industry, which include discretionary and quantitative. As has been discussed previously in this book, discretionary allocation is a process that uses a combination of tools such as performance and the experience of the management team to form a view on potential allocation. The amount that will be allocated is usually discretionary in nature, but will likely conform to a range.

Many discretionary managers have a sector fund of funds where capital is allocated to numerous

managers that focus on the same strategy. For example, a credit fund of funds could allocate capital to 10 different hedge funds that focus on credit.

Quantitative fund-of-funds managers rely on specific quantitative-allocation methodologies to generate a strategy. These could include portfolio optimization such as the efficient frontier, which uses covariance and variance methodologies to find the hedge fund that produce the best risk-adjusted returns.

Fee Structure

The fund-of-hedge-funds manager will not manage the fund for free, of course; investors must pay a fee for the services that the management team is performing. The fee structure varies by fund of fund, but the industry standard is 1 and 10, or half of the 2 and 20 that single-manager hedge funds often charge investors. In the 1 and 10 model, the fund of hedge funds' general partner charges limited partners a 1 percent management fee and a 10 percent performance fee. Some funds of hedge funds will only charge a management fee (usually higher than 1 percent) while others will charge a smaller management fee and a hefty performance fee (usually higher than 10 percent). The management fee is an annual fee on the assets managed by the fund. The management fee is used to cover operational expenses of the fund that occur regardless of the fund's performance, such as compliance, accounting, and other back-office costs associated with managing an investment fund. This management fee is most often paid in either quarterly or monthly installments of the total annual fee. As we learned in previous chapters, investors may begin to resent the management fee if performance sours because the performance-neutral nature of the fees creates the impression that an investor is paying to lose money—an unattractive scenario for any investor.

The performance fee (also known as *carried interest* or *incentive fee*) is a percentage of the return on investment generated by the fund. Like in single-manager hedge funds, the performance fee is seen as a way of aligning the general partner and limited partners' interests by incentivizing the former to produce gains for the latter. Some funds of hedge funds may include a hurdle-rate provision that guarantees a certain rate of return before the general partner collects any performance fee. A high-water mark is another important provision that is often included in the limited partnership agreement (LPA) allowing the general partner to collect a performance fee only on new profits. The hurdle rate and the high-water mark provisions aim to ensure that the general partner only takes a cut of performance that truly benefits the investor and also serves to guard against excessive fees in the fund-of-hedge-funds universe. If you have been paying close attention in this book, you will notice that the fees charged by funds of funds mirror those charged by the underlying hedge funds. This dual layer of fees is a major focus of criticism from investors.

Active Portfolio Management and Monitoring

For many investors it can be time consuming, stressful, and difficult to manage a portfolio of hedge fund investments. Funds of funds thus present a solution to this issue since the fund of funds' management team will actively monitor and manage the portfolio and make decisions based on regular analysis of their managers and overall market factors. It is reasonable for even experienced investors to feel uncomfortable investing in the alternative-asset class, so many outsource this responsibility to funds of hedge funds. The management team will analyze the reports from managers, compare against relevant benchmarks, analyze risks in the portfolio, and do other day-to-day portfolio management activities that most investors lack the time or skill to perform. This is a key advantage to fund-of-funds investing and one reason that funds of funds have grown alongside the remarkable expansion of hedge funds and private equity.

To give readers insight into how a fund of hedge funds manages a portfolio and monitors performance, we spoke with two executives from SAIL Advisors Group, a hedge fund research and investment specialist. Wayne Yi is an Executive Director and Senior Analyst responsible for global credit and event driven investments. He is a member of the firm's investment committee and has over 12 years of experience in the financial industry. Jason Filiberti is a Senior Vice President responsible for Business Development in

North America and has over 11 years of experience in the financial industry.

Richard Wilson: What is your process for screening a hedge fund manager before allocating to the strategy?

Jason and Wayne: The SAIL team implements a comprehensive and rigorous due diligence process designed to identify manager candidates with strong investment skills and proven investment expertise, as well as those who have demonstrated a high level of integrity and business acumen to operate an investment management firm successfully. Additionally, we seek to determine whether the manager has the requisite skill and sufficient capacity to generate alpha while controlling losses within the confines of the stated strategy.

Regarding the manager's investment skills, we utilize quantitative and qualitative procedures to assess the quality of returns and expectations for future performance. We examine the manager's performance expectations (including returns, drawdowns, and volatility) given prevailing market conditions, and confirm by team consensus whether these expectations are reasonable given the manager's past performance and prevailing strategy-wide conditions. It is important to analyze the manager's history of volatility, drawdowns, correlations, consistency of returns, and compare these to peer group funds, market indices, and current investments in the funds. We also employ proprietary risk analyses to determine potential risks within a manager's portfolio and verify these with the manager.

Our manager research involves a dual process—investment due diligence and operational due diligence, where the operational due diligence is truly an independent review as the ODD team has veto right of any fund in the investment committee. The ODD team reports to the Chief Risk Officer and is distinct from the research/investment team. The objective of the operational due diligence process is to independently assess the operational processes and infrastructure of the underlying hedge funds and to verify the backgrounds and integrity of the key investment professionals. This is ensured by a thorough due diligence process that is implemented through calls, onsite visits, communications with third party service providers and a review of relevant documents.

Richard Wilson: Can you explain how you build a portfolio of hedge fund investments? How do you monitor those positions and make adjustments to the portfolio?

Jason and Wayne: We are constructing our portfolios with a core/satellite approach that aims to control losses, limit volatility and generate attractive absolute returns over an investment cycle. By combining core and satellite managers across different strategies, we ensure that our portfolios are positioned in line with the current market environment and the overall risk/return objectives of our funds.

Core managers are defined as managers that are very experienced, usually run lower net exposures and generate more predictable returns with lower volatility; thus those managers are sized bigger. Satellite managers receive smaller allocations as they tend to manage their strategy with higher volatility and a higher expected return. We use satellite managers as either "right tail" managers that would benefit our portfolios in a positive market environment or as "left tail risk protection" managers that serve as an implicit hedge in our funds during adverse market conditions.

The allocation to core and satellite managers depends on each of our fund's risk/return objective.

Thank you to Jason Filiberti and Wayne Yi of SAIL Advisors Group for their insights on how their fund of hedge funds identifies hedge funds and manages the portfolio.

Improved Communication with Managers

Funds of hedge funds often represent a larger portion of a hedge fund's assets under management than what is allocated by an individual investor. Although most hedge funds would argue that they do not give preference to any limited partner over another in terms of regular communication and availability, smaller investors would argue that this is a problem, especially when investing in large funds of over a billion dollars in assets under management. Funds of funds therefore have an advantage over smaller individual investors in hedge funds, as they may be more likely to have their concerns addressed or receive more consistent attention from investor relations and fund management staff.

Lower Barriers to Entry

Top-performing hedge funds and those with long, impressive track records often have limited space available for new limited partners. Investors are often frustrated that they cannot invest in the brand name hedge fund firms like Bridgewater Associates due to limited capacity. In the latest hot hedge funds and for those who have built reputations as strong hedge fund managers, demand often outpaces supply, meaning that there are more investors than space available in the particular hedge fund. The hedge fund may launch a new fund or expand its capacity, or, as often is the case, the fund will restrict access to its preferred investors. These preferred investors are simply those investors that the hedge fund prefers over others; these investors are typically larger, more institutional investors with whom the fund has a strong relationship. This tends to leave smaller, less-connected investors out in the cold wanting to get inside.

Funds of hedge funds may have a relationship with these top hedge funds and can act as an intermediary between smaller investors and hedge funds. This makes sense for hedge funds; they can then limit the amount of reporting, compliance, and coordination by only having to work with one party instead of multiple smaller investors that would have to invest individually without the fund-of-funds vehicle pooling the investments. Indeed, there are some funds of hedge funds, known as feeder funds, which only act as a fund collecting capital to invest in exclusive hedge funds.

This leads to a related advantage of funds of hedge funds: lower minimum investments. While hedge funds often require $500,000 or more as a minimum investment, funds of hedge funds will typically have lower investment requirements. This lowers the barrier to entry for investors who may want to dip their toes in the hedge fund pool without risking $1 million or more. It is also great for smaller investors who would like to gain exposure to hedge funds but do not have the capital to allocate significantly to a fund. Many hedge funds—either by policy or by preference—will not accept investment below $1 million, and feeder funds or funds of hedge funds can enable smaller investors to participate in the hedge fund investor community, although in a more limited capacity.

Additional Layer of Due Diligence

Hedge funds are complicated investments, which is part of the reason that investing in hedge funds is restricted only to qualified, sophisticated investors. Even with that initial filtering, there are still some investors who lack sufficient knowledge of or expertise in hedge funds and thus assume a great deal of risk without realizing that they have done so. Furthermore, there are brilliant, sophisticated investors who do not have the skill or resources to do proper analysis and due diligence of hedge funds. Fortunately for these investors, funds of hedge funds are typically staffed with seasoned investment professionals who have expertise in multiple hedge fund strategies.

By investing in a fund of hedge funds, an investor can essentially outsource a substantial amount of the due diligence and homework required of hedge fund investors. Funds of hedge funds often perform substantial due diligence and have regular communication with managers and even perform frequent onsite visits to help guard against fraud or mismanagement. This provides funds-of-hedge-funds investors with greater peace of mind to help to ensure that hedge fund investors are well informed and aware of the risks in investing in hedge funds.

Diversifying within the Hedge Fund Sector

It is often frightening and risky to allocate to a single hedge fund manager in a single hedge fund strategy: putting all your eggs in one basket, so to speak. Funds of hedge funds enable investors to allocate across several managers without the headache of monitoring each individual allocation, as well as perform much of the requisite due diligence and analysis on each fund. For the average investor with only $1 million to invest in the hedge fund sector, it may be inefficient to allocate across multiple managers. Instead, these investors will allocate that $1 million to a fund of hedge funds that will pool that capital allocation among that of others and then invest among multiple managers, often in different, less correlated strategies. This provides a welcome level of diversification for investors worried about entrusting too much capital to one manager or one strategy. An investor can then invest the aforementioned $1 million across several strategies from emerging markets to small-cap, long/short, and convertible arbitrage.

The fund-of-hedge-funds structure also allows investors to more comfortably allocate to emerging managers. An individual investor will often be wary of committing too much capital to an emerging manager or start-up because of the associated risks, as well as the fear of making up too much of that manager's capital base. A fund of hedge funds will often be in a better position than an individual—or even institutional investor—to perform analysis and due diligence. The fund-of-hedge-funds vehicle allows the smaller investor to invest alongside others in an emerging manager and spread the risk out among other investors. Otherwise, the emerging manager may be overly dependent on a single investor and exposed to the risk of a significant redemption in a bad quarter or due to that investor's personal capital needs, so this is often a good thing for the hedge fund as well.

Economies of Scale

The final advantage of funds of hedge funds that I would like to touch on in this section is the economies of scale for this vehicle. As you have read, there are many challenges to investing in hedge funds as a smaller investor; one such challenge is the costs (in terms of both time and financial expenses) associated with investing in hedge funds. The costs of performing due diligence, analysis, accounting, and compliance reporting on multiple hedge fund investments can start to cut into the returns of these investments, thus making it an inefficient use of capital. Funds of hedge funds provide economies of scale that help alleviate this problem by spreading the costs of performing these duties across multiple investors. Of course, investors will pay a fee for these services—that is how the fund of hedge funds are compensated—but investors often find this model to be more cost-efficient than directly investing in hedge funds.

Disadvantages

While funds of hedge funds can help investors realize great returns while outsourcing the due diligence required of intelligent investing, there are many disadvantages associated as well. Problems that arise with funds of funds can include limited liquidity, exposure to industry-wide trends, and less control and customization. As you will see in the section that follows, funds of hedge funds can have multiple shortcomings.

Limited Liquidity

An important aspect of investing is liquidity, the ability to transfer your money in and out of one investment.

For hedge fund investors, this can be particularly problematic because hedge funds often have limited liquidity. This means that a fund will only allow its investors to redeem their investment at certain times during the year; the most common intervals being monthly, quarterly, and annually. In order to cash out the investment, an investor must submit a redemption notice to the fund for the next available redemption date, and funds will often require that you submit this notice at least 30 days prior to that date.

Liquidity may seem like a minor concern but it can quickly become a big problem for investors. In addition to the more common reasons for withdrawals, such as poor performance or a rebalancing of the investor's portfolio, there are a number of hard-to-predict events that can arise. To name just a few possibilities, the investor could have a medical or financial emergency that requires the money allocated to the fund; the fund manager could become seriously ill or die unexpectedly; or a significant part of the management team could leave the fund to start their own fund. All of these events could place your capital at significant risk and will probably make you wish that you could redeem your money as easily as you can in a common stock investment. Funds of hedge funds are similar in their limited liquidity because they have allocated to hedge funds with varying redemption dates and many funds of funds thus impose similar redemption requirements

and even lock-ups. Investors should take liquidity into account when considering a hedge fund or fund-of-hedge-funds investment.

Exposure to Industrywide Trends

A fund of hedge funds can diversify an investor's exposure to single-manager or single-strategy risks, but investors will likely still have some exposure to hedge fund industry-wide trends. For example, hedge fund performance was sluggish in 2011 to 2012 with many analysts pointing to volatility in the markets as a primary cause of the lackluster returns. A struggling global economy, the European sovereign debt crisis, and fiscal negotiations in the United States all helped contribute to extreme volatility in recent years. Such widespread trends can have an impact on hedge funds, even those in otherwise minimally correlated strategies. Thus, we can see that overall economic or industry-related trends can affect the returns of even a highly diversified portfolio of hedge fund investments.

Less Control and Customization

For those who prefer to have complete control and transparency with their investments, a fund of hedge funds presents a few problems. For one, in most cases, the fund of hedge funds is actively managed for the benefit of multiple investors and the management team may make decisions that are contrary to what the investor would prefer. For example, the investor may have a greater risk appetite than the other investors in the fund or than the fund of hedge funds management team thinks is appropriate given the market conditions. This lack of customization and control can be frustrating, especially for seasoned investors who are used to having complete control over the management of their investments. Still, for many fund-of-hedge-fund investors, this hands-off approach to investing is a benefit as it allows greater peace of mind knowing that a team of investment professionals is responsible for the performance of the fund.

Less Transparency

In a fund of hedge funds, the investor does not have a relationship with the hedge funds that make up the portfolio. This is seen as a disadvantage because the investor is less engaged with the investment and may have less insight into the operations and management of each hedge fund. This oversight is delegated to the fund of hedge funds and the investor is largely expected to trust the judgment and abilities of the fund-of-funds management team. For investors, this can be a frightening prospect, especially in light of recent scandals and frauds where many investors were only vaguely aware that their fund-of-funds or feeder-fund vehicles had invested in risky or fraudulent investments. It is therefore incumbent on the investor to only select a fund of hedge funds that he feels can adequately perform the due diligence, compliance, monitoring, and other duties required of hedge fund investing.

The Current State of Funds of Hedge Funds

The fund-of-hedge-funds sector was hit particularly hard in the Great Recession, with many funds suffering extraordinary losses and a subsequent wave of redemptions. As the dust from the financial crisis settled, a good number of fund-of-hedge-funds investors were left with less money as well as questions for managers. Namely, does the fund-of-funds model need to be reexamined? Do funds of funds justify the extra fees? Are investors better off selecting hedge funds on their own? In the end, most investors, concerns come down to an essential question: Where is the value?

Fortunately, funds of hedge funds have since answered many of these questions. Those that could not provide their investors with enough value to justify the additional layer of fees fell by the wayside or are now emerging with significantly less capital than their pre-crisis levels. The fund-of-hedge-funds model has undergone a number of important changes that benefit the investor.

One such shift in the model is a push toward greater transparency with better, more frequent reporting and improved communication between management and investors. In light of the Bernard Madoff scandal that rocked the investor community, many investors are demanding more transparency and stepping up due-diligence procedures. Those funds of hedge funds that have survived the industry changes have embraced the new demands from investors and accepted that investors want more transparency if they are to trust a fund manager with their money.

Another significant change in the fund-of-hedge-funds model is an industry-wide lowering of fees. This did not only occur for funds of hedge funds—which have always faced skepticism from investors as to whether the additional layer of fees justifies the returns and the benefits of a diversified hedge fund investing platform—but for all hedge funds. Investors are increasingly demanding lower fees, with only a few exceptions for managers like Renaissance Technologies and SAC Capital—both of which have historically charged fees greater than the industry standard 2 percent management and 20 percent performance fees. Investors who suffered losses on their hedge fund investments in recent years came out of the crisis looking for hedge funds to respond with a more generous fee structure.

According to a survey conducted by Preqin in 2009 and released in April 2010, hedge funds responded to the difficult post-crisis fundraising climate by lowering fees and conceding that the 2-and-20-fee model would have to change, at least temporarily. As many funds of hedge funds faced extreme dissatisfaction from investors in the wake of the financial crisis, many funds lowered their fees below the standard management fee of 2 percent and made other concessions to investors in order to regain their confidence. The 2010 Preqin report revealed that the mean management fee charged by funds of hedge funds was 1.44 percent and the mean performance fee was 11.54 percent (Preqin, 2010).

Today, the fund-of-hedge-funds industry has emerged from the crisis smaller but arguably stronger as a sort of natural selection occurred, eliminating many of the managers who could not consistently outperform. Furthermore, today's funds of hedge funds have largely adapted to the current demands from investors in terms of performance, transparency, compliance, and reporting.

Industry Insight

For this chapter we interviewed two fund-of-funds managers, each with over 15 years of experience, Amanda Haynes-Dale and Richard Travia. Our first interview is with Amanda Haynes-Dale of Pan Reliance Capital Advisors.

Richard C. Wilson: Can you please briefly describe the type of fund you work at and your role there?

Amanda Haynes-Dale: Pan Reliance Capital Advisors is a boutique fund-of-hedge-funds group that has been advising high-net-worth, family-office, endowment, foundation, and pension clients since January 1991. I am a founder and managing director of Pan Reliance Capital Advisors, which is an SEC-registered investment advisor and WOBE (woman-owned business enterprise).

Richard C. Wilson: Is there a typical background for a fund-of-funds manager? How did you get to your current position?

Amanda Haynes-Dale: Fund-of-funds managers have typically come from varied backgrounds.

Generally, the managers with the longer and more successful track records have come from an investment background, as opposed to investment banking, consulting, or marketing. I was trained as a money manager at Wertheim & Co. (now part of Morgan Stanley); shortly thereafter I started a broker–dealer, which included hedge funds as clients and subsequently formed the fund of funds.

Richard C. Wilson: Do you identify more on the GP-fund-management side or the LP-investor side? How do you navigate those two roles as a fund of fund?

Amanda Haynes-Dale: I have evaluated many managers in my career, and one of the most important elements of my analysis is alignment of interests. I am one of the largest investors in our funds and feel it's important to "eat your own cooking." I feel that this prevents me from having to identify with one side or the other and helps me avoid potential conflicts of interest.

Richard C. Wilson: What do you tell investors who question paying the additional layer of fees for funds of funds? Why has the fund-of-funds model endured?

Amanda Haynes-Dale: You get a lot for the extra layer of fees: (1) Instant diversification amongst multiple managers. (2) Reasonable entry minimums to hedge funds with $1 to 5 million minimums. (3) Ongoing monitoring. (4) Administrative relief of tracking multiple managers on a monthly basis. (5) Only one K-1 and year-end audited financials.

The FoHF model has endured because it affords investors who don't have a large asset base or hedge fund expertise to access multiple hedge fund managers; when added to long-only portfolios, they can bring down the volatility and improve the overall performance.

Richard C. Wilson: Do you foresee further consolidation in the fund-of-funds industry? What about the hedge fund industry as a whole?

Amanda Haynes-Dale: I do expect further consolidation of the fund-of-funds industry. There are many economies of scale that can be generated by larger firms. However, investment management is based on trust between manager and client, creating a barrier to classic M&A in the industry. There will always be room for managers that provide value to clients or specialize in specific areas of the markets.

I expect the industry as a whole to continue growing. On average, institutional allocations to hedge funds are still quite small relative to traditional investment strategies. This bodes well for the future of the industry as does increasing demand from retail investors. Growth however is predicated on hedge funds' continued ability to produce superior, uncorrelated, risk-adjusted returns. The incremental AUM will migrate to the funds that perform and the fund-of-funds managers that can identify them.

Richard C. Wilson: What are the strategies that are most attractive to you? Is there an AUM size or length of track record that you target? Do you invest in emerging managers and startups or is there a minimum threshold for AUM or the age of the fund?

Amanda Haynes-Dale: In our 22-plus-year history of investing in hedge funds, we have gravitated toward fundamentally based strategies and stayed away from CTAs, quantitative strategies, and short-term traders. This lends itself to traditional long/short equity, long/short credit, and event-driven strategies. We have no hard and fast rules about AUM and track record. We opportunistically invest in emerging managers but tend to let others bear the startup risk.

Richard C. Wilson: What is your process for screening a hedge fund manager before allocating to the strategy?

Amanda Haynes-Dale: Our investment process has been refined over the past 22 years to efficiently weed out managers that do not meet our investment or operational criteria. It involves numerous meetings with the portfolio manager and staff to develop a deep understanding of the investment strategy and how he or she operates the business. The process is highly qualitative with some quantitative elements. The detailed process is much too involved and nuanced to describe in full here.

Richard C. Wilson: Can you explain how you build a portfolio of hedge fund investments? How do you monitor those positions and make adjustments to the portfolio?

Amanda Haynes-Dale: Our investment process determines the individual funds that are available for us to invest in. The construction of each portfolio depends on the mandate it is expected to fulfill. Our flagship fund, Pan Multi Strategy, L.P., which launched in 1991 is designed to provide historical, equity-like returns with volatility normally associated with bonds. To achieve this goal we invest in a portfolio of 17 to 20 funds at any given time. Generally, half of the portfolio has been long/short equity, and half has been a mixture of other strategies that are less correlated to equity markets.

Richard C. Wilson: How do you guard against style drift in your managers?

Amanda Haynes-Dale: After allocating, we typically maintain an active dialogue with our managers and their staffs. We monitor all reports produced by the fund itself and consistency with the fund's stated objective. In addition we seek out secondary and tertiary sources of information, including public filings, other investors, service providers, and the sell-side community. Ultimately we seek to triangulate as many data points as possible to constantly reevaluate our thesis on a manager.

Richard C. Wilson: How has your business and industry changed since the financial crisis?

Amanda Haynes-Dale: A great deal has changed in the past five years but just as much remains the same. Clients still look to us to provide attractive risk-adjusted returns with low correlations to other investment alternatives. Significant changes include the level and cost of the new regulatory environment and the focus on operational due diligence. These trends existed prior to the crisis, but were very much accelerated by it.

Richard C. Wilson: What are some significant trends you are seeing in the fund-of-hedge-funds industry or hedge fund industry as a whole?

Amanda Haynes-Dale: Within the FoHF industry, we have seen a broad move toward customization of products for investors. Whether you call it a "managed account" or "fund of one," the desire to have a specific product is part of the reason for the consolidation of the FoHF industry. In the industry as a whole, the concentration of assets in the hands of the largest managers seems to be driven by the consultant community, as well as the size of the allocations from large plan allocators.

Richard C. Wilson: What is a typical day for you and your management team? We want to give our readers a sense of what it's like to run a fund of hedge funds, so any and all details are welcome.

Amanda Haynes-Dale: I would say that there is no typical day. The scope of our investment universe requires a great deal of reading and a healthy intellectual curiosity. We spend the majority of our research time on managers with whom we currently have capital and a smaller portion of our time meeting with prospects. In addition, we spend time speaking with our investors to keep them apprised of developments within our fund. We have been fortunate over time to have very loyal investors, which is a competitive advantage for Pan Reliance.

Our second industry insight interview is with Richard Travia of Tradex Global Advisors.

Richard C. Wilson: Can you please briefly describe the type of fund you work at and your role there?

Richard Travia: Tradex Global Advisors focuses on identifying, researching, and investing in small, niche hedge fund strategies. We affect that through portfolios of hedge funds, funds of managed accounts, and single hedge fund vehicles. I am a partner and the director of research for Tradex and primarily focus on risk management and due diligence, both from an investment and operational perspective on all hedge fund strategies.

Richard C. Wilson: Is there a typical background for a fund-of funds-manager? How did you get to your current position?

Richard Travia: I do not think there is a typical background for a fund-of-funds manager. That being said, the fund-of-funds-manager recipe should likely include an analytical side, a bit of intuition, and a healthy portion of skepticism. I have been allocating to hedge funds for a very long time, and cofounded Tradex Global Advisors with my partner, Michael Beattie, in 2004. I have had the good fortune of being put in senior positions in the hedge fund industry very early on in my career, allowing me to learn from and work alongside Michael, who is one of the most intuitive hedge fund allocators in the business.

Richard C. Wilson: Do you identify more on the GP-fund-management side or the LP-investor side? How do you navigate those two roles as a fund of funds?

Richard Travia: Personally, I identify more from a very interested LP perspective. My role certainly has elements of marketing and fundraising in order to build our brand and business, and to manage the funds and operations in the most profitable and efficient ways possible, but at the end of the day, I invest in hedge fund managers and strategies with a fiduciary duty and ethical responsibility to be the best LP investor on behalf of our clients.

Richard C. Wilson: What do you tell investors who question paying the additional layer of fees for fund of funds? Why has the fund-of-funds model endured?

Richard Travia: I do not presume to know what every investor's expertise is or what their infrastructure looks like. What I do know is what it takes to be an effective and profitable allocator to hedge funds. Investors who have requisite infrastructure, employees, knowledge, experience, and dedication to pre-investment and ongoing monitoring and due diligence likely should be allocating to hedge funds on their own. Those who don't should be comfortable enough to recognize their deficiencies, and if hedge fund exposure is desired the investor should hire an expert. The fund-of-funds model has endured because conducting a proper due diligence and monitoring a portfolio of hedge funds is a full-time job, and hedge fund exposure adds alpha for investors. I think the traditional, large, multi-strategy, diversified fund-of-hedge-funds portfolio is antiquated and adds very little value, but strategy-specific and/or concentrated portfolios of hedge funds can be created to take intelligent risk and can add a tremendous amount of value.

Richard C. Wilson: What are the strategies that are most attractive to you? Is there an AUM size or length of track record that you target? Do you invest in emerging managers and startups or is there a minimum threshold for AUM or the age of the fund?

Richard Travia: Strategies that are able to make absolute returns on a consistent basis are typically most attractive. That being said, markets are efficient and no trade makes money forever. We focus on identifying trades and strategies that have asymmetric-return profiles, that are relatively simple to understand and implement, and that are liquid. Large AUM has never been a prerequisite for us. We like to invest in hedge funds and strategies that have very experienced managers but in some cases may be off the radar and therefore more flexible and nimble. Generally, we do not seed hedge funds, but I have been an early investor with quality managers consistently throughout my career.

Richard C. Wilson: What is your process for screening a hedge fund manager before allocating to the strategy?

Richard Travia: We have a proprietary screening process, which includes several factor models that incorporate both quantitative and qualitative data points. That being said, the discretionary overlay is likely the most important part of the process. Once we have determined that we want to speak with a hedge fund to learn more about their business, we will initiate a series of calls and meetings to best understand the philosophy, process, strategy, experience, risk management, and trade. If we determine that an investment could be made based on the viability of the strategy and opportunity set for the trade, we will initiate a lengthy, in-depth operational due diligence that helps to understand every aspect of the fund and business outside of the investment strategy. We then can view the fund from an objective angle, using quantitative inputs, investment-strategy comprehension, operational understanding, layer in a macro view of some sort, and take on intelligent risk if it makes sense.

Richard C. Wilson: Can you explain how you build a portfolio of hedge fund investments? How do you monitor those positions and make adjustments to the portfolio?

Richard Travia: It really depends on the type of fund that is being managed. We currently have a multi-strategy fund of hedge funds that attempts to be diversified within super-liquid underlying hedge funds, a concentrated single-strategy fund of hedge funds that focuses on mortgage-focused hedge funds, and a single hedge fund that focuses on shorting highly levered, unsecured, low-quality, high-yield debt. Regardless of the vehicle, we focus on allocating in a way that allows the underlying manager's strategy to best reflect the objective of the fund. We tend to monitor funds both from an active and passive perspective. We use market data, macroeconomic information, fund correspondence, and regular detailed conference calls and/or meetings with the hedge fund to ensure that we understand how performance was derived, what opportunities are available, how the portfolio is exposed, and what the liquidity is in the underlying portfolio. With this information we can make informed dynamic allocation and redemption decisions.

Richard C. Wilson: How do you guard against style drift in your managers?

Richard Travia: This really is a process that starts from understanding the return profile of a fund, the liquidity of the underlying assets, the strategy of the manager, the exposures in the portfolio, and tends to be rounded out by regular and regimented correspondence with the underlying hedge fund managers.

Richard C. Wilson: How has your business and industry changed since the financial crisis?

Richard Travia: The industry has changed a great deal since 2008, with investors putting a tremendous amount of more work into their allocation decisions. Investors are naturally more skeptical of the industry as a whole, and a demand for liquidity and transparency is evident. These are all positive steps forward for hedge funds as an asset class, and our business has specifically refocused its efforts on providing liquid and transparent, strategy-specific opportunities to investors that require alpha-production and absolute returns.

Richard C. Wilson: What are some significant trends you are seeing in the fund-of-hedge-funds industry or hedge fund industry as a whole?

Richard Travia: Specifically we are seeing a renewed desire for small, niche, alpha-producing hedge funds and strategies. Additionally, we are seeing a shift away from the large, traditional, multi-strategy, diversified fund-of-hedge-funds vehicles, and a focus on strategy-specific opportunities. Also, with the passing of the JOBS Act, and the imminent clarification and adjustment to the General Solicitation rules, the hedge fund industry will soon no longer only be an allocation choice for institutional investors.

Richard C. Wilson: What is a typical day for you and your management team? We want to give our readers a sense of what it's like to run a fund of hedge fund so any and all details are welcome.

Richard Travia: A typical day for me includes several hours of reading market research and manager letters, several hours of conversations with hedge fund managers and service providers, and several hours of conversation with current or prospective clients.

I enjoyed having Richard Travia of Tradex Global Advisors and Amanda Haynes-Dale of Pan Reliance Capital Advisors contribute to this fund-of-hedge-funds chapter. It is always great to hear from executives who understand the challenges from both the LP and the GP side.

Conclusion

In this chapter, you have seen the positive aspects of funds of hedge funds but also the disadvantages associated with funds of hedge funds, like the additional layer of fees, limited liquidity, and less customization for the investor. The point of this chapter is not to argue either in favor or against funds of hedge funds but rather to give you a better understanding of the industry as a whole. The model's endurance is a testament to the value of funds of hedge funds, but the recent outflows from these funds show that there are real risks and costs to investing in funds of hedge funds, just as there are with any investment.

Test Yourself

Answer the following questions.

1. True or False: A passively managed fund is where a firm or firm manager manages a portfolio with the objective to beat or exceed industry benchmarks or indexes.

2. True or False: Feeder funds are funds of hedge funds that invest directly in stocks and securities.

3. A struggling global economy, the European sovereign debt crisis, and fiscal negotiations in the United States all helped contribute to _____ in recent years.
   A. Conservatism
   B. Volatility
   C. Steady growth
   D. A rise in the federal funds rate

4. True or False: Discretionary allocation is a process that uses a combination of tools, such as performance and the experience of the management team, to create a view on potential allocation.

5. Funds of hedge funds utilize the due-diligence process to:
   A. Just detect fraud or compliance issues.
   B. Understand how a sector is changing and to accurately predict the risk associated with that sector.
   C. Obtain valuable information on a competing fund of funds.
   D. Detect fraud or compliance issues and to sort potential hedge funds and determine what is most likely to produce alpha.

Answers can be found in Appendix B.

Appendix A: Bloomberg Functionality Cheat Sheet

Throughout this book, several BLOOMBERG PROFESSIONAL® functions are used. For each Bloomberg function, type the mnemonic listed on the Bloomberg terminal, then press the <GO> key to execute.

Bloomberg Mnemonic	Technical Study	Bloomberg Mnemonic	Technical Study
NI HEDGE	Scrolling News: Hedge Funds	HFR	CTRB Hedge Fund Research
HEDN	Hedge Fund News	FL	Fund Look-Up
HFND	Hedge Fund Home Page	FMAP	Fund Map
FSRC	Fund Screening	FSCO	Fund Scoring
TAG	Hedge Fund Tag Manager	DCHF	CTRB Dow Jones Credit Suisse Hedge Fund Indexes
WHF	Hedge Fund Ranking		
FREP	Fund Reporting	HBOX	Hedge Fund In a Box
NI NEWHEDGE	Scrolling News: New Hedge Funds	HDGE	CTRB Eurekahedge Hedge Fund Indices
HFNI	Hedge Fund Indices	FLNG	13F Filing Summaries

SBHFCTRB	Standard Bank Commodities Hedge Fund Group	STNI HEDGETAX	Suggested News Filter: Hedge Fund, LBO Tax Legislation
NI HEDGEBRIEF	Scrolling News: Hedge Fund Newsletter	STNI NEWHEDGE	Suggested News Filter: Hedge Fund Launches
NI QFND	Scrolling News: Quantitative Hedge Funds	STNI HEDGE13DS	Suggested News Filter: Hedge Fund 13D Filings
NI HFEBRIEF	Scrolling News: Hedge Funds Europe Newsletter	STNI HEDGE13FS	Suggested News Filter: Hedge Fund 13F Filings
CHWI	CTRB Canadian Hedge Watch Hedge Fund Indices	STNI HEDGE13XS	Suggested News Filter: Hedge Fund 13D and 13G Filings
NH HFR	News from Hedge Fund Research	STNI FUNDSUSPEND	Suggested News Filter: Hedge Fund Closures, Withdrawal Suspensions
NH VAN	News from Van Hedge Fund Advisors International	STNI HEDGE13F	Suggested News Filter: 13F Alerts
STNI HEDGEREG	Suggested News Filter: Hedge Fund Regulation	XLTP	Excel: Risk Measures for Funds

Appendix B: Answers to Test-Yourself Quizzes

Chapter 1

1. B
2. False
3. C
4. False
5. True
6. A
7. False
8. D
9. False
10. True

Chapter 2

1. False
2. True
3. A

4. True
5. C
6. B

Chapter 3

1. D
2. True
3. False
4. B
5. False

Chapter 4

1. A
2. True
3. False
4. C
5. False

Chapter 5

1. D
2. True
3. False
4. A
5. True

Chapter 6

1. D
2. A
3. True
4. False
5. True

Chapter 7

1. True
2. False
3. B
4. True
5. B

Chapter 8

1. True
2. False
3. A
4. True
5. B
6. True

7. B, D
8. False
9. D

Chapter 9

1. B
2. False
3. False
4. True
5. A

Chapter 10

1. D
2. True
3. True
4. False
5. B

Chapter 11

1. B
2. False
3. False
4. C
5. True

Chapter 12

1. B
2. True

3. False
4. A
5. True
6. D
7. True

Chapter 13

1. A
2. False
3. False
4. A,C
5. D

Chapter 14

1. False
2. False
3. B
4. True
5. D

References

Altegris. n.d. "Long/Short Equity: Seek Equity-like Returns with Potentially Lower Volatility." *Long Short Equity*. www.altegris.com/en/Alternatives/Strategies-available/Long-short-equity.aspx.

Bank for International Settlements 2013. "Statistical Release: OTC Derivatives Statistics at End-December 2012." www.bis.org/publ/otc_hy1305.pdf.

Barclay Hedge, Ltd. "Barclay CTA Index." www.barclayhedge.com/research/indices/cta/sub/cta.html#.

Battalio, Robert, Hamid Mehran, and Paul Schultz. 2012. "Market Declines: What Is Accomplished by Banning Short-Selling?" New York Federal Reserve. *Current Issues in Economics and Finance* 18 (5). www.newyorkfed.org/research/current_issues/ci18-5.pdf.

Burton, Katherine. 2008. "Simons, Mandel Post Their Biggest Drops in Fund Slump." *Bloomberg* (April 8). www.bloomberg.com/apps/news?pid=newsarchive&sid=a4i5haSt2ECw.

Commercial Finance Association. 2013. "2013 Annual Asset-Based Lending and Factoring Survey." https://www.cfa.com/eweb/DynamicPage.aspx?Site=CFA&WebKey=2f388eee-12cc-441b-9584-986d6261fc51.

Hedge Fund Research, Inc. 2013. "HFRI Indices— USD." *HFRI Indices, Hedge Fund Indices—Hedge Fund Research, Inc.* (August). www.hedgefundresearch.com/mon_register/index.php?fuse=login_bd&1379011766.

Horejs, Mallory. n.d. "Long Short Equity Handbook." Morningstar Advisor. http://advisor.morningstar.com/uploaded/pdf/Alt_Long-ShortEquity.pdf.

Litterick, David. 2002. "Billionaire Who Broke the Bank of England." *The Telegraph* (September 13). Telegraph Media Group Limited. www.telegraph.co.uk/finance/2773265/Billionaire-who-broke-the-Bank-of-England.html.

Mallaby, Sebastian. 2010a. "'Go for the Jugular.'" *The Atlantic* (June 4). www.theatlantic.com/business/archive/2010/06/go-for-the-jugular/57696/.

Mallaby, Sebastian. 2010b. *More Money than God: Hedge Funds and the Making of a New Elite.* New York: Penguin.

Preqin. 2010. "Hedge Funds: The Fee Debate—An End to '2 & 20'?" Preqin Research Report (April). www.preqin.com/docs/reports/Preqin_Hedge_Fund_Terms_and_Conditions_April2010.pdf.

Shane, Scott. 2010. "How Dodd's Reform Plan Hurts Startup Compliance." *Businessweek* (March 19). www.businessweek.com/smallbiz/content/mar2010/sb20100318_367600.htm.

United States Securities and Exchange Commission. 1972. *General Rules and Regulations under the Investment Company Act of 1940.* Washington, DC: United States Securities and Exchange Commission.

About the Author

Richard C. Wilson is Founder and CEO of the Hedge Fund Group association, the number1 largest hedge fund association at more than 115,000 global members. With a background in capital raising, Richard has built a following by providing the industry with consulting-quality thought leadership, articles, videos, and over 100 speeches in 15-plus countries around the world. Over the past 10 years, through Richard's capital raising, advisory, and full-day training workshops (CapitalRaising.com) and family office conferences, he has met face-to-face with well over 2,500 fund managers and at least as many hedge fund investors. The Hedge Fund Group, Certified Hedge Fund Professional training program, Family Office Database (FamilyOffices.com) and CapitalRaising.com assets are owned and operated under the Wilson Holding Company, a global holding company with over 60 products and services and several media assets in the finance industry. To join the Hedge Fund Group association for free and to learn more about the hedge fund certification program please see http://HedgeFundGroup.org and http://HedgeFundCertificaiton.com.

The Wilson Holding Company has a weekly reach to over 1 million professionals through its leading media assets in the venture capital, hedge fund, commodities, private equity, and family office industries including the #1 private equity community http://PrivateEquity.com and most popular websites on family offices (http://FamilyOfficesGroup.com and http://FamilyOffices.com).

Richard's team is perhaps best known for their work in the secretive world of family offices, where Richard advises on single family office formation and formalization, provides advisory board and investment committee participation services, and assists with direct investment deal flow and co-investment opportunities for wealthy families. Richard has met face-to-face with more than 1,000 family offices and has relationships with over 50 families managing $1B or more in assets. In this space, his global team has founded the Single Family Office Syndicate, Billionaire Family Office, and Family Office Database. To learn more about these areas please visit http://SingleFamilyOffices.com, http://BillionaireFamilyOffice.com, and http://FamilyOffices.com.

Richard has authored a number of books including *The Hedge Fund Book: A Training Manual for Capital Raising Executives & Professionals*, *The Family Office Book: Investing Capital for the Ultra-Affluent*, and the upcoming title in 2014: *The Single Family Office: Creating, Operating, and Managing the Investments of a Single Family Office*.

Index